THE RISE AND
FALL OF THE
MURDOCH
EMPIRE

THE RISE AND FALL OF THE
MURDOCH EMPIRE

JOHN LISNERS

JOHN BLAKE

Published by John Blake Publishing Ltd,
3 Bramber Court, 2 Bramber Road,
London W14 9PB, England

www.johnblakepublishing.co.uk

www.facebook.com/Johnblakepub   facebook
twitter.com/johnblakepub   twitter

First published in hardback in 2012

This edition published in paperback in 2013

ISBN: 978-1-78219-427-9

British Library Cataloguing-in-Publication Data:

A catalogue record for this book is available from the British Library.

Design by www.envydesign.co.uk

Printed in Great Britain by CPI Group (UK) Ltd

1 3 5 7 9 10 8 6 4 2

Papers used by John Blake Publishing are natural,
recyclable products made from wood grown in sustainable forests.
The manufacturing processes conform to the environmental
regulations of the country of origin.

All pictures from the author's collection except where indicated.

CONTENTS

PROLOGUE

*Force void of judgment falls by
its own weight – Horace*

In January 2009 I had planned to write about the corporate
culture of Rupert Murdoch's News Corporation under the
tongue-in-cheek working title: *In Bed with Rupert Murdoch*.
Although I was never intimately involved with the world's
most powerful media mogul I closely observed his modus
operandi and witnessed his growing influence through
working inside the organisation on three different continents
for lengthy spells over a period spanning 45 years, the major
part of it in Fleet Street. I was on first name terms with many
of his top executives, although I declined to join the team of
Murdoch's UK newspaper operation, News International,
preferring to remain a freelance journalist. Nevertheless I was
afforded a unique opportunity at NI where I had carte blanche
to pursue investigations and feature stories of my own choice

or to accept commissions on behalf of the company. I was able to take advantage of NI's seemingly limitless resources to engage in widely differing projects. There were no borders. I could travel wherever I pleased in pursuit of a good tale. And there were many of those.

In September 2010, it became apparent that activities at the *News of the World* over hacking and other serious forms of malfeasance were far wider than had originally been believed. The mighty vehicle created by Murdoch was in deep trouble, particularly as it had moved its headquarters from Australia to America where stringent laws applied to companies and overseas subsidiaries for which they were accountable under US legislation. The fallout from News International's UK holdings dramatically unfolded, each revelation building on the last. A mountain of killer revelations was finally exposed to the world which now threatened a global organisation, built, controlled and powered by its central figure – Rupert Murdoch.

Was this the beginning of the end of the world's most powerful newspaper mogul and his empire? Unlike other press barons whose fiefdom was restricted to national borders, Murdoch's kingdom circled the globe and my working title now needed rethinking to embrace the cataclysmic changes. News International appeared to have succumbed to the myth of its seemingly impregnable position and had stepped on landmines of its own planting. One by one they were now exploding before a global audience.

I write this book from the view point of a working journalist and newspaper lawyer advising editors and journalists on the limitations dictated by law, convention, codes and ethics. As a journalist I had a clear window into the culture and workings of journalists and senior executives at

Murdoch newspapers. A number of them have been arrested but not charged and I make no comment on the outcome of police inquiries into their behaviour. The purpose of this book is to share with the reader my view from the window and also my own experiences undertaking commissions from News International and other relevant newspapers. Any view I express about employees or former employees of News Group Newspapers is a personal view only and does not relate to anything else.

Within News Group, as in most other large organisations, there were in my opinion a number of loose cannons who were given authority beyond their capability or judgment. As a general rule from my own observation, NI journalists who abused that authority or judgment were unlikely to be punished where it led to a positive result. In fact, abuse of authority leading to publication of a 'good story' could have quite the opposite effect and be rewarded by the journalist's line manager or editor who might for whatever reason not wish to know the full background of how that journalist obtained the story or if the story was correct.

Village Fleet Street was a fascinating mix of personalities and talent. It promoted talent and enterprise and despised failure. It allowed unimaginable excesses among its denizens and overlooked their personal failings providing they produced results. It was a place where prejudices could be aired and criticised in the same newspaper and where reputations could be ruined overnight by vindictive writers with personal prejudices. Supreme power of newspapers lay with the proprietor and the daddy of them all was Rupert Murdoch: Australian-born, anti-establishment to a degree, educated in England, citizen of America by choice and media billionaire through being the smartest operator of them all and hardnosed beyond imagination.

I joined Murdoch's *Daily Mirror* in Sydney in 1966. One of his key executives, Frank Shaw, employed me on the basis that I had studied law and under the false impression that I had been junior chess champion of South Australia (I did not disillusion him). When the *Mirror*'s Chief of Staff discovered I had been a university student and knew nothing about reporting I was given the dubious title of interstate editor and provided with a desk in the telex room which fortunately gave me valuable access to editors in regional offices and correspondents overseas. I would also see messages exchanged between Rupert Murdoch and interested parties outside his organisation.

The paper's news editor was known as Macca and opened my eyes to an exciting media world where travel and adventure came to men and women who were markedly different from the norm. People like Macca himself who had been hired, fired and re-hired by Murdoch on several occasions and eventually made editor of the *Sunday Mirror*. He considered it de rigueur to benefit from overcharging expenses and told the story of how he had made a killing when sent to New Guinea to find an Asmat village where Michael Rockefeller, missing heir to his family's billions, was last seen alive. By chance, Macca found what he was looking for on the first day of searching but kept the details to himself. Tragically, young Rockefeller had either been eaten by cannibal tribes or killed by a crocodile. After two weeks Macca decided it was an appropriate time to break the news. He got his scoop and two weeks of expenses. At one morning's conference during a dustmen's strike Macca's news list contained the acronym SARE. Rupert Murdoch happened to drop by and queried what the letters stood for. 'Shit and rubbish everywhere,' came the response. Macca was unashamedly fearless.

Before long I was writing a TV column for the *Sydney Mirror* and a weekly political column in *The Australian*, neither of which impressed Murdoch. I shared an office with the *Mirror*'s showbiz writer Matt White who was to become my mentor and close friend. Matt had returned to Sydney from London and been offered the editorship which he declined, preferring instead to write about movies. Sean Connery would stay with him when visiting Sydney and, according to Matt, rarely bothered to get dressed because of the queue of eager women begging to meet him. Matt had been a fighter pilot in the Second World War and later became a journalist and film producer. When he was in London, he had rented a flat in Hampstead with his friend the Earl of Coventry, a lover of cricket, gambling and high living. As a result, Matt was one of the few journalists to share the services of a butler while working for Associated Newspapers.

In Sydney, competition between the two evening newspapers was fierce. The *Sun*, part of the Fairfax group, was gradually overtaken by Murdoch's *Mirror*, which he purchased soon after inheriting the *Adelaide News*. In order to overtake the *Sun*, he took the *Mirror* downmarket, publishing sensational stories under huge headlines and offering rich prizes to attract readers. Journalists on the two opposing newspapers would think nothing of engaging in dirty tricks to beat their rival. It was real Front Page stuff. Not pretty, but effective.

Reporters would impersonate doctors or policemen in pursuit

of an exclusive. There was an outcry after a photographer donned a doctor's coat and snatched a photograph of Mick Jagger's former girlfriend Marianne Faithfull. She had taken a drug overdose and been rushed to the intensive care unit of St Vincent's hospital in Sydney. Despite the unlawful means used, the Sunday Mirror splashed on the story with the headline: SCOOP! MARIANNE IN A COMA. It showed the singer lying in bed with tubes stuck in her mouth and a caption which read, 'First exclusive picture of Marianne Faithfull, Mick Jagger's girlfriend, as she lies in hospital fighting for life after an overdose of drugs.' Although the Australian Journalists Association condemned the tactics used, newspapers in Australia and in Britain were happy to publish the dramatic photograph. Sydney provided an excellent training ground for Fleet Street.

Ron Boland, Murdoch's right-hand man in Adelaide, offered me a job with the *Adelaide News* and its sister paper the *Sunday Mail* in 1968. I spent some weeks putting together a campaigning story about the large number of fatalities discovered among workers inhaling asbestos dust. Extensive research on the subject had been made available to me by Adelaide University, which had investigated different kinds of cancers arising from exposure to asbestos dust. Despite pleas from the features editor, Ron Boland refused to print the story to avoid offending major advertisers. Suppression of that kind would not happen to me again. Once I had arrived in Fleet Street, I found that refusal to publish by one newspaper group normally opened opportunities with another.

I joined the *Melbourne Sun*, part of the Herald and Weekly Times group once led by Rupert's father Sir Keith Murdoch and whose ethos was markedly different to the brash culture of his son's News Limited. Journalists were treated with civility and pay and conditions were a considerable improvement although one missed the go-getting excitement that existed at News Limited. But that was soon to return when I arrived penniless in London in January 1970, having just spent five glorious months on a mountain between Malaga and Ronda in Spain where I wrote my still-unfinished play and drank wine delivered in large casks strapped to the back of a donkey. But reality soon set in and the Press Association in Fleet Street beckoned. Impressed by my knowledge of law (from the results of a written test given to employees) editor-in-chief Sir David Chipp personally welcomed me to the organisation. But David held far greater expectations of me than I did for the pace of life at the PA with the result that I left some six months later and joined a notorious press agency run by a Fagin character who looked as if he had just emerged from a Charles Dickens novel. Tommy Bryant was outrageous and compelling with an unlimited supply of chutzpah.

Tommy's Fleet Street News Agency was suitably based in subterranean premises in Red Lion Court off Fleet Street. Tommy (whose catchphrase was, 'Jesus Christ, why aren't you earning me money?') hired young freelance journalists keen to break into Fleet Street. Several of his protégés were to become London editors and first class executives. He supplied stories to every newspaper and kept his wife pregnant most of the time to inhibit her passion for shopping.

Tommy was a master at 'buying' crime stories and had acquired a series of tipsters, most of them police officers, who he would regularly suborn with the promise of £5 for each publishable tip received. He was not the only one doing so. A former Labour MP and cabinet minister Shirley Williams recently made light of the fact on television that when as a young reporter she worked for the *Daily Mirror* police were regularly given a fiver for their assistance. But that was small beer compared to police on the make in the 1970s. They were paid thousands, stashed in brown envelopes and left on the bar of an Old Compton Street pub in Soho where pornographers and police exchanged pleasantries on a Friday evening.

Although it was against press council policy, Tommy would not hesitate to break rules or ethics when it came to getting a story. The press council had ruled that newspapers should not pay convicted criminals for their stories unless in exceptional circumstances. Tommy had no inhibitions. He promised criminals the world for their stories and promptly reneged on the deal once it was published. His police contacts in the City of London gave him adequate protection against disillusioned and unhappy criminals.

Across the way from Tommy's den in Red Lion Court were the offices of News Limited of Australia, home of Murdoch's London correspondents. One of his long-serving London editors, Peter Gladwin, had been given a seat on the board of directors of the newly acquired *News of the World*. Peter said he'd alerted Murdoch to rumours that Robert Maxwell had put in a bid for the newspaper but was modest about his role. 'I was made a director simply to agree with whatever Rupert wanted.'

Apart from the Press Association and Fagin, the doors to the major newspapers were difficult to batter down for a young reporter from Australia. Fleet Street was a mecca for talented and clever journalists who could drink to excess and yet turn in superb prose. Battering rams were not the answer. The big money and recognition would come from acquiring exclusives and that is how I came to be offered considerable incentive from the *News of the World* to give it first refusal on my stories. I began chasing big stories, which at that time sold for small fortunes. It was at the height of relentless competition between the Sunday and daily newspapers in London, much of it generated by Murdoch's acquisition of the *News of the World* and the *Sun*. On two different occasions, I had front-page splashes in all three of the Sunday populars on the same day. Editors began taking notice of this and within two years of arriving broke in London, I had acquired an Aston Martin DB5, two substantial properties, and the use of an office on the second floor of Bouverie Street, London EC4.

The combined circulation of the three Sunday newspapers – *News of the World*, *Sunday Mirror* and *Sunday People* – exceeded 10 million and the total readership was in the region of 30 million. It was an exciting change from the smaller newspapers on which I had worked in Australia, although the culture within the Murdoch camp was much the same in both countries. While the *NoW* provided ready cash, enabling Murdoch to quickly expand his empire, it was the *Sun* in which he showed most interest. He had bought a failing, left-wing newspaper and turned it into a huge money-spinner, eventually beating its main competitor the *Daily Mirror*. Murdoch had recognised the *Mirror*'s mistake in trying to be too upmarket while catering mainly to a blue-collar audience and made sure the *Sun* would have no such pretensions. His paper was working class but pandered to entrenched, right-wing opinions. It was bigoted, brash, angry about immigration, critical of homosexuals and interested in sex, sensation, and money. The *Mirror* would never again catch up with the *Sun*'s simple but effective formula. Much of its early success was due to the genius of advertising whizz kid Graham King who had proved his worth with Channel 9 TV in Adelaide and the *Daily Mirror* in Sydney. King's golden touch would later increase sales of the *Sunday Times* and Murdoch's *Star* magazine in America.

Murdoch paid his executives well. For the journalist or editor who could produce the results Murdoch demanded, there would be ample riches. For those who failed, early dismissal was on the cards. This approach ensured an editor would adapt the same hardnosed approach as the proprietor to avoid the risk of being moved sideways or sacked. Murdoch allowed no slack. His treatment of staff was rarely based on sentiment or emotion. Generally, the fate of an employee would be determined only by business considerations, although there have been some significant exceptions.

Rupert Murdoch's approach to politics and politicians has been along similar lines. A politician who might be sympathetic to his organisation would be given a good press while otherwise he or she would be regarded as an enemy. And a prime minister's term in office was finite while Rupert Murdoch was there for life. So it was they who usually sought favour with the press mogul and not the other way around. In fact, Murdoch bluntly told politicians questioning him about his friendship with politicians and access to prime ministers, 'I wish they'd leave me alone.' But neither side could leave the other alone for too long. When it helped his business, Murdoch could be at ease with either political party or, if necessary, support a dictatorship. His minions would also show deft footwork in nurturing friendships with people in power.

Politicians, police and public servants should be free to

speak to the press providing they understand their boundaries. To limit that freedom in any way is tantamount to state censorship and that is unacceptable in a genuine democracy. The range of voices that are able to speak in the UK has been entrenched in the national psyche and must be preserved at all costs. The extent to which those boundaries have been compromised – and there is little doubt that they have been – is now the subject of a major investigation that will impact heavily on future relationships with the press. Journalism can be entertaining and enjoyable and hugely satisfying. Competition is healthy and there are already laws in place to prevent criminality. All that is needed is enforcement. The press should not be gagged.

Proprietors would do well to remind themselves of Kingsley Martin's comment in the *New Statesman* in 1932. He wrote: 'Every newspaper lives by appealing to a particular public. It can only go ahead of its times if it carries its public with it. Success in journalism depends on understanding the public. But success is of two kinds. [*Daily Mail* founder Alfred Harmsworth, 1st Viscount] Northcliffe had a genius for understanding his public and he used it for making money, not for winning permanent influence. He became a millionaire because he was his own most appreciative reader; he instinctively appealed in the most profitable way to the millions of men and women whose tastes and prejudices were the same as his own. He lived by flattering. He did not educate or change his public in any essential; he merely induced it to buy newspapers.'

1

CAUGHT

New York, Friday, 11 March 2011. Rupert Murdoch's 80th birthday. Breaking news carried reports of a major disaster. Japan's most powerful earthquake ever recorded had struck the country's north-east coast, triggering a massive tsunami destroying everything in its path. More than 20,000 people were dead or missing and the Fukushima Daiichi nuclear power plant was in meltdown.

A cataclysmic event of this magnitude was a heady reminder to take stock of one's own situation. For Murdoch, it was an unwelcome portent of dangerous times ahead, just as he was planning a multi-billion takeover in Britain and putting finishing touches to dynastic strategies for the Murdoch family. The last thing he needed was a tsunami affecting his own empire.

News Corporation dominated the world, as the largest and most successful multimedia organisation. It owns the most

1

prestigious newspapers and magazines on three continents. Its TV stations and satellite broadcasters reach nearly every nation on Earth. Among its subsidiaries are film companies, movie studios and book publishers. Its tentacles are legion. Rupert Murdoch, a visionary and business genius, had laid the foundations of his empire in Adelaide, Australia, more than 50 years ago and is now one of the most powerful men on the planet. He is widely admired as a corporate giant, yet has many detractors who have condemned his tabloid newspapers and the influence he wields among politicians worldwide. Left-of-centre politicians have been particularly scathing of his modus operandi and neo-conservative leanings.

Murdoch created a unique culture within News Corporation and its international subsidiaries. The prime objective for his executives has been to embrace the corporation's ambitious drive for success. Murdoch's DNA is shared by a large number of executives among his 52,000-strong global work force. To succeed, they have to follow the corporation's aim of beating the competition at all costs. Colleagues must be part of the cult of the 'Mini-Me', a cloned version of Rupert Murdoch. For their dedication, staff receive generous salaries but the corporation's political philosophies and morality have always been dictated by need. And the major needs have been growth and capital. Bedtime reading for the boss is the bottom line of the company's income statement.

In the UK, News International is the most powerful media group bar none. It is the largest single shareholder in British Sky Broadcasting and its subsidiaries include the *Times*, the *Sunday Times*, the *Sun*, and until its dramatic closure in July 2011, the *News of the World*. The *Sun on Sunday* has now replaced its toxic predecessor to take up the slack that left

News International presses idle for more than seven months. Annual profits from BSkyB alone have topped £1 billion and it wasn't until the phone hacking scandal broke big in the summer of 2011 that Murdoch dropped his bid for all of its shares. The family had wanted full control of this satellite goldmine. With all six of his children by three different wives already on their way to becoming billionaires, adding BSkyB to their portfolio would have assured their fabulous status quo in perpetuity.

But the cracks in the Murdoch empire had begun to show as early as 2000. Eventually they would open wide enough to form a devastating condemnation of News International and threaten the foundations of its far-reaching empire. Murdoch's own tsunami was dangerously imminent.

When Murdoch won his battle for the *News of the World* in 1968, few people were aware of the true nature of the man. To many, the young Australian millionaire appeared to be a rank outsider. A gambler looked upon as unsophisticated and brash, showing little respect for the establishment or British royalty and without pretensions or social aspirations. But social climbing was hardly an issue. Murdoch had been born into privilege. He stood to inherit wealth, influence, and a first class pedigree among the Australian elite. When Murdoch eventually appeared before parliament at Westminster in July 2011, he stated that his father was not a wealthy man. By comparison to his own wealth, now counted in billions, there was some truth in that. But his father was far from average either in terms of wealth, social standing or political influence.

Sir Keith Murdoch had been head of the Melbourne Herald Group of newspapers and owned the *Adelaide News* (inherited by Rupert on his father's death) and the Brisbane *Courier-Mail*. Murdoch's mother Elisabeth was a Dame, having been honoured by the Queen for her charity work. The family lived in the wealthy Melbourne suburb of Toorak and owned a country estate, Cruden, and famous works of art. Sir Keith had himself been able to wield considerable political influence with Australian politicians, including prime ministers who had provided introductions to political leaders and newspaper magnates in England and America.

Young Rupert was sent to Geelong Grammar, an independent school whose alumni included Prince Charles, the King of Malaysia and John Gorton, a former Australian prime minister. He completed his education at Oxford. But the steely resolve Murdoch possessed was inspired by an admirable quality possessed by many down to earth Aussies – an egalitarian and courageous spirit which refused to be held back by social convention or conservatism. Murdoch was born with bags of this spirit. Despite his background, or perhaps because of it, he cared little about the class system in Britain and even less for the royal family. But that lack of interest in itself would be a contradiction. The royal family in Britain is one of the most successful dynasties ever created and the hereditary principle is one that Murdoch has perpetuated with his own family.

How ironic then that the British newspaper which had bankrolled his global buying spree and the royal family would both figure so highly in the first visible cracks of his empire. The royals had been an important source of revenue for his newspapers. Readers showed interest in every aspect of their lives and royal reporters were among the most highly paid journalists in Fleet Street. Competition for exclusive stories involving even minor royalty has been fierce, no matter how mundane the member and while their expense accounts were enviable, royal reporters were under continual pressure to produce the goods.

Clive Goodman had been the *News of the World*'s royal reporter for some years when he was asked to write the newspaper's Blackadder column, previously edited by former royal spin doctor Mark Bolland. Goodman had broken a host of exclusives but could not afford to rest on his laurels. It is axiomatic among newspapers that a journalist is only as good as his or her last story and Andy Coulson, then editor of the *NoW*, was singularly unimpressed with past glories.

In 2005, Goodman wrote two totally bland stories about Britain's Crown Prince William. On 6 November he reported the prince pulling a tendon in his knee and seeing his doctor. The second, published a week later, was even more trivial. It was about Prince William borrowing a television station's editing suite from a journalist friend, Tom Bradby, who would help him edit some home movies. This was small beer for Goodman but it would prove fatal for the newspaper.

Prince William and Tom Bradby concluded that information used by the *NoW* was obtained through illegal means, probably by someone accessing their voicemails – the practice that in the ensuing scandals became popularly known as 'phone hacking' – rather than from leaks by royal courtiers. This set in train a high-powered Scotland Yard investigation conducted by an assistant deputy commissioner in counter terrorism who reported to assistant commissioner Andy Hayman, head of the specialist operations directorate responsible for royalty protection. *News of the World* offices at Wapping were searched during the inquiry and on 8 August

2006, Clive Goodman and private detective Glenn Mulcaire, a former Wimbledon footballer, were arrested under the Regulation of Investigatory Powers Act 2000. The following day, the two men were charged under the Act for intercepting telephones and also under the Criminal Law Act 1977 for conspiring to commit the offence.

The royal family was determined to put an end to journalists snooping on them and hoped the law would make an example of the reporter. It was no coincidence that Goodman and Mulcaire were brought before the Central Criminal Court, better known as the Old Bailey. It was the ideal venue for attracting maximum attention. Normally the Old Bailey tries major criminal cases. Hacking phones would in comparison be considered a minor offence, had royals not been victims.

Now Goodman appeared before the illustrious court, on 29 November 2006, for what may have seemed to him and some of his Fleet Street colleagues to have been a rather trivial misdemeanour. He and Mulcaire pleaded guilty to intercepting telephones belonging to three members of the royal household, assistants to Princes William and Harry. Mulcaire also pleaded guilty to accessing the voicemail of other people between 16 February and 16 June 2006. They included: Simon Hughes, Liberal Democrat MP; Gordon Taylor, chairman of the Professional Footballers' Association; Max Clifford, the publicist; Australian model and actress Elle Macpherson and Andrew Skylet, a football agent also known as Sky Andrew.

The method used to hack phones had been quite simple. Goodman would ring the mobile phone of a royal aide and if the answer message came into play he would punch in a security code which came as standard for most mobile phones. This would normally consist of a series of four repetitive digits. Provided that the owner of the mobile had either forgotten or not bothered to change their security code (this was quite common), it would allow him to access the messages left on the phone. Goodman, the court was told, made 487 calls and Mulcaire 122. The reporter's response was that he was driven to break the law because of pressures to perform. On 26 January 2007, Goodman was jailed for four months and Mulcaire for six months.

Mr Justice Gross told Goodman the case was not about press freedom. 'This was low conduct, reprehensible in the extreme. It is about grave, inexcusable and illegal invasion of privacy.' To Mulcaire, who had a contract with *NoW* for the considerable sum of £104,988 and who had received a further £12,300 paid in cash by Goodman, the judge said: 'This was serious criminal conduct to which we must not become numbed. It is to my mind [of] the very first importance to the fabric of our public life that such intrusive, sustained criminal conduct should be marked by immediate loss of liberty ... neither journalist or private security consultant are above the law. What you did was plainly on the wrong side of the line.'

But of greater import than the judge's contempt for their actions was his observation made during his summing up that the hacking might not be limited to the two men he was about to jail. He said to Mulcaire: 'As to Counts 16 to 20 [relating to the phone hacking of Max Clifford, Simon Hughes MP, Andrew Skylett, Elle Macpherson and Gordon Taylor], you had not dealt with Goodman but with others at News International.'

Lawyers' fees for representing Goodman and Mulcaire

were paid by the newspaper and Andy Coulson, accepting responsibility as editor of the *NoW* while denying any knowledge of what had taken place, resigned from the newspaper. Some months earlier, the editor had declared: 'Clive Goodman's actions were entirely wrong and I have put in place measures to ensure that they will not be repeated by any member of staff.'

With Coulson's departure from the *NoW* Murdoch may have lost one of his best editors but he had not, at that time, lost one of his best men. Coulson was highly regarded among friends and foe alike and he was still very much in the Murdoch camp as a good friend of the *Sun*'s editor Rebekah Brooks, who held enormous sway with Murdoch. Brooks was Coulson's predecessor at the *NoW* and at 32 had been the youngest editor of a national newspaper when appointed by Murdoch in 2000. Within four months Coulson would be working as an aide to the leader of the Conservative party, David Cameron MP. Brooks and Cameron had already forged a strong connection.

Brooks herself was more highly regarded for her skills as a supreme charmer and networker rather than as a journalist. She was a striking redhead with pre-Raphaelite looks and impressed Murdoch to the extent that glass ceilings were removed to ease her passage up the corporate ladder. After editing the *Sun* she was made chief executive of News International, a role previously entrusted only to longserving, tried and tested employees such as Murdoch's right-hand man, Les Hinton.

Both Brooks and Coulson exuded an aura of power and influence after the fashion of their guru and boss. They were young, motivated, successful and attractive and, above all, they had Murdoch's ear and the future Conservative prime minister's admiration. Staff at News International were either in awe or feared making a blunder. Very little mercy would be shown to those who failed to produce. Jobs were becoming scarce in Fleet Street and well-paid journalists were expected to be on call and prepared to do everything asked of them, even if it meant dressing up in silly costumes to satisfy an editor's whim. An epigram written by Humbert Wolfe in the 1920s rings as true for them today as for many Fleet Street reporters: 'You cannot hope to bribe or twist/Thank God! The British journalist/But seeing what the man will do/unbribed, there's no occasion to.'

Following Goodman's and Mulcaire's imprisonment, News International bosses hoped they could draw a line under the hacking and that it would soon be forgotten. Scotland Yard and the Press Complaints Commission (PCC) were also satisfied that the incident was a one-off, committed by a rogue reporter and his private investigator. If others had been involved, there was insufficient evidence to pursue them further. Police had seized a large number of documents from Mulcaire but apparently had not considered them actionable. The PCC's own investigation conducted in 2007 concluded that 'No evidence has emerged ... of a conspiracy at the newspaper going beyond Messrs Goodman and Mulcaire to subvert the law or the PCC's Code of Practice ... and that no one else at the *News of the World* knew that Messrs Goodman and Mulcaire were tapping phone messages for stories.'

To a News International optimist, it would appear that the newspaper was now in the clear. But that would have been wide of the mark. The tsunami was slowly gathering strength and one of the main protagonists, the *Guardian*, was like a terrier refusing to let go of its bone. Unfortunately for News International, some of its activities had left it highly vulnerable and sufficiently open to criticism and attack.

Normally, one can take stock of possible threats to a company but it would virtually be impossible to predict precisely what damage could be done to a super-rich multinational with an astute visionary like Murdoch at its head. On inheriting the *Adelaide News* some 60 years earlier, Murdoch had steadily expanded the company by careful plotting, planning, and risk-taking. His greatest enemy was government or state regulation against which he continually battled to avoid restrictions. His constant business goal has been *laissez-faire* and his British newspapers have consistently campaigned against European control and the Euro. Battling against the odds and winning is what Murdoch has always done best.

In the early 1990s his conglomerate was on the brink of bankruptcy but with determination, some luck and brilliant tactics he avoided disaster. A cut-throat business like media demands constant change, innovation and incisive leadership and there is nobody better equipped than Rupert Murdoch. His own testament to this was reinforced when making a guest appearance on *The Simpsons*. He parodied himself to millions of viewers as that 'Billionaire tyrant Rupert Murdoch'.

In 2007 it was thought that Murdoch had achieved his ultimate ambition with the successful takeover of the *Wall Street Journal* (*WSJ*). It was the jewel in his crown and he had fought hard against his detractors to win. Once again, as with his battle for the UK *Times*, there were those who loudly voiced opposition, declaring that he was unfit to run such a prestigious and influential newspaper and that he was bound to take it downmarket. Dow Jones and its *WSJ* subsidiary are the largest and most influential financial information provider and newspaper in America. It is the supreme powerbase from which to assert influence with the country's elite. Murdoch's aggressive battle to achieve victory came at a high price. He paid more than $5 billion for the privilege but while that may have satisfied him it did not please all of his shareholders. There was considerable rumbling among a large number of News Corporation investors who considered Murdoch had paid well over the odds for a trophy at a time when the print industry was being overshadowed by digital media.

But what may seem like an unprofitable investment at first instance can very soon bring greater dividends. In monetary terms, what Murdoch loses on the swings he mostly gains on the roundabouts. This may come about in gaining a political advantage concerning regulation or by smoothing a path to a future takeover. He has proved this time and again, despite the occasional bad investment. He started *The Australian*, a national newspaper, in the mid-1960s and, despite years of loss-making, it proved to be a great asset considering the leverage it has given him in his country of birth. There he still controls the majority of newspapers. Murdoch's influence on Australian politics is unbelievably powerful. He can make and break prime ministers as will be seen in a later chapter on the sacking of Gough Whitlam, a former Labour PM of Australia whom Murdoch had initially supported.

As with *The Australian* newspaper, Murdoch has continued to support influential loss-makers like the *Times* of London and the *New York Post*. It is a given that the proprietor of a national newspaper is granted access to politicians and governments apart from any social cachet such ownership brings.

In his 80th year, Murdoch focused on taking full ownership of British Sky Broadcasting. It was a prize Murdoch felt entitled to, in spite of a minority holding of 39.1 per cent, which gave him the controlling interest. Murdoch had nearly bankrupted News International companies through his belief in the future of Sky. His then managing director in London, Australian Bruce Matthews, urged his boss against funding Sky. Bruce, with whom I had shared many a drink in Fleet Street, told me, 'I warned Rupert it wouldn't work and that it could bring the whole organisation to its knees.' And, to a degree, Matthews, who had managed the London newspapers' move from Fleet Street to Wapping, was right. The crisis of the early 1990s came close to bankrupting the group. But Murdoch had faith in his vision and urged his shareholders to 'hang on in there'. Those who supported Murdoch's vision were not disappointed. By 2011 BSkyB had become a cash cow.

Bringing the whole of BSkyB into the News Corporation fold was also part of Murdoch's dynastic planning strategy. Murdoch had always made it clear that his family would inherit his vast fortune. He had scoffed at public declarations made by Robert Maxwell, his old adversary in the battle for *News of the World*, who boasted he would leave nothing to his sons. True to his word, Maxwell's toxic legacy was written in red. His sons Ian and Kevin Maxwell were left a massive company debt and endured years of agony, having to account to police and financial regulators for their father's fraudulent stewardship of London's Mirror Group Newspapers.

Murdoch launched his £7.8 billion bid for full control of the satellite broadcaster in June 2010, although BSkyB rejected the offer as being too low. The cost, however, would be the least of the bid's problems. The primary considerations were EU and UK regulations and opposition to Murdoch's dominance of the media by interested parties, including Parliament and members of the public. The first hurdle to overcome was Europe but anti-trust regulators at the European Commission in Brussels gave clearance for the bid in December 2010. The next hurdle was a possible intervention by the UK business secretary, Vince Cable. He could prove difficult and was expected to intervene on grounds of media plurality and to demand that the press regulator Ofcom investigate the bid before granting approval. In the meantime, some of Murdoch's competitors, including the *Telegraph*, the *Daily Mail*, Trinity Mirror – whose interests include the *Daily Mirror* – and executives at the BBC and Channel 4 wrote to Cable urging him to block the takeover.

At this juncture good fortune smiled on Murdoch. David Cameron became prime minister in the Conservative-Liberal coalition government following the general election of 6 May 2010. His director of communications was Murdoch's former editor Andy Coulson, who remained a close pal of Rebekah Brooks. James Murdoch, as head of News International, had given his newspapers' backing to Cameron, as had Rebekah Brooks when she was editor of the *Sun* and then as chief executive officer of News International. She had by now become a member of the influential social and political circle known as the Chipping Norton set. This was made up of high fliers with country houses in the Cotswolds. Brooks was on first name terms with Cameron, as she had been with the two preceding prime ministers, Tony Blair and Gordon Brown. Such was her political clout that both Brown and Cameron had been guests at her wedding to racehorse trainer and author Charlie Brooks who, like Cameron, had been educated at Eton. The elite circle of friends of the PM extended to Murdoch's daughter Elisabeth, a successful independent TV company owner and film maker, and her PR guru husband Matthew Freud, a great-grandson of Sigmund Freud and who in earlier times had pedalled PR tidbits to the *NoW*. With such an astonishing power group rooting for the Murdoch takeover of Sky, business secretary Vince Cable would have to tread carefully if his intention was to stop News Corporation taking over. Whatever Cable's private views he would have to appear neutral. In the event, what happened can only be described as media mayhem bordering on comedy, despite the seriousness of the business at hand.

The *Daily Telegraph* has always been a solidly conservative newspaper catering to an affluent centre-right readership. It has an enviable record for excellent news coverage. In recent years it has become more adventurous in its content and won wide acclaim for its exposé of the expenses scandal involving Westminster politicians. In the past, however, it has often looked down from its lofty perch on the red-top newspapers and their undercover operations. It was surprising, then, that the *Telegraph* was to write to the business secretary imploring him to reject News International's bid and barely a week later devised a newspaper trap for the politician in the best underhand tradition of *News of the World* reporters.

Employing a classic scam, the *Daily Telegraph* sent two attractive women reporters in their twenties pretending to be concerned mothers, one blonde, the other brunette, to speak to Cable at his constituency meeting. The purpose of their sting was to elicit information on how the coalition was getting along. Cable sang like a canary. Unbelievably, the government minister felt compelled to give vent to his innermost feelings to two women who minutes previously had been complete strangers. Commenting on the state of the coalition government, he offered, 'Well, there is a constant battle going on behind the scenes. We have a big argument going on about tax and that is party political because I am arguing with Nick Clegg [the deputy prime minister and Lib Dem leader] for a very tough approach and our Conservative friends don't want that.'

When the conversation turned to Rupert Murdoch's takeover bid, the business secretary hurled discretion to the wind. 'I am picking my fights, some of which you may have seen ... and I don't know if you have been following what has been happening with the Murdoch press, where I have declared war on Mr Murdoch and I think we are going to win. Majority control [of BSkyB] would give them a massive stake. I have blocked it using the powers that I have got and they are legal powers that I have got. I can't politicise it but from the people that know what is happening this is a big, big thing. His whole empire is now under attack...' As if to emphasise his own might as a cabinet minister, Cable boasted of a 'nuclear option' available to him. 'Can I be frank with you? And I am not expecting you to quote this outside. I have a nuclear option. It's like fighting a war. They know I have nuclear weapons but I don't have any conventional weapons. If they push me too far then I can walk out of the Government and bring the Government down. And they know that.'

A report of his conversation with the reporters was published in the *Daily Telegraph* but notably omitted his views on Murdoch. Executives at the newspaper must have been well aware that to reveal his antipathy to the takeover would have been counterproductive. Such disclosure would have resulted in Cable's removal from the bid process – which is exactly what eventually happened. To their credit, the BBC, which also opposed the bid, nevertheless broadcast details of Cable's diatribe against Murdoch and News Corporation leaked to them by a *Telegraph* employee. Cable suffered public ridicule and shame and was instantly replaced by culture secretary Jeremy Hunt, an impartial colleague who was not opposed to NI. In different circumstances, Cable could quite properly have been sacked for his indiscretion but for the sake of the coalition it was expedient for him to remain, despite his offer to resign.

The method used by the *Telegraph* to get their story was condemned by the PCC, which ruled, 'On this occasion, the commission was not convinced that the public interest was such as to justify this level of subterfuge.' It said it had advised newspapers not to go on 'fishing expeditions' in the hope of finding stories. *Daily Telegraph* editor Tony Gallagher, while accepting the adjudication, said it had 'alarming implications for the future of investigative journalism'.

Following the BBC leak, the story was published in full by the *Daily Telegraph,* which also released on the web the secretly recorded conversation with Cable. But the *Daily Telegraph* fiasco only served to give a brief respite from the very serious position NI and its parent company News Corporation faced. Financially, the company was in a strong position but problems over the acquisition of Sky were mounting and Murdoch's dynastic plans for the future had not yet been resolved. Worst of all, the scandal over hacking and their misuse of private information would not go away.

The Data Protection Act, 1998, came into force in England on 1 March 2000 and was to have particular application to the media, especially newspapers. Section 55 of the Act makes it an offence to obtain, disclose or procure the disclosure of confidential personal information knowingly or recklessly without the consent of the organisation holding the data. The information commissioner, Richard Thomas, whose office was responsible for enforcement of the Act, published a report in 2006 entitled, 'What price privacy? The unlawful trade in confidential personal information.' It found, 'records of information supplied to 305 named journalists working for a range of newspapers...' They included the *Daily Mail*, the *Observer*, the *Times*, and the *Daily Mirror*.

The report was based in part on findings from the information commissioner office's own investigation, Operation Motorman, which was begun in 2002 and uncovered large-scale trade in personal information. Private investigators and corrupt officials were involved, with access to personal records relating to police and vehicle ownership. The information commissioner estimated that thousands of offences had taken place that related to Section 55 outlined above and he urged for tougher penalties to face those who carried out such crimes.

In 2003, the House of Commons Select Committee on Culture, Media and Sport inquired into privacy and media intrusion. Among those giving evidence was Murdoch's favourite editor Rebekah Brooks (then editor of the *NoW*) and her deputy Andy Coulson. Curiously, it took place on 11 March 2003, Rupert Murdoch's 72nd birthday. Had she not been such a favoured 'daughter' of the press magnate, it is doubtful she would have held on to her job after returning to

Wapping from Westminster. Under questioning by the committee, she claimed that self-regulation under the PCC had changed the culture in Fleet Street and 'in every single newsroom in the land'. This was so wide off the mark that one could be forgiven for thinking she was simply naive or totally delusional. Asked if she or her newspaper ever used private detectives, bugged people, paid the police or others for information, she sensibly replied that subterfuge was only ever used in the public interest. But pressed further by Chris Bryant MP on whether she ever paid the police for information, she surprisingly admitted: 'We have paid the police for information in the past.'

Coulson, seated beside her, acted quickly to correct Brooks' astonishingly frank admission that NI had paid police for information. Incredibly, it was tantamount to a confession that police had been suborned and surely would have led to instant dismissal by Murdoch had it been anybody else. When Brooks was asked if she would continue to pay the police in future, Coulson swiftly replied on her behalf, stating, 'We operate within the law and if there is a clear public interest, then we will.' However, the damage had been done, leaving the newspaper wide open to further investigation. Brooks was furious. She would not readily forget nor forgive Bryant for interrogating her and that would not augur well in the future. The *Guardian* had carefully noted these proceedings.

Brooks's conduct during the questioning led some executives at NI to question whether she had been appointed as editor too early in her career or whether she was at all suitable to lead the world's largest-selling Sunday newspaper. But she had charm and been given power and most of all, she had Rupert Murdoch's ear. At 35 she had a good relationship with Tony Blair, the prime minister. At press charity functions, she would be one of the first to greet the PM and accompany him, arm-in-arm, during his walkabout before making his short speech to the assembled editors and journalists. On one such occasion at the Australian High Commission, I watched with amusement as Brooks and the *Times* political columnist Mary Ann Sieghart 'captured' Tony Blair, one on each side of him, arms locked as they led him around the grand reception area, closely followed by the News International chairman Les Hinton as rear guard. But even more important than the influence the editor wielded and her elevated role at the newspaper was the protection afforded her by the most powerful media baron in the world. Who would dare attack her in the face of such might?

If Rebekah Brooks lacked a certain amount of journalistic savvy, she more than made up for it with her ability to charm and network. From humble beginnings as a secretary at the *News of the World* magazine, she was swiftly promoted to features editor of the newspaper and then editor. She conducted a controversial campaign against paedophiles by instigating a policy of naming and shaming. The idea was to alert mothers in case they were unaware that a paedophile lived nearby. Her action provoked a lynch mob mentality among some readers and backfired when people incited by the campaign vandalised a doctor's house after failing to understand the difference between 'paedophile' and 'paediatrician'. The chief constable of Gloucestershire damned the campaign as 'grossly irresponsible' journalism.

During Brooks's editorship at the *NoW* from 2000 to 2003, two unrelated murders of young children were to play a defining role in the future of News International. The first was the murder of eight-year-old Sarah Payne. On 1 July 2000, Sarah disappeared after playing with her siblings in a cornfield at Kingston Gorse, West Sussex. The child's body was discovered on 17 July some 24 miles away. She had been murdered by Roy Whiting, a known child sex offender with previous convictions who had been listed on a sex offenders register. The case attracted national headlines and was the catalyst for Brooks's campaign of naming and shaming under the proposed 'Sarah's Law'. This was modelled on the American 'Megan's Law', to give parents of young children access to the sex offenders register. A limited trial of Sarah's Law later proved successful. Brooks developed a strong relationship with the murdered girl's mother, Sara, and the pair embarked on an effective, if controversial campaign. A close liaison continued between Sara Payne and News International until July 2011 amid the allegations that Sara's own mobile, given to her by the newspaper, had also been hacked.

The second murder was that of Milly Dowler, a 13-year-old who had gone missing on her way home from school in Surrey on 21 March 2002. Her body was found on 18 September 2002. This case received nationwide publicity and a home video of Milly ironing clothes and playing to the camera was given saturation coverage. Detectives who had worked on Sarah Payne's case were asked for their assistance in finding her. The *Sun* offered a £100,000 reward for information about her disappearance. Until her body was found, her parents kept sending text messages to Milly's mobile in the vain hope that she might still be alive. On 23 June 2011, Levi Bellfield, a serial killer, was convicted of the teenager's murder. At the time of his arrest, he was already serving a life sentence for two other murders and one attempted murder.

By April 2008, Gordon Taylor, the Professional Footballers' Association chairman, had obtained indisputable evidence that his phone had been hacked by Glenn Mulcaire and that others in the *News of the World*, apart from Goodman, were involved. Taylor had begun his action shortly after Goodman and Mulcaire were arrested but it had taken his legal team, led by solicitor advocate Mark Lewis, some months to obtain details from police. This was done by obtaining third-party disclosure – which meant Scotland Yard had to open the files of their original investigation into hacking and provide full details to the lawyer. In fact, the police had an Aladdin's cave of illegally obtained information documented by the private detective, who had been a meticulous note-taker, logging thousands of entries. Later there would be a re-opening of the investigation and further arrests made but that was only after the police had been publicly criticised for limiting their enquiries to one single case of a 'rogue' reporter.

But News Group Newspapers now had a dilemma. The previous December, James Murdoch had been appointed News Corporation's chief executive for operations in Europe and Asia and the Murdochs' long-term plans appeared to be in place. James had done a good job at Sky and Brooks had settled in well as editor of the *Sun* and would soon become chief executive of News International. A lack of controversy would guarantee NI's eventual takeover of BSkyB and Rupert Murdoch's dynastic ambitions would be fulfilled. Politically, the firm was on good terms with the Labour Party and Murdoch, sharing Scottish ancestry with Gordon Brown – who had at last succeeded Tony Blair as prime minister – enjoyed cordial relations with Downing Street. Labour's prospects for re-election looked bleak but Brooks had charmed the Tories so bets were hedged either way. Andy Coulson had also excelled in his job as the Conservative leader's advisor and the last thing News International needed was a revival of the hacking scandal.

When Mark Lewis first set out Gordon Taylor's case to the *News of the World*'s legal team in April 2008, Tom Crone, the newspaper's legal manager, expressed surprise, saying he thought Lewis had suggested settling the case for £250,000. Yet evidence included a much discussed email with the words '...transcript for Neville' [believed to refer to Neville Thurlbeck, chief reporter, although there was no proof of this] with tape transcripts concerning 35 voicemail messages to 'GT' (Gordon Taylor) and 17 to his advisor 'JA' (Jo Armstrong). They had been sent to Mulcaire by reporter Ross Hindley.

Taylor's lawyers also presented further damning evidence of a contract between Glenn Mulcaire using the alias Paul Williams and assistant news editor Greg Miskiw agreeing that *News of the World* would pay a minimum of £7,000 if it printed a story about Gordon Taylor provided by Mr 'Williams'. Scotland Yard had also provided an audiotape on which Mulcaire was heard giving instructions to a journalist, believed to be from another newspaper but moonlighting for the *News of the World*, on how to access Gordon Taylor's voicemail. The clincher came when Mr Lewis applied to the High Court and successfully argued for an order that Mulcaire identify the journalist and provide further information. News International lawyers immediately contacted him to negotiate a settlement. The newspaper agreed to pay Gordon Taylor £700,000, which included his legal expenses. Additionally, two further sums were paid to his colleagues whose phones were hacked, bringing the total payout to around £1 million.

To avoid public disclosure, the settlement contained a gagging clause and it was not until a year later that news of the deal leaked out. Journalist Nick Davies broke the story in the *Guardian* newspaper on 8 July 2009, stating that 'Rupert Murdoch's News Group Newspapers has paid out more than £1 million to settle legal cases that threatened to reveal evidence of his journalists' repeated involvement in the use of criminal methods to get stories.' Putting the boot in, the article suggested, '...the suppressed evidence ... may open the door to hundreds more legal actions by victims of News Group.' That was an invitation that couldn't be resisted.

Public relations supremo Max Clifford, who for years had been selling stories to News International on behalf of clients and had also been on Mulcaire's list of hacking victims, immediately announced that he would sue the newspaper. The case never came to court. Clifford had lunch with Rebekah Brooks, who had been made chief executive of News International in June 2009, and a deal was sorted out in 'no time' at all. Clifford would be paid £1 million, in return for which he would supply exclusive stories to the newspaper for several years. Other named victims, and people who thought they might have been victims followed his example. News International set aside a multi-million pound fund to deal with individual and class actions.

With the *Guardian*'s disclosure, the hacking scandal resurfaced and further serious considerations arose that would prolong the agony for News Corporation and raise questions over whether its directors were fit to run a global concern. Coulson's role as advisor and aide to David Cameron would also come under scrutiny, as would the relationship between News Group newspapers and the Metropolitan Police, including senior Scotland Yard officers. An inevitable consequence would be that NI executives would be recalled for further appearances before the parliamentary committee unimpressed with answers they had previously given.

The second report of the Culture, Media and Sport Committee session was published in February 2010. It included an assessment of the 'persistent libelling' of the McCann family following the disappearance of their daughter Madeleine in Portugal in May 2007; the case brought by F1 racing boss Max Mosley against the *News of the World* (invasion of privacy and breach of confidence); and press standards, following the *Guardian* allegations that the *News of the World* had paid over £1 million to settle three civil actions relating to the phone hacking. The latter item, the committee stated, 'cast doubt on assurances we had been given during our 2007 inquiry ... that the phone-hacking at *News of the World* had been limited to one "rogue reporter", Clive Goodman.'

The committee criticised 'the silence of Clive Goodman and Glenn Mulcaire, their confidentiality settlements with the *News of the World* and the "collective amnesia" at the newspaper group which we encountered during our inquiry ... We find ... the newspaper group did not carry out a full and rigorous inquiry, as it assured us and the Press Complaints Commission it had. The circumstances of payoffs made to Messrs Goodman and Mulcaire, as well as the civil settlements with Gordon Taylor and others, also invite the conclusion that silence was effectively bought. The readiness of all concerned – News International, the police and the PCC – to leave Mr

Goodman as the sole scapegoat without carrying out full investigations is striking. The verdict of the PCC's latest inquiry, announced last November, we consider to be simplistic, surprising and a further failure of self-regulation ... Throughout we have repeatedly encountered unwillingness to provide the detailed information that we sought, claims of ignorance or lack of recall, and deliberate obfuscation. We strongly condemn this behaviour which reinforces the widely held impression that the press generally regard themselves as unaccountable and that News International in particular has sought to conceal the truth about what really occurred.'

The report was good news for Andy Coulson, particularly at a crucial time with election fever gathering pace. It said that it did not see 'evidence that Andy Coulson knew that phone hacking was taking place. However, that such hacking took place reveals a serious management failure for which as editor he bore ultimate responsibility, and we believe that he was correct to accept this and resign.' Les Hinton had also given further evidence and told the committee: 'There had never been any evidence delivered to me that suggested the conduct had spread beyond one journalist. If others had evidence that wrongdoing went further, I was not told about it.' Three months later, in May 2010, David Cameron was elected prime minister and rewarded Coulson's work by appointing him to the role director of communications at No 10 Downing Street.

In the meantime, the *Guardian*, whose stories on the hacking had received little follow up by other UK newspapers, had been in touch with the *New York Times* to give their continuing investigation a wider audience. The American newspaper was happy to oblige and sent reporters to the UK to investigate the story. They interviewed some 12 former

NoW staff members and alleged in their report that hacking had been widespread at *NoW*. Some critics argued their report was biased as they were in competition with News Corporation newspapers in New York where Murdoch owned the *New York Post* and the *Wall Street Journal*. Murdoch would certainly have put the *NYT* on his wish list of newspapers despite finding it stuffy and pompous, but it was not for sale. He had known its owners, the Sulzberger family, as a very young man when he and his father Sir Keith visited the USA. Since buying the *Post* in 1977 Murdoch had been a formidable competitor.

Former *News of the World* showbusiness journalist Sean Hoare told the *New York Times* and the *Guardian* that he had engaged in phone hacking while working for the Murdoch press. He alleged the practice was widespread and that he had been actively encouraged to do so by Andy Coulson. The then editor strongly denied his allegations. Interviewed under caution by police, Hoare refused to repeat his claim. The *NYT* also reported claims by Hoare that journalists would pay police officers money for locating a target by 'pinging' their phones to pinpoint the target's whereabouts. Friends of Hoare described him as an old-style Fleet Street journalist who drank a lot, took drugs, but always managed to get the stories. He insisted that under Coulson he could do as he liked so long as he produced the goods. The *Guardian*, delighted with his 'confession', described Hoare as a brave and 'courageous whistleblower'.

Hoare had moved from the *Sun* to the *Sunday People* under Neil Wallis, a former deputy editor at the *Sun*. He then moved to the *News of the World* in 2001 under Rebekah Brooks and then Andy Coulson, who sacked him in 2005 because of his drink and drug problems. It was drug-taking and excessive alcohol which led to Hoare's chronic illness and early death in July 2011 at the age of 48. Some months before he died, he blamed his deterioration on the newspaper. He was quoted as saying, ' I was paid to go out and take drugs with rock stars – get drunk with them, take pills with them, take cocaine with them. It was so competitive. You are going to go beyond the call of duty. You are going to do things that no sane man would do. You're in a machine.' *Guardian* columnist Marina Hyde, who had worked as a secretary at the *Sun* when she met Hoare, reported, 'My friend's benders with the stars were legendary, but his courage on the phone hacking story must be his lasting legacy.'

But was his action really so courageous? While not defending News International, which accepted phones had been hacked by its reporters, it is difficult to see Hoare as being courageous by admitting to his criminal activity years after the event. He had been sacked in 2005 but some five years had elapsed before he confessed to illegal practices for the greater part of his career. Further, he blew the whistle while terminally ill. Had he done so earlier, when he was being paid top wages and leading a life of Riley, snorting cocaine and drinking to excess, that could have been described as being courageous. He might also have saved many victims of hacking from serious stress. As for blaming the newspaper for pushing reporters to drink and drugs, that is a total nonsense. I have worked with most Fleet Street newspapers and, while over-indulgence in drink and more exotic substances was common, it was never imposed or necessarily encouraged by editors or management. That was always a matter of personal choice. There was no doubt that journalists were pushed to sometimes extraordinary lengths to get stories, but that is to be expected in the media where the ability to break an exclusive story excites passion and healthy competition.

Another colourful Fleet Street character 'came out' a week after Hoare's account was published in New York. Paul McMullan, a former deputy features editor at *News of the World* and now the landlord of a local pub in Dover, Kent, told the *Guardian* that telephone hacking at the newspaper was widespread. The *Guardian*'s report on 8 September 2010 said, 'Paul McMullan, a former features executive and then member of the newspaper's investigations team, says that he personally commissioned private investigators to commit several hundred acts which could be regarded as unlawful, that use of illegal techniques was no secret at the paper ... McMullan's decision to speak publicly about illegal techniques at the paper came as the Commons speaker John Bercow paved the way for a second, powerful committee of MPs to investigate the scandal.'

The *Guardian* report appeared to be a little economical with the reason for McMullan's willingness to make his confession public. In an amusing article published in *The New Statesman* on 6 April 2011, actor Hugh Grant revealed how he had 'bugged the bugger' after a chance meeting with McMullan. In a serendipitous encounter, Grant's car broke down just as McMullan was driving past. The reporter, sensing a story, wasted no time in taking photographs of the actor, who then reluctantly accepted a lift to the nearest town. On arrival, McMullan asked Grant if he would pose for a picture with him 'not for publication, just for the wall of the pub'. According to Grant's account, McMullan followed the best tradition of Fleet Street insincerity and broken promises by promptly selling the picture to the *Mail on Sunday* for £3000. He also invited Grant to visit him at the pub and it was then that the actor decided it would be fun to bug the journalist with a hidden tape recorder. During their taped meeting McMullan, who no longer worked for the *NoW*, revealed he had worked as a freelance for the *Guardian* and had hidden in bushes to take photographs of his ex-boss Rebekah Brooks, hoping she might be out riding with David Cameron. He said the purpose of his paparazzi expedition was to show that Murdoch was backing the future prime minister.

Grant said, 'I tell you the thing I still don't get – if you think it was all right to do all that stuff [hacking and using private investigators] why blow the whistle on it?'

McMullan considered his answer. 'Erm... Right. That's interesting. I actually blew the whistle when a friend of mine at the *Guardian* kept hassling me for an interview. I said, "Well, if you put the name of the Castle [pub] on the front page of the *Guardian*, I'll do anything you like." So that's how it started.'

Despite Hoare's after-the-event whistle-blowing and McMullan's quid pro quo interview with the *Guardian*, 2010 ended on a positive note for News International. The Crown Prosecution Service announced that no further charges would be brought over the *News of the World* hacking scandal. But any joy that might have brought for those concerned would be short lived.

2

THE MOST HUMBLE
DAY OF MY LIFE

Plus ça change, plus c'est la même chose – the more
things change the more they stay the same.

Publisher John Bell, born in the 18th century and
considered to be one of the founders of popular
journalism in Britain, was hardly distinguishable in his
aspirations from Rupert Murdoch. Bell published a variety of
magazines and newspapers, including *Bell's New World*, the
Oracle, and the *Messenger*. His publications were light-
hearted, sophisticated, easily read and gossipy.

The *Messenger* was described by Francis Williams in his
book *Dangerous Estate – The Anatomy of Newspapers* as a
summary of the news of the week with feature articles that
catered to every taste from sport to scandal and politics: 'Bell
was not much concerned with principles. He was an
entertainer and populariser, not a prophet: a pathfinder for the
popular journalism of the future. But he has a place in the

struggle for the freedom of the press larger than that of some more serious-minded men because he showed the way to that popular appeal upon which such freedom rests.' His son, John Browne Bell, founded the *News of the World* in 1843. Murdoch closed it 168 years later, publishing its last edition on 10 July 2011.

Its closure was a sad day for British journalism. Most of the staff were decent and law-abiding and it had been the most successful Sunday newspaper in the land. It was an institution. Its illustrious former editor, Stafford Somerfield, once told Murdoch it should remain 'as British as roast beef and Yorkshire pudding', which to an extent it did, but not with the same editor. Because of a personality clash (Summerfield didn't like taking orders from the proprietor) Murdoch sacked him shortly after he bought the paper in 1969 for a price then estimated at no more than £6 million.

Purchasing the *NoW* was a turning point in the News Corporation story. Cash poured in from sales of more than six million newspapers every week and it was the *NoW* milch cow which enabled Murdoch to fund his his global buying spree as quickly and effectively as he did. The visionary mogul had come to London with empty pockets and bought a goldmine on borrowed money. For good measure he had also tossed in a cheap Australian scandal sheet known as the *Melbourne Truth*, which Rupert's mother wished he'd never owned. Eventually he sold the *Truth* for peanuts to two of his favourite Sydney editors, Owen Thomson and Mark Day.

The *News of the World* enabled Murdoch to acquire the *Sun*, whose profitability would add to his war chest for US purchases. The Mirror Group had sold the *Sun* as a losing proposition and hoped that would thwart his ambitious plans with its debts but the paper became Britain's most successful daily. Murdoch was so proud of his acquisition that he would sometimes travel to work on the underground just to enjoy the thrill of watching so many people read his morning newspaper.

An apocryphal story relayed to me by then managing director Bruce Matthews concerned Murdoch's urgent need for a suitably large printing press for the *Sun*. The only press available at the time was owned by the Mirror Group and they would certainly not have helped their deadly rival. Murdoch sent an Indian negotiator to the Mirror Group, which apparently assumed the poor chap had arrived from the subcontinent to buy the press for an ailing Indian newspaper group and wanted desperately to ship it over to his country. No competition there, then. As a result, they sold it to him at a hugely discounted price to help their third world colleague. They were furious to discover that the printing press had made a journey by lorry to Bouverie Street just a few hundred yards away.

One-upmanship was considered fair game in the newspaper industry and the victor was to be applauded rather than condemned. Murdoch outsmarted countless rivals. The more his business grew the greater his reputation became, provoking admiration and hostility in equal measures. Less successful rivals insisted his achievement was entirely due to his downmarket approach. But critics often lost sight of the fact that a newspaper is a business and the primary object of any business is survival. Nobody forced readers to buy a particular newspaper and just as John Bell's formula has proved successful over the past 200 years it will no doubt continue to do so for a further 200. Murdoch was aware of this from the time he sat on his father's knee and he has continued mining that rich seam.

Apart from the shocking antics exposed at News International, the greatest criticism levelled at Murdoch is that there has been an abuse of the massive power and influence he is able to wield through majority ownership of the media. But it is not just proprietors who can wield the power. Newspaper editors are delegated considerable power that can be open to abuse. Fortunately in Britain there are still sufficient media groups who will criticise each other or be subject to some scrutiny by the PCC. But the PCC has been too ineffective in some areas and laws governing criminal behaviour by the press or their agents have not been sufficiently enforced.

Long before the phone hacking scandal, Richard Stott, an editor of the *Daily Mirror*, was so outraged at the *Sun*'s handling of a story that he accused it of being Fleet Street's whore. By contrast with the *Sun*, the *Daily Mirror* considered it had a social conscience, although its stature was later badly affected by the criminality surrounding its proprietor Robert Maxwell. Stott's editorial invoked Rudyard Kipling's aphorism: 'power without responsibility – the prerogative of the harlot throughout the ages'. In spite of Stott's attack, Murdoch hired him in 1993 as editor of *Today*, a tabloid which closed down in 1995.

This whole issue of conscience in the press was at the time of writing being explored by the Leveson inquiry into the culture, practice and ethics of the press. Lord Leveson was appointed by the Prime Minister and given the following wide terms of reference:

'Part one: to inquire into the culture, practices, and ethics of the press, including: a. contacts and the relationships between national newspapers and politicians and the conduct of each; b. contacts and the relationship between the press and the police and the conduct of each; c. the extent to which the current policy and regulatory framework has failed including in relation to data protection; and d. the extent to which there was a failure to act on previous warnings about media misconduct.

'To make recommendations: a. for a new more effective policy and regulatory regime which supports the integrity and freedom of the press, the plurality of the media and its independence, including from government, while encouraging the highest ethical and professional standards; b. for how future concerns about press behaviour, media policy, regulation and cross-media ownership should be dealt with by all the relevant authorities, including parliament, government, the prosecuting authorities and the police; c. the future conduct of relations between politicians and the press; and d. the future conduct of relations between the police and the press.

'Part two: to inquire into the extent of unlawful or improper conduct within News International, other newspaper organisations and, as appropriate, other organisations within the media, and by those responsible for holding personal data.

'To inquire into the way in which any relevant police force investigated allegations or evidence of unlawful conduct by persons within or connected with News International, the review by the Metropolitan police of their initial investigation and the conduct of the prosecuting authorities.

'To inquire into the extent to which the police received

corrupt payments or other inducements or were otherwise complicit in such misconduct or in suppressing its proper investigation and how this was allowed to happen.

'To inquire into the extent of corporate governance and management failures at News International and other newspaper organisations and the role, if any, of politicians, public servants and others in relation to any failure to investigate wrongdoing at News International.

'In the light of these inquiries, to consider the implications for the relationships between newspaper organisations and the police, prosecuting authorities, and relevant regulatory bodies – and to recommend what actions, if any, should be taken.'

Yet Murdoch has far too much at stake to have approved or even turned a blind eye to the type of criminality that allegedly took place at the *NoW*, though stories of his single-minded determination in business are legion. Bert Hardy, the chief executive at News International, was invited to spend Christmas in New York with the Murdoch family. Bruce Matthews said that Hardy arrived at Heathrow with his family and telephoned Murdoch to say they were on their way. Murdoch is alleged to have said words to the effect of, 'Sorry, Bert, there's been a change of plan. You're fired.' Like other top executives, Bert received adequate compensation but his execution was painful.

There was much for which Murdoch could be criticised, but not criminal wrongdoing. Certainly, as a newspaper man he would allow corners to be cut and be prepared to publish dubious stories but illegality was not his style. His success came from a deep understanding and appreciation of journalism. He would have had absolutely nothing to gain but dishonour had he allowed his organisation to engage in criminal activities. Nothing could have been more counterproductive for his intended move to take over BSkyB. He owned the most prestigious newspapers in the world and to sacrifice that position for a red top whose popularity and circulation were in decline would hardly make sense, particularly as his other media interests were turning over billions each year.

However, that did not excuse his executives and Murdoch, as their boss, for not exercising rigorous control over the staff and for adopting a head-in-the-sand approach to their methods. There should have been sufficient internal controls to flag up concerns at payments made to informants and who was making them. These are matters that will be explored throughout this book.

Murdoch inspired great loyalty among his staff. But there were degrees of worship and the extent to which some of his worshippers went could be embarrassingly comic, even for the boss. At a conference for News executives in Cancun, Mexico in March 2004, Murdoch was to deliver his keynote speech to a global audience. Guests included Condoleezza Rice and Norman Schwarzkopf from the US and Michael Howard MP, then leader of the Conservative party. One of Murdoch's executives, Roy 'Rocky' Miller, had been nominated to introduce the magnate.

Bruce Guthrie, a Melbourne editor, described the event in his book *Man Bites Murdoch*: 'Miller typified the sort of executive Murdoch prefers: hard-driving, hard-partying, a doer rather than a thinker.'

But it was the introduction by Rocky Miller and not Murdoch's address that stayed in Guthrie's mind. Miller had begun well enough. 'Good evening, ladies and gentlemen. My name is Roy Miller and I have the great honour tonight of introducing a very great man, Rupert Murdoch.' At this stage, continued Guthrie, 'He certainly had everyone's attention, particularly those who picked up on a certain uneven rhythm in his speech patterns. Then he got emotional. 'Just before you come up here, Rupert, I want to say one thing though; you're my fucking hero.' The Australians guffawed, the Brits merely shook their heads... and the earnest Americans couldn't believe it. Miller went on repeating his key phrase. 'No, no,' he said to an increasingly rowdy audience. 'You are my fucking hero, Rupert.'

Murdoch was prepared to put up with idiosyncratic staff or court jesters, providing they made him money or he found them amusing. In the right circumstances it would amuse him to see one of his staff cock a snook at convention. He admitted to his US biographer, Michael Wolff, that he was drawn to the 'larrikin' in Rebekah Brooks. A larrikin is an Australian expression for a much-loved rogue. But it goes deeper than that, meaning to have an anti-authority streak. Someone who is not frightened to step outside of social norms or to take chances which others might not. In America, Australian Col Allan at the *New York Post* fitted the bill admirably and in the UK qualifying editors were Kelvin Mackenzie of the *Sun* and Wendy Henry of the *News of the World*.

Editors were given virtual autonomy and could sometimes be in danger of misreading Murdoch's signals and believing they had been given a wider authority than was intended. Such a signal could translate into an assumed authority to do as they pleased, providing they maintained a healthy circulation and did not upset Rupert. Sensibly, Murdoch would wine and dine his more important editors and bring them home to meet the family. Social engagement with the boss would ensure they could absorb his views and gave them an idea of his political leanings, which could vary from country to country and usually involved backing the likely winner at an election. From then on, they would be left to get on with the job but could take advice from Murdoch's trusted lieutenants like Les Hinton. If Murdoch was displeased with their performance he would soon let them know by telephone. One London editor was ordered to fly to America by Concorde for a dressing down because she had published an article that offended a leading actor in a News Corporation-funded movie.

Newspapers, particularly nationals, are in a powerful position to influence members of the public, local authorities, and government. Unlike a public authority, whose actions can be challenged by judicial review, there are few checks on the way that power is exercised by editors and journalists. Separation of powers has long been recognised as an essential element in democracy and for maintaining checks and balances against unacceptable behaviour. Unfortunately, a number of Fleet Street journalists working at national newspapers were in a position to abuse their power in the belief that friends in the police force and in parliament would provide a shield against investigation. In the absence of clearly defined parameters from management, they were able to assume authority had been granted or approved, perhaps even to the extent of engaging in unchecked criminal practices. And instead of being punished for obvious abuse, such behaviour might have been rewarded in the event of a successful outcome.

OPERATION WEETING

In January 2011 the police launched Operation Weeting over phone hacking at the *News of the World*. The investigation began only weeks after the CPS had said that no further hacking charges would be brought. The police also ran Operation Elveden to inquire into allegations of inappropriate payments to police by those involved in hacking and Operation Tuleta into allegations of computer hacking. All three were led by Sue Akers, a deputy assistant commissioner at Scotland Yard and head of organised crime and criminal networks in the specialist crime directorate. An internal inquiry by the *News of the World* led to the sacking of news editor Ian Edmondson.

With continued pressure coming from all quarters, Andy Coulson resigned as Cameron's director of communications in the same month. Cameron was sorry to see Coulson go but, with so much publicity surrounding his position, Coulson had found it impossible to continue. High profile figures, including a former deputy prime minister, were now issuing claims against the newspaper and in June, actress Sienna Miller accepted a payment of £100,000 from the newspaper after it accepted her phone had been hacked.

On 4 July lawyer Mark Lewis – who had acted for Gordon Taylor – broke the news that was to herald the death sentence for the *News of the World*. Milly Dowler's phone was believed to have been hacked after she went missing. Calls had been intercepted and messages deleted, raising hopes in her parents that she might still be alive. The nation was horrified. Such was the outrage that advertisers immediately withdrew from the newspaper and overnight the brand became toxic. Three days later, James Murdoch made the astonishing and unexpected announcement that the world's largest and oldest Sunday newspaper would print its final edition on 10 July, the same day that Rupert Murdoch was due to fly to London and manage the crisis.

But the saga was far from over. David Cameron appointed a high court judge to inquire into the scandal and to examine the question of regulation and relationships between the press, the public and state authorities including parliament. The Sky bid would also have to be set aside. Further allegations were made, but not supported by evidence, that News International reporters had targeted former prime minister Gordon Brown. Brown then mistakenly accused the *Sun* of hacking into his son's medical records, a claim denied by the newspaper. Unconfirmed reports suggested that telephones of relatives of September 11 victims may also have been hacked. Had it been true it would have had a devastating result for the whole organisation.

Journalists at the *News of the World* and editor Colin Myler – appointed when Coulson resigned – were devastated that they had been given three months notice to quit. Many of them had not been at the newspaper during the critical periods and blamed Rebekah Brooks for not resigning as head of News International. They thought that if she had done the 'honourable' thing and gone, the newspaper could have been saved.

Arriving in London, Rupert Murdoch had Brooks at his side. On being asked what his priority was, he turned to her and said, 'This one.'

The final issue of the *News of the World* made an abject apology: 'We praised high standards, we demanded high standards but, as we are now only too painfully aware, for a period of a few years up to 2006 some who worked for us, or in our name, fell shamefully short of those standards. Quite simply, we lost our way. Phones were hacked, and for that this newspaper is truly sorry.'

Some £20 million was set aside to pay victims for the intrusion. The highest individual payments were agreed with Milly Dowler's parents, who were to receive £2 million as compensation for their 'hurt'. Full-page advertisements had been taken out in national daily and Sunday newspapers apologising for the NoW's 'serious wrongdoing' and pledging that its parent organisation was 'committed to change'.

Contrition by the newspaper and News Corporation did not mean an end to inquiries by Scotland Yard and a flood of damaging disclosures continued throughout 2011. Operation Weeting then comprised a team of more than a hundred full-time detectives and support staff examining every aspect of the case. By the end of October some 16 arrests over alleged hacking had been made, among them editor Andy Coulson, his boss Rebekah Brooks and Neil Wallis, a former deputy editor who became a PR consultant advising Scotland Yard. Five journalists and senior editorial staff had all worked as news editors – Greg Miskiw, James Weatherup, Clive Goodman (arrested a second time), Ian Edmonds and Neville Thurlbeck. All 16 denied the charges. Of the 3,870 names of possible victims of hacking which had appeared on Glen Mulcaire's list, fewer than 200 had been notified by police and more than 60 victims had launched civil damages claims against News International.

PARLIAMENT AND THE POLICE

An unexpected fallout of the hacking scandal was the resignation on 17 July of Sir Paul Stephenson, the Metropolitan police commissioner and Britain's most senior police officer. The Scotland Yard chief had had an unblemished career but resigned because of speculation about his connection with Neil Wallis. Stephenson's judgment was questioned over his decision to hire Wallis as a media consultant at Scotland Yard. The Met paid Wallis £24,000 to work as a two-day-a-month PR between October 2009 and September 2010 and the contract was cancelled less than six months before the launch of Operation Weeting. As a consultant at Scotland Yard, it was alleged that Wallis was also paid more than £25,000 by News International and that he had supplied 'crime exclusives' to the *News of the World*. He was reported as having received £10,000 for one of his stories despite the fact that his contract contained confidentiality and conflict of interest clauses.

Wallis's reputation in Fleet Street had been that of an aggressive taskmaster who would berate colleagues in front of other staff while asserting his dominance. If Coulson wanted to reprimand a reporter he would set Wallis on them. Wallis had also been a member of the PCC and its editors' code of practice committee. He had also acted as PR to Champneys, a luxury health spa where Stephenson had stayed as a non-paying guest for five weeks. But the police chief denied Wallis had anything to do with his stay, saying that he was a friend of the spa's managing director.

News International had a long-standing relationship with Scotland Yard officers, as did other Fleet Street newspapers. There was nothing wrong with that in itself. The press could be helpful to police and favours would be returned. However, care had to be taken on the extent of that relationship and the nature of any exchanges. A former commissioner, Lord Stevens, was reported to have been one of the most highly paid columnists to write articles for the *News of the World* after he had retired from the job. There was nothing improper about that but it served to demonstrate the continuing good relationships with former policemen and the high regard the newspaper group had for them.

Sir Paul Stephenson had shared some 18 dinners with News International executives, eight of them with Wallis while officers at Scotland Yard were investigating the newspaper. Wallis also had a good relationship with assistant commissioner John Yates. Yates himself resigned from Scotland Yard on 18 July. There had been criticism of his handling of a review of the initial investigation. But he insisted he was leaving with a clear conscience and his integrity intact.

Previously, the Metropolitan Police Authority disciplinary committee had announced it had decided to suspend him pending an inquiry into allegations following the phone hacking. Yates, who had appeared before the home affairs committee a week earlier, said he regretted his 2009 decision not to reopen the hacking investigation and suggested the *News of the World* had failed to co-operate with the police inquiry. He said, 'They have only recently supplied information and evidence that would clearly have had a significant impact on the decisions that I took in 2009 had it been provided to us.'

The serious business of MPs' interrogation of senior police officers took a comic turn when it came to former assistant commissioner and head of counter-terrorism Andy Hayman. He appeared on 14 July, having been responsible for the hacking inquiry between 2005 and 2006. The answers he gave to a number of questions exposed him to public ridicule and led to one MP accusing him of being a 'dodgy geezer', which he thought was 'a really poor show'.

The committee's chairman, Keith Vaz MP, said he was 'more Clouseau than Columbo'. Vaz asked Hayman to comment on the fact that in 2008, following his retirement from the Met, he had taken a job as a columnist with News International.

Hayman replied: 'That is a private matter for me and the *Times*.' Asked how it looked to the public that both he and the former director of public prosecution were now working for News International he commented, 'It could look bad.' Criticised for having dinner with NI executives during the inquiry into hacking he said, 'Not having the dinner would have been potentially more suspicious than to have it.' Asked if he had ever received payment, Hayman theatrically threw up his arms and exclaimed, 'Good God. Absolutely not. I can't believe you suggested that! That is a real attack on my integrity.'

Vaz concluded the session saying: 'Normally I would sum up the evidence, but on this occasion, it speaks for itself.'

SUMMONED TO PARLIAMENT

The Murdochs were not keen to appear before the culture, media and sport committee on 19 July. In days gone by, editors and publishers who displeased MPs would be dragged before Parliament by the serjeant at arms. If found guilty, the next stop would normally be the Tower of London and a period of enforced penitence. But it was far more civilised in 2011. The committee chairman, John Whittingdale, MP, had been friendly with Les Hinton and had been invited to his wedding (which he did not attend). The proceedings were conducted in a firm but courteous fashion except for a shock interruption. Two hours into the questioning an activist calmly walked down to the press magnate and hit him with a plate of shaving cream in the face. Quick as a flash, Wendi Deng, Murdoch's third wife, who had been sitting behind her husband alert to his every move, leapt with the fury of an attacking rottweiler and smacked the attacker's head with her right hand while grabbing the foam plate with her left. Activist Jonathan May-Bowles was handcuffed and led away. Murdoch's composure was praised by his interrogators and his wife won instant plaudits from TV viewers and press who were glued to the proceedings.

Neither Rupert nor James was comfortable in their temporary surroundings at the Palace of Westminster. Submitting to interrogation by ordinary MPs was not really a press baron's style. It was more usual for politicians and prime ministers to pay court to Murdoch as the kingmaker. However, he had flown to Britain to sort out the mess and accepted his fate with stoicism. At times during the questioning he could appear a little vague, an old man slow to answer a question, wondering what it was all about. But the toughness and sharp intellect shone through, revealing much. James Murdoch, on the other hand, appeared more like a college graduate who'd just completed his MBA and enjoyed business-speak. There was some hesitation over important questions but overall the pair accounted well enough for themselves and their American shareholders appeared satisfied with the result.

Rupert and James had been well prepared by lawyers and personal advisers. Rupert told the committee he wanted to say something before he started. 'This is the most humble day of my life,' he ventured. It came pretty close to saying he was sorry for what had happened, but humble? The most powerful media man in the world 'humble'? That was hard to believe and analysing his words the emphasis appeared to me to be a reflection of the circumstances of the day, rather than a deeply personal regret. Nevertheless the MPs appeared suitably reassured that this was an expression of regret, particularly when James elaborated.

John Whittingdale told the Murdochs, 'When this committee took evidence in 2009, we heard from the managing editor of the *News of the World*, Stuart Kuttner; the legal manager of News International, Tom Crone; the *News of the World* editor, Colin Myler; the former editor Andy Coulson and Les Hinton, the former chairman of News International. All of them told us that there had been a thorough investigation and no evidence had ever been found that anybody else was involved. That clearly was not correct. Were any of them lying to this committee?'

James Murdoch responded that the company had relied on a police investigation in 2007, the PCC findings, and legal opinion of outside counsel that 'it was not clear that there was a reason to believe that those matters were anything other than settled matters and in the past.'

Labour MP Tom Watson, a leading protagonist against News International, suggested to Rupert Murdoch that someone at the paper had lied and that he had been misled. Murdoch agreed. Watson then asked him, 'Can I take you back to 2003? Are you aware that in March of that year Rebekah Brooks gave evidence to this committee, admitting paying police?'

Murdoch replied, 'I am now aware of that. I was not aware

at the time. I am also aware that she amended that considerably, very quickly afterwards.'

Watson: 'I think that she amended it seven or eight years afterwards.'

Rupert Murdoch: 'Oh, I'm sorry.' Murdoch admitted that nobody investigated Brooks' statement because, 'I didn't know of it. I'm sorry. Allow me to say something. This is not an excuse. Maybe it is an explanation of my laxity. The *News of the World* is less than one per cent of our company. I employ 53,000 people around the world who are proud and great and ethical and distinguished people – professionals in their line. Perhaps I am spread, watching and appointing people whom I trust to run those divisions.'

Watson was keen to know how much Rupert Murdoch knew about wrongdoing at the *News of the World*, when was he was made aware of it and what News International subsequently did about it. 'You are ultimately responsible for the corporate governance of News Corp.'

Rupert Murdoch explained that the organisation had worked with the police on further investigation and that he had spoken to Les Hinton about the matter. The Labour MP asked why Mr Murdoch had not dismissed chief reporter Neville Thurlbeck following the Mosley case. Murdoch replied, 'I had never heard of him.'

Mr Watson: 'A judge made it clear Thurlbeck set out to blackmail two of the women involved in the case.'

Rupert Murdoch: 'That is the first I have heard of that.'

Mr Watson: 'Do you agree with Mr Justice Eady when he said that the lack of action discloses a remarkable state of affairs at News International?'

Rupert Murdoch: 'No.'

Mr Watson: 'Mr Murdoch, a judge found a chief reporter guilty of blackmail. It was widely reported. He says it was a remarkable state of affairs...'

Rupert Murdoch: 'Why didn't he put him in jail?'

Mr Watson: 'Because it was a civil case. Were you aware that News International commissioned an investigation into News International emails by Harbottle & Lewis [a law firm employed to assist in the phone hacking investigation]? ... You are aware that Lord Macdonald QC [former director of public prosecutions who became a regular contributor to the *Times*] has since reviewed the emails again on behalf of News International, are you not?'

Rupert Murdoch: 'Yes.'

Mr Watson: 'You are aware that he stated he found evidence ... And you are aware that he stated to the board that he found evidence of indirect hacking breaches of national security and evidence of serious crime in the Harbottle & Lewis file.'

Rupert Murdoch: 'He did indeed.'

Mr Watson: 'Who was aware of Harbottle & Lewis findings at News International?'

Rupert Murdoch: 'It went to the senior officials of News Corp. Certainly the top legal officer.

James Murdoch: 'Mr Jon Chapman was the top legal officer of News International. Mr Crone was the head of legal affairs at News Group Newspapers.'

Mr Watson: 'Were you informed about the findings by your son, Mr Murdoch, or by Rebekah Brooks?'

Rupert Murdoch: 'I forget, but I expect it was my son. I was in daily contact with them both.'

Mr Watson: 'Mr Murdoch, at what point did you find out that criminality was endemic at *News of the World*?

Rupert Murdoch: 'Endemic is a very hard, wide-ranging word. I also have to be extremely careful not to prejudice the course of justice, which is taking place now. It has been disclosed. I became aware as it became apparent. I was absolutely shocked and appalled and ashamed when I heard about the Milly Dowler case, only two weeks ago, eight days before I was graciously received by the Dowlers.'

Mr Watson: 'Did you read our last report into the matter, where we referred to the collective amnesia of your executives who gave evidence to our committee? ... A parliamentary inquiry found your senior executives in the UK guilty of collective amnesia and nobody brought it to your attention. I do not see why you do not think that that is very serious.'

Rupert Murdoch: 'But you're not really saying amnesia, you're really saying lying.'

Mr Watson: 'In April the company admitted liability for phone hacking and nobody took responsibility for it then. No one was fired. The company admitted that they had been involved in criminal wrongdoing and no one was fired. Why was that?'

Rupert Murdoch: 'There were people in the company who apparently were guilty. We have to find them and we have to deal with them appropriately.'

Mr Watson: 'Mr Murdoch, why did you decide to risk the jobs of 200 people before pointing the finger at those responsible for running the company at the time of the illegality – your son and Rebekah Brooks? ... We found your executives guilty of collective amnesia. I would have thought that someone would like to bring that to your attention – that it would concern you. Did they forget?'

Rupert Murdoch: 'No.'

Mr Watson: 'Did you close the paper down because of the criminality?'

Rupert Murdoch: 'Yes, we felt ashamed at what had happened and thought we ought to bring it to a close.'

Mr Watson: 'People lied to you and lied to their readers.'

Rupert Murdoch: 'We had broken our trust with our readers; the important point was that we had broken our trust with our readers.'

Labour MP Jim Sheridan wanted to know why Mr Murdoch had entered the back door of No 10 Downing Street to visit the Prime Minister after he was elected. 'Because I was asked to,' the press baron responded, adding that he and his family had often been asked to visit No 10. Sheridan asked if Murdoch had ever imposed any pre-conditions on a party leader in the UK before giving them support in his newspapers. Murdoch replied: 'I never guaranteed anyone the support of my newspapers. We had been supporting the Thatcher government and the Conservative government that followed. We thought it had got tired and we changed and supported the Labour party 13 years ago, or whenever it was, with the direct loss of 200,000 circulation [readers].' But he was emphatic that no preconditions on either Labour or the Conservatives had been imposed. However, he did admit to arguing with Tony Blair about the euro.

Jim Sheridan: 'You must be horrified by the scandal and the fact that it has cost you the BSkyB transaction and led to the closure of the *News of the World*. Who do you blame for that?'

Rupert Murdoch: 'A lot of people had different agendas, I think, in trying to build this hysteria. All our competitors in this country formally announced a consortium to try and stop us. They caught us with dirty hands and they built the hysteria around it.'

Jim Sheridan: 'I know this is a very stressful time for yourselves, but Mr Murdoch, do you accept that ultimately you are responsible for this whole fiasco?'

Rupert Murdoch: 'No.'

Jim Sheridan: 'You are not responsible. Who is responsible?'

Rupert Murdoch: 'The people that I trusted to run it and then maybe the people they trusted. I worked with Mr Hinton for 52 years and I would trust him with my life.'

Conservative Dr Therese Coffey, MP, asked Rupert Murdoch who recommended to close down the *News of the World*.

Rupert Murdoch: 'It was the result of a discussion between my son and I and senior executives. Miss Brooks one morning called the whole board of the News Corporation to seek their agreement.'

Questioned about the company's future intentions and whether or not they would start a new Sunday newspaper, it would have been better for James to leave the question entirely to his father. The chair asked, 'Is it your intention to launch a new Sunday tabloid newspaper?'

James Murdoch: 'No, there are no...'

Rupert Murdoch: 'We have made no decision on that.'

James Murdoch: 'There's no decision on that.'

Chair: 'So for the moment there are no plans to have a News International title coming out on Sunday at the tabloid end of the market?'

James Murdoch: 'There are no immediate plans for that.'

Rupert Murdoch: 'But no guarantee that we won't.'

Chair: 'Fine. You have talked in the past about moving to seven-day newsrooms. There was speculation that the title *The Sun on Sunday* had been reserved.'

Philip Davies, Conservative MP, asked what sort of coaching the Murdochs had received before attending the present hearing. 'Who has advised you on how to handle this session and what was their advice?'

James Murdoch: 'With respect to today, after scheduling this appearance, we took some advice around the context of this sort of setting – it is my first time and, I think, my father's first time in a committee meeting like this – mostly on logistics, what sort of questions you would ask and so on. We were advised, fundamentally, to tell the truth and to come and be as open and transparent as possible. That is my and my father's intent and intention and we hope that we can show you that that is what is happening.'

Philip Davies: 'Mr Murdoch senior, in answer to some questions from Mr Watson, you seemed to indicate that you had a rather hands-off approach to your company. The point you made was that the *News of the World* was less than one per cent of your entire worldwide business, so you would not really be expected to know the ins and outs of what was going on. Could you just give us an illustration of how many times or how often you would speak to the editor of your newspapers – for example, how often you would speak to the editor of the *Sun* or to the editor of the *News of the World*?

Rupert Murdoch: 'Very seldom. Sometimes, I would ring the editor of the *News of the World* on a Saturday night and say, 'Have you got any news tonight?' But it was just to keep in touch. I ring the editor of the *Sunday Times* nearly every Saturday – not to influence what he has to say at all. I am very careful always to premise any remark I made to him by saying, "I'm just inquiring." I'm not really in touch. I have got to tell you that, if there is an editor that I spend most time with, it is the editor of the *Wall Street Journal*, because I am in the same building. But to say that we are hands-off is wrong. I work a 10 or 12 hour day and I cannot tell you the multitude of issues that I have to handle every day. The *News of the World* perhaps I lost sight of, maybe because it was so small in the general frame of our company, but we are doing a lot of other things too.'

Asked by Philip Davies why Les Hinton resigned, Rupert Murdoch said, 'Les Hinton resigned, sadly, last Friday [15 July] following Rebekah Brooks's resignation, saying, "I was in charge of the company during this period that we are under criticism for and I feel I must step down."'

Philip Davies: 'Were either Rebekah Brooks or Les Hinton asked to leave or did they ask to leave?'

Rupert Murdoch: 'They both asked to leave.'

Philip Davies: 'Why did you not accept Rebekah Brooks's resignation when she first offered it?'

Rupert Murdoch: 'Because I believed her and I trusted her and I do trust her.'

Philip Davies: 'It seems on the face of it that the *News of the World* was sacrificed to try and protect Rebekah Brooks' position at News International. In effect, instead of her departure being announced, the *News of the World* was offered up as an alternative to try to deal with the whole thing. Do you now regret making that decision? Do you regret closing the *News of the World* to try to save Rebekah Brooks? In hindsight, do you wish that you had accepted her resignation to start with so that that paper with a fine tradition could continue and all the people who are now out of work or are struggling to find a job could still be in work?'

Rupert Murdoch: 'I regret very much the fate of people who will not be able to find work. The two decisions were absolutely and totally unrelated.'

Philip Davies: 'So when you came into the UK and said that your priority was Rebekah Brooks, what did you mean?'

Rupert Murdoch: 'I am not sure I did say that; I was quoted as saying that. I walked outside my flat and had about 20 microphones stuck at my mouth, so I'm not sure what I said.'

Philip Davies: 'You were misquoted, so to speak.'

Rupert Murdoch: 'I am not saying that. I just don't remember.'

Conservative Damian Collins, MP, wanted to know where limits of privacy in a transparent society lay: 'To what extent do you think the use of confidential, private information –

even phone records and phone hacking – is permissible in the pursuit of a news story?'

Rupert Murdoch: 'I think phone hacking is something quite different. But I do believe that investigative journalism, particularly competitive, does lead to a more transparent and open society, inconvenient though that may be to many people. And I think we are a better society because of it. I think we are probably a more open society than even the United States.'

Damian Collins: 'Where do you draw the line with that? Where are the boundaries of legitimate investigation? What is that about?'

Rupert Murdoch: 'There was a great – well, if we'd done it there would have been a terrible outcry... I'm sorry to say this and I don't know your circumstances or those of anyone else around here, but when the *Daily Telegraph* bought a series of stolen documents of all the expenses of MPs it caused a huge outcry, one which I feel has not been properly addressed. I think there is an answer to it and we ought to look at the most open and clear society in the world, which is Singapore, where every minister gets at least $1 million a year and the prime minister a lot more and there is no temptation and it is the cleanest society you would find anywhere.'

Damian Collins: 'Do you think you have a cultural problem within your organisation in that people only tell you things that they think you want to hear and that even people who have been your trusted advisers and worked with you for years simply withhold information because they want to curry favour?'

Rupert Murdoch: 'No, not my trusted advisers certainly.

You should hear the conversations in my office. They are coming in all the time and arguing. Most people say I've got crazy ideas and fight against me.'

Damian Collins: 'Do you think there was a pressure on editors of your newspapers that leads them to take risks and break boundaries? In the *News of the World*, there was illegal action and wrongdoing and people broke the law in order to get scoops.'

Rupert Murdoch: 'No, I think that's totally wrong. There is no excuse for breaking the law at any time. There is an excuse, if I may say so, and I think rightful, for all newspapers when they wish to, to campaign for a change in the law, but never to break it. I just want to say that I was brought up by a father who was not rich but who was a great journalist and he, just before he died, bought a small paper, specifically in his will saying that he was giving me the chance to do good... I remember what he did and what he was most proud of and for which he was hated in this country by many people for many, many years, was exposing the scandal at Gallipoli, which I remain very, very proud of.'

Damian Collins: 'I think that all students of history are well aware of that.'

Rupert Murdoch: 'That just addresses the question of it being a family business. I would love to see my sons and daughters follow if they are interested.'

Commenting on the fact of his frequent meetings with prime ministers during his career, Mr Murdoch said, 'I wish they would leave me alone.' But he regretted falling out with one. 'The politician I met most in those days [after the arrest of

Clive Goodman] was Mr Brown when he was chancellor of the exchequer. His wife and my wife struck up quite a friendship and our children played together on many occasions. I am very sorry that I am no longer... I thought he had great values, which I shared with him and I am sorry that we have come apart. I hope one day that we'll be able to put it together again.'

Asked by Damian Collins if he stood by his earlier statement that the crisis had been handled very well with only a few minor mistakes, he replied: 'I don't believe that either he [James Murdoch] or Mr Hinton made any great mistakes. Were mistakes made within the organisation? Absolutely. Were people that I trusted, or that they trusted, badly betrayed? Yes.'

Conservative Louise Mensch, MP, put it to him that, 'this terrible thing happened on your watch. Mr Murdoch, have you considered resigning?'

'No,' said Rupert Murdoch, 'because I feel that people I trusted – I am not saying who, and I don't know what level – have let me down. I think that they behaved disgracefully and betrayed the company and me and it is for them to pay. Frankly, I think that I am the best person to clean this up.'

Murdoch had been given permission by the chair to make a closing statement: 'Thank you, Mr Chairman. Members of the committee, I would like to read a short statement now. My son and I came here with great respect for all of you, for parliament and for the people of Britain, whom you represent. This is the most humble day of my career. After all that has happened, I know that we needed to be here today. James and I would like to say how sorry we are for what has happened, especially with regard to listening to the voicemail of victims of crime. My company has 52,000 employees. I have led it for 57 years and I have made my share of mistakes. I have lived in many countries, employed thousands of honest and hard-working journalists. I own nearly 200 newspapers of very different sizes and have followed countless stories about people and families around the world. At no time do I remember being as sickened as when I heard what the Dowler family had to endure – which I think was last Monday week – nor do I recall being as angry as when I was told that the *News of the World* could have compounded their distress. I want to thank the Dowlers for graciously giving me the opportunity to apologise in person. I would like all the victims of phone hacking to know how completely and deeply sorry I am.

'Apologising cannot take back what has happened. Still, I want them to know the depth of my regret for the horrible invasions into their lives. I fully understand their ire, and I intend to work tirelessly to merit their forgiveness. I understand our responsibility to co-operate with today's session as well as with future inquiries. We now know that things went badly wrong at the *News of the World*. For a newspaper that held others to account, it failed when it came to itself. The behaviour that occurred went against everything that I stand for – and my son, too. It not only betrayed our readers and me, but also the many thousands of magnificent professionals in other divisions of our company around the world. Let me be clear in saying: invading people's privacy by listening to their voicemail is wrong. Paying police officers for information is wrong. They are inconsistent with our codes of conduct and neither has any place in any part of the company that I run. But saying sorry is not enough. Things must be put right. No excuses. This is why News International is co-operating fully with the police, whose job it is to see that justice is done. It is our duty not to prejudice the outcome of the legal process. I am sure the committee will understand this. I wish that we had managed to see and fully solve these problems much earlier. When two men were sent to prison in 2007, I thought this matter had been settled. The police ended their investigations, and I was told that News International conducted an internal review.

'I am confident that when James later rejoined News Corporation, he thought the case had closed too. These are subjects you will no doubt wish to explore and have explored today. This country has given me, our companies and our employees many opportunities. I am grateful for them. I hope our contribution to Britain will one day also be recognised. Above all, I hope that we will come to understand the wrongs of the past, prevent them from happening again and, in the years ahead, restore the nation's trust in our company and in all British journalism. I am committed to doing everything in my power to make this happen. Thank you.'

The committee's questioning of Rupert Murdoch's 'hand-maiden' – as former *Sun* editor Kelvin Mackenzie had cheekily described Rebekah Brooks, did not run as smoothly as that of her mentors. Although she too had been advised and attended by top solicitors, her answers at times appeared hesitant or subject to memory lapses. Welcomed to the hearing by chairman John Whittingdale, she was invited to comment on whether she now accepted 'that the statement issued saying that *News of the World* journalists had not accessed voicemails or, indeed, instructed investigators to do so, is actually untrue.'

Brooks responded: 'We have appointed Sir Charles Gray [a retired high court judge and former libel QC] so that victims of phone hacking, if they feel they want to come directly to us and don't want to incur expensive legal costs, can come directly and be dealt with very swiftly.' Like other top Murdoch executives, she had believed phone interception was the work of a single rogue reporter until 2009, 'when the Gordon Taylor story appeared in the *Guardian*', at which time she was chief executive of News International. But even at that time, information unravelled very slowly and, she said, 'It was only when we saw the Sienna Miller documentation that we realised the severity of the situation.'

Had she been aware of the arrangement News Group had with Mr Mulcaire while she was editor at the *News of the World* and the *Sun*? 'No,' she said.

Mr Watson: 'So you didn't know what he did?'

Rebekah Brooks: 'I didn't know particularly that Glenn Mulcaire was one of the detectives that was used by the *News of the World*, no.'

Mr Watson: 'You didn't know he was on the payroll?'

Rebekah Brooks: 'In fact, I first heard Glenn Mulcaire's name in 2006... I didn't know Glenn Mulcaire. I had never heard the name until 2006. There were other private investigators I did know about and had heard about, but he wasn't one of them.' But she admitted having contact with another private detective, Steve Whittamore, who she thought had formed the principal target or 'the major part of Operation Motorman'.

Mr Watson: 'I would like to know what you did with him.'

Rebekah Brooks: 'In the main, my use of private

investigators while I was editor of the *News of the World* was purely legitimate and in pursuit in the main, as you know, of the addresses and whereabouts of convicted paedophiles through Sarah's Law. That is my majority – if not almost my exclusive use of private investigators. But I accept that the *News of the World* also used private investigators for other stories.'

Brooks was reminded by the committee that she was editor at the *News of the World* during Milly Dowler's abduction and subsequent murder.

Damian Collins: 'The phase of your time at the *News of the World* is particularly pertinent to our hearing today. Would you say that ... was a story you were more heavily involved in than other stories?'

Rebekah Brooks: 'Not particularly... under my editorship we had a series of terrible and tragic news stories, starting with Sarah Payne, Milly Dowler's disappearance and subsequent murder and then of course the Soham cases [the murder of schoolgirls Holly Wells and Jessica Chapman in Soham, Cambridgeshire]. As you know, part of the main focus of my editorship of the *News of the World* was convincing Parliament that there needed to be radical changes to the Sex Offenders Act 1997 which came to be known as Sarah's Law and were very similar to laws imposed in America under Megan's Law. So I suppose, if I had a particular extra involvement in any of those stories, then it would have been on the basis that I was trying to push and campaign for readers' rights on the ten pieces of legislation that we got through on Sarah's Law and campaigning for those to be put forward.'

Damian Collins: 'When you gave evidence to the committee in 2003, you referenced the Milly Dowler case as an example of how you thought that the press had worked particularly well with the police and the family liaison officers and it was a view that was supported by Andy Coulson, who gave evidence with you on that day. I appreciate that this is quite a long time ago, but is that something you stand by now? You spoke about it when you gave evidence, but did you have a particular knowledge of the details of the case?'

Rebekah Brooks: 'When I spoke about it in 2003, I was unaware of what I now know... Clearly, these allegations that came out two weeks ago, if true, are appalling and obviously contradict the statement I made.'

Damian Collins: 'As you say, in the context of what we now know, it does appear ridiculous, to use your word. When were you first aware that Milly Dowler's phone had been hacked?'

Rebekah Brooks: 'I think it was last Monday or the Monday before.'

Damian Collins: 'Nothing was ever said to you at the *News of the World* to suggest that Milly Dowler's phone had been hacked, and that that may have been carried out or authorised by an employee of *News of the World*?'

Rebekah Brooks: 'Of course not, no... We saw the story at the same time that you all saw the story. My instant reaction, like everybody else's, was one of shock and disgust that a family who had suffered so much already had heard these allegations that clearly added immeasurably to their suffering. The first thing I did was write to Mr and Mrs Dowler with a full apology to say that we would get to the bottom of the allegations and whether anyone, either representing the *News of the World* or authorised by a professional journalist at the *News of the World*, which I still find staggering to believe, was involved. If we find out that is true, I have every confidence that News International and the police will get to the bottom of that, which they should, as a priority.'

Damian Collins: 'I appreciate your statement. But what I asked was when were you aware that the information that was passed to Surrey police resulted from the hacking of Milly Dowler's phone? Are you saying you were not aware of that until it was reported recently in the newspapers?'

Rebekah Brooks: 'Yes.'

Damian Collins: 'It would seem to us incredible that, potentially allegedly, someone employed by *News of the World* would take the decision themselves to pass information to the police that, however obtained, was the result of a newspaper investigation of which they were part and that they did not consult the editor or senior members of staff. That seems incredible.'

Rebekah Brooks: 'In some ways, I think the opposite. I don't know anyone in their right mind who would authorise, know, sanction or approve of anyone listening to the voicemails of Milly Dowler in those circumstances. I just don't know anyone who would think it was right and proper thing to do at this time or at any time. I know we know a lot more now, but that is all I can tell you.'

Labour Paul Farrelly, MP, a former *Observer* journalist suggested to Brooks that News International was peddling two myths following the conviction of Goodman and Mulcaire.

Paul Farrelly: 'One was that it was just a rogue reporter and the second was that Mulcaire was not really active or doing this sort of stuff until 2005. You had gone by then, and the myth was not to make any link between the two activities – his activities and the sorts of activities that were going on under Motorman. The Milly Dowler case comprehensively demolished both of those myths, didn't it?'

Rebekah Brooks: 'But it wasn't a myth; it was what everyone believed at the time.'

Paul Farrelly: 'Thanks to a partial leak – a good description of the paper that was left in the safe in the office of Harbottle & Lewis – we have had an account through the *Sunday Times* in the last few days that there were a number of gatekeepers on news desks both in your time at the *News of the World* and under Andy Coulson. The names were Alex Marunchak, Greg Miskiw, Clive Goodman, Neville Thurlbeck, James Weatherup and Ian Edmondson – if the *Sunday Times* is accurate – and yet we are still being asked to believe that you as a hands-on editor and Andy Coulson simply did not know what your news desk was up to.'

Rebekah Brooks: 'I cannot comment on what others knew, when they knew it and how they knew it. I can only tell this committee what I knew while I was editor of the *News of the World* and subsequently editor of the *Sun* and as chief executive I can account for my actions in trying to get to the bottom of this story.'

Conservative Philip Davies MP quizzed Brooks on News International's relationship with politicians and the prime minister. 'Could you tell us how often you either spoke to or met the various prime ministers? How often would you speak to or meet Tony Blair, Gordon Brown and David Cameron respectively?'

Rebekah Brooks: 'Gosh. On Prime Minister David Cameron, I read the other day that we had met 26 times. I don't know if that is absolutely correct. I can do my best to come back to you on an exact number. I am sure that it is correct if that is what the prime minister's office say. The fact is I have never been to Downing Street while David Cameron has been prime minister, yet under Prime Minister Gordon Brown and Prime Minister Tony Blair, I did regularly go to Downing Street... On Prime Minister Gordon Brown, in the time that he was in Downing Street and also while he was chancellor, I would have gone maybe six times a year.'

Philip Davies: 'And with Tony Blair, something similar?'

Rebekah Brooks: 'Probably similar. Maybe in the last few years a little more... Strangely, it was under Labour prime ministers that I was a regular visitor to Downing Street and not the current administration.'

Philip Davies: 'How often would any of those prime ministers ask you – if ever – as either editor or chief executive, not to publish a story?'

Rebekah Brooks: 'I can't remember an occasion where prime ministers asked us to not run a story... I can remember many occasions when a cabinet minister, a politician or a prime minister, was very unhappy at the stories we were running but not that they have ever pleaded directly for one not to run.'

Philip Davies: 'And if they had, you would not have been interested anyway, presumably?'

Rebekah Brooks: 'As long as the story was true and accurate or was part of a campaign, then no. There is no reason for a prime minister... that is exactly why we have a free press.

Philip Davies: 'This is my final question. There has been a feeling that, in some way, you had a close relationship with the current prime minister. The allegation goes – it seems to me that it is no different to your relationship with previous prime ministers, but just for the benefit of what people may perceive – that you had a close relationship with the prime minister which was helpful to him and certainly News International's support was helpful to him politically. But that in return News Corporation was hoping that that would in some way grease the wheels for the takeover of BSkyB. Was any of that part of the wider strategy of News Corporation? Were you encouraged to get closer to the prime ministers with that in mind? '

Rebekah Brooks: 'No, not at all. I have read many, many allegations about my current relationship with the prime minister, with David Cameron, including my extensive horse riding with him every weekend up in Oxfordshire. I have never been horse riding with the prime minister. I don't know where that story came from. I was asked three days ago to disclose the racehorse that I owned with the prime minister, which I do not, and I was asked a week ago to explain why I owned some land with the prime minister, which I do not. I am afraid, in this current climate, many of the allegations that are put forward I am trying to answer honestly, but there is a lot out there that just isn't true and particularly around this subject of my relationship with David Cameron. The truth is that he is a neighbour and a friend but I deem the relationship to be wholly appropriate and at no time have I ever had any conversation with the prime minister that you in the room would disapprove of.'

Liberal Adrian Sanders, MP, asked Ms Brooks her reaction to a newspaper report that she had advised David Cameron on who to appoint as a press spokesman and suggested it should be Andy Coulson.

Rebekah Brooks: 'I think it is a matter of public knowledge that it was the chancellor George Osborne's idea... The first time I heard of him being approached was from Andy Coulson and not from the Prime Minister.'

Mr Sanders: 'So you had no conversation with David Cameron, who was not prime minister at the time?

Rebekah Brooks: 'The piece that you – no. The answer is that the allegation, which I have read, is that I told the prime minister to hire Andy Coulson and that is not true and never was true. The idea came from George Osborne.'

Mr Sanders: 'So you had no conversation with David Cameron about Andy Coulson being suitable for that position?'

Rebekah Brooks: 'No.'

Mr Sanders: 'None whatsoever?'

Rebekah Brooks: 'No – obviously, you are talking before his appointment?'

Mr Sanders: 'Yes.'

Paul Farrelly: 'Would you agree, Ms Brooks, that part of the public concern here is about the closeness of the police and now politicians to *News of the World* and News International?'

Rebekah Brooks: 'I think the public's concern overwhelmingly, on the interception of voicemails, is the idea that anybody could intercept the voicemails of victims of crime. I think that is their overwhelming concern.'

Paul Farrelly: 'But there has been a lot of concern voiced over the closeness of police and politicians and *News of the World* and News International. Would you agree as a matter of fact?

Rebekah Brooks: 'I have seen that the *News of the World* has been singled out for that closeness. I think you were going to address it – you know this more than anyone on the committee because of your career as a journalist – it is wholly unfair in discussing the closeness of police and politicians to the media to single out the *News of the World*.'

Some committee members felt that Clive Goodman's letter of 2 March 2007, sent to the group human resources director Daniel Cloke and copied to *News of the World* managing editor Stuart Kuttner and Les Hinton, executive chairman of News International, should have been acted on as part of NI's investigation. Sections of the Goodman letter were blanked out and a copy of the redacted letter is set out below:

Dear Mr Cloke,
Re: Notice of termination of employment

I refer to Les Hinton's letter of February 5 2007 informing me of my dismissal for alleged gross misconduct.

The letter identifies the reason for the dismissal as 'recent events'. I take this to mean my plea of guilty to conspiracy to intercept the voicemail messages of three employees of the royal family.

I am appealing against this decision on the following grounds:

i The decision is perverse in that the actions leading to this criminal charge were carried out with the full knowledge and support of [BLANKED OUT]. Payment for Glen (sic) Mulcaire's services was arranged by [BLANKED OUT].

ii The decision is inconsistent, because [BLANKED OUT] and other members of staff were carrying out the same illegal procedures. The prosecution counsel, the counsel for Glen (sic) Mulcaire, and the judge at the sentencing hearing agreed that other *News of the World* employees were the clients for Mulcaire's five solo substantive charges. This practice was widely discussed in the daily editorial conference, until explicit reference to it was banned by [BLANKED OUT]. As far as I am aware, no other member of staff has faced disciplinary action, much less dismissal.

iii My conviction and imprisonment cannot be the real reason for my dismissal. The legal manager, Tom Crone, attended virtually every meeting of my legal team and was given full access to the Crown Prosecution Service's evidence files. He, and other senior staff of the paper, had long advance knowledge that I would plead guilty. Despite this, the paper continued to employ me. Throughout my suspension, I was given book serialisations to write and was consulted on several occasions about royal stories they needed to check. The paper continued to employ me for a substantial part of my custodial sentence.

iv Tom Crone and [BLANKED OUT] promised on many occasions that I could come back to a job at the newspaper if I did not implicate the paper or any of its staff in my mitigation plea. I did not and I expect the paper to honour its promise to me.

v The dismissal is automatically unfair as the company failed to go through the minimum required statutory dismissal procedures.

Yours sincerely,
Clive Goodman

Les Hinton, now living in the US, appeared again before the committee by satellite on 25 October 2011 to explain why he had told them two years earlier that NI had found nothing that indicated a 'suspicion' of hacking. Tom Watson praised Hinton for 'only' saying seven times he couldn't remember an answer. Mr Hinton said NI's investigation had been thorough despite the subsequent arrests. He said there was no reason for James Murdoch to resign over the company's handling of the scandal. In relation to answers previously given by NI to the Committee, he admitted, 'It's clear some of the answers were not accurate. Whether you would call them untruthful, I don't know.' Commenting on Goodman's letter he said, 'I don't think I'd regard Mr Goodman's letter as evidence of anything,' adding that it had been handed by the company to Harbottle & Lewis which found no evidence to support Goodman's claims.

Paul Farrelly compared Mr Hinton to a mushroom for the reason that 'You seem to have been kept in the dark by a lot of people.'

In October 2011, the *Independent* reported: 'Senior Surrey police detectives investigating the disappearance of Milly Dowler held two meetings with journalists from the *News of the World* and were shown evidence that the newspaper held information taken from the voicemails of the murdered schoolgirl. An investigation by the *Independent* which focuses on this crucial period of the phone hacking scandal reveals that the force subsequently failed to investigate or take action against the News International title. One of the officers who attended the meetings was Craig Denholm who was the deputy chief constable of Surrey. He was also the DCS in charge of Operation Ruby, the code name for the investigation launched following the disappearance of the teenager on 21 March 2002.'

3

RICH MAN
POOR MAN

'My father was not a rich man,' Rupert Murdoch told the Westminster committee when he appeared before them on 19 July 2011. By comparison to Rupert's billions he might not have been. But neither was he, to any extent of the imagination, a poor man, at least not by the time he retired.

During an illustrious career as a journalist, editor and proprietor, Sir Keith had become a confidant of prime ministers and politicians and been befriended by Lord Northcliffe, the British press baron who had owned the *Times* and *Daily Mail*. As head of the Melbourne Herald, Australia's most powerful newspaper group, Sir Keith's influence was considerable and he personally owned two profitable newspapers, one in Adelaide and the other in Brisbane.

By the time Rupert was a year old the family had moved to Toorak, an exclusive suburb of Melbourne, and owned farms and art works including paintings by Australia's most celebrated artist, Sir Sidney Nolan. Rupert Murdoch was privileged from birth. He was looked after by a nanny and governess and was sent to exclusive schools in Victoria and then to university in Oxford, England. He was also lucky enough to learn the newspaper business on his father's knee. Sir Keith, who shared Rupert's desire for power and influence, was an excellent teacher. As an older father, he had patience and wisdom and was the ideal person to instruct his son on how to harness the power that would come from ownership of the press and to understand its interaction with politics – vital ingredients that would eventually make Rupert the most powerful press baron in the world.

On his father's death in 1952, Rupert inherited the major part of his father's estate. Rupert had three sisters. His older sister Helen was born in 1929 and the pair often played together on the family estates, more so than with their younger sisters Anne, born in 1935, and Janet, born in 1939. Both Helen and Anne were later appointed by Rupert to executive positions at News Limited publications in Australia.

Keith Murdoch had been born in Melbourne in 1885 and was one of seven children. His father, Patrick John Murdoch and mother, Annie, had been given a Free Church posting to Melbourne in 1884 from Aberdeenshire. Before emigrating, he had been the minister of a small church at West Cruden Bay, a fishing village. Rupert's maternal grandfather was Rupert Greene, an engineer in the wool trade who was regarded as a Jack the Lad type of character. Rupert Greene had charisma and was popular among his colleagues. He was also a great cricketer and enjoyed gambling and drinking, the very opposite of Sir Keith whose Presbyterian upbringing had been strict. Rupert's mother, Elisabeth, was born in 1909 and was only 19 when she married Keith when he was 43.

Sir Keith had begun his career as a journalist with the *Melbourne Age* newspaper, owned by David Syme, a member of his father's congregation. Although his father would have wanted him to continue with his education, Patrick acceded to Keith's overriding interest in becoming a journalist. For Keith it was a brave move as he had a bad stutter that could prove a drawback. But he overcame this and showed an aptitude for his work. The Murdochs were a pioneering family. They were among the educated classes in Australia and had access to influential people among the small select communities that flourished in a young country awash with immigrant workers, prospectors, miners, and families descended from convicts sent to build the emerging colonies.

Patrick Murdoch had also been interested in politics and was a friend of Andrew Fisher, a former Australian prime minister. In 1904, Patrick was elected moderator of the General Assembly, the Presbyterian Church of Australia's highest office. He had also been invited to serve on the royal commission on religious education in state schools and was a keen supporter of the press, stating that it was 'the strongest foe of tyranny'.

By 1908 Keith Murdoch had honed his skills as a reporter and was looking to extend his horizons. He was keen to overcome his stutter, which he had already controlled to an extent, but he also wanted to study further and enrolled at the London School of Economics. Two years later he returned to Melbourne and was given a permanent job by the *Age* as parliamentary reporter. In 1912 Keith became political correspondent for the *Sydney Sun*. There he met up with and supported his father's friend Andrew Fisher who had been elected prime minister. In 1915 Murdoch was promoted to managing editor of the United Cable Service of the *Sun* and Melbourne *Herald* and was transferred to London, a move that was to give him a place in Australian military history in relation to the Gallipoli campaign of the First World War.

Before leaving for London, Keith Murdoch was asked by Andrew Fisher to stop over in Egypt where Australian troops were stationed prior to being sent to Gallipoli. His purpose was to inquire about problems with post office mail. There had been many complaints about non-delivery of letters and cables between Egypt and Australia. Keith carried with him an important introductory letter from Australia's defence minister George Pearce to General Sir Ian Hamilton, commander of the Mediterranean expeditionary force. On meeting Murdoch on 2 September 1915, Hamilton gave the journalist an introduction to General Sir William Birdwood, commander of the Australian and New Zealand Army Corps (ANZAC). The handwritten note read, 'My dear Birdwood. This gentleman is duly authorised. Help him in any way you can. Yours ever, Ian Hamilton.' The signed note was to lead to Hamilton's dismissal because it enabled Murdoch to report back to Andrew Fisher the dire circumstances and conditions of the ANZAC forces who suffered heavy casualties at Gallipoli, much of which was blamed on Hamilton and British leadership. He also sent a copy of the report to the British prime minister, Herbert Asquith.

The Melbourne *Herald* many years later commented on Murdoch's letter. 'It was an astonishing document, a compound of truth and error, fact and prejudice, serious charges against Hamilton and the British general staff... Mr Asquith, without consulting Kitchener or Hamilton, had it printed as a state paper and circulated it to the members of the Dardanelles committee. They decided that Hamilton ... would have to go.'

Keith Murdoch's report to Fisher is a striking example of the influence and familiarity he enjoyed with the prime minister of the day and one that is remarkably similar to the influence wielded by his son Rupert. Keith's letter dispensed in one sentence the original object of his task, which was to investigate postal services in Egypt. He then continued: 'It is of bigger things I write you now. I shall talk as if you were by my side, as in the good days ... I now write of the unfortunate Dardanelles expedition ... it is undoubtedly one of the most terrible chapters in our history.'

Murdoch based his findings on a despatch written by Ellis Ashmead-Bartlett, a London journalist whose report he tried to smuggle into London to overcome war censorship rules. It was confiscated by officials and Murdoch then sent his own report. Murdoch's own version is littered with purple prose: 'When the autumn rains come and unbury our dead, now lying under a light soil in our trenches', 'Alas, the good human stuff that there lies buried, the brave hearts still, the sorrow in our hard-hit Australian households.' Describing the 'finer spirit of some Australian boys – all of good parentage,' he adds, 'It is stirring to see them, magnificent manhood, swinging their fine limbs as they walk about Anzac. They have noble faces of men who have endured. Oh, if you could picture Anzac as I have seen it, you would find that to be an Australian is the greatest privilege the world has to offer.'

There was little praise for British officers: 'At Mudros are countless high officers and conceited young cubs who are plainly only playing at war. What can you expect of men who have never worked seriously, who have lived for their appearance and for social distinction and self-satisfaction and who are now called on to conduct a gigantic war? Kitchener has a terrible task in getting pure work out of these men, whose motives can never be pure, for they are unchangeably selfish. I want to say frankly that it is my opinion and that, without exception of Australian officers, that appointments to the general staff are made from motives of friendship and social influence. Australians now loathe and detest any Englishman wearing red.'

Rupert Murdoch, on being asked about his father's letter commented, 'My father's letter from Gallipoli to Fisher was a highly emotional, important and nationalistic piece of reporting. He described in graphic detail how British officers were sitting five miles behind the lines drinking iced gins and directing our Australian boys down in the thick of fighting without even a lump of ice for their wounds.'

Years later Rupert Murdoch financed a film on Gallipoli starring Mel Gibson and depicted his father as a hero who 'stopped a war'. Even more remarkable is the fact that Murdoch referred to his father's letter 96 years after the event when facing questions at Westminster in 2011.

Keith Murdoch's letter and his part in the sacking of General Hamilton gave him instant kudos on his arrival in London while back home it made him a hero for his patriotic concern for the 'diggers', as the ANZAC soldiers came to be known. In London, his criticism of Hamilton was a useful political tool for those opposed to the Gallipoli campaign, particularly Lord Northcliffe and David Lloyd George, MP, who was to become prime minister. For Murdoch it also helped seal a friendship with Lord Northcliffe who became mentor and teacher.

Northcliffe, born Alfred Charles William Harmsworth, began contributing to newspapers as a schoolboy. Soon he was made editor of *Bicycling News* and at 21 he launched *Answers*, 'a weekly storehouse of interesting information', which made sufficient money to launch other periodicals, eventually giving him sufficient funds for ownership of several national newspapers including the *Daily Mail*, the *Times*, the *Daily Mirror* and the *Evening News*. He aimed at the mass market, exactly the same formula used by popular newspapers today and one that Keith Murdoch was to embrace in Australia as editor of the Melbourne *Herald*.

One of Keith Murdoch's first tasks in taking over the *Herald* was to popularise the newspaper and take advantage of new technology, such as faster cable services which meant he could bring world news to the nation in afternoon newspapers because of the time difference between Australia and the other side of the world, stealing a march on the morning papers. His newspaper was also one of the first to bring in new printing presses. In the Second World War Keith Murdoch had the foresight to avoid newsprint shortages by creating Australia's own paper mills in an area of forest in Tasmania. He was instrumental in starting up the Australian Associated Press agency. To the chagrin of conservative Melbournians he also staged the first beauty contest in Australia, which did much for increased circulation and expanded the Herald empire with more newspapers and radio stations, creating one of the most powerful media conglomerates in Australia.

Rupert Murdoch's mother has described in the past how

she would often find Keith and Rupert poring over papers, with her husband advising young Rupert to learn all he could. Dame Elisabeth would suggest to her husband that at nine or ten years of age it might be too early talking business to their son. Keith would reply that it was never too early. Rupert later remembered how his father could never stop meddling with his newspapers even when he had other projects on the go. While he was in semi-retirement Keith would still mark up the various stories that appeared every morning, advising and criticising. Keith Murdoch absolutely lived for his newspapers.

The Murdoch children all got on well with their father and considered Dame Elisabeth as the strict parent in their family. The role of caring for them fell to her as Sir Keith was often away from the home, but he spent as much time with them as he could whenever he was around. Because there was such an age gap between Murdoch's parents the children didn't always find a peer group. Rupert was considered to be a shy child whose older sister Helen had a great influence on him, particularly with her views on the poor and underprivileged, resulting in him being called 'Red Rupert' at school for spouting socialist principles. Rupert would irritate his father by discussing Lenin in positive terms at the dinner table and describing him as 'the great teacher'. At Oxford, Murdoch continued his rebellious flirtation with Lenin while enjoying the fruits of capitalist wealth.

Dame Elisabeth has spoken with pride about Rupert's achievements when reflecting on the relationship between Keith and her son: 'Many of the things which Keith was able only to toy with have come to fruition under Rupert. One of his great ambitions, for instance, was to start a national newspaper. He always loved the idea of getting involved with politicians and he was a great one for Australianism. A lot of people have probably told Rupert, "Your father wanted to do so and so." This is a great mistake. My husband would have wanted Rupert to do what he had to do. I have always been very careful never to quote the dead. Too many people like the idea of saying someone said something when they are no longer around to confirm it.'

Despite his huge achievement in building up the Herald group, Keith Murdoch had reluctantly to accept the hard reality that despite his accumulated wealth and exalted position he was nevertheless an employee and not a proprietor. The power he could exercise as managing director of the group would only last for a finite period. Once he retired he would lose his power base. He did not have enough shares in the company to influence editorial policy or to be a king maker in the future. In the words of an Australian politician, JT Lang, 'Murdoch had one very simple idea. He wanted to be the most powerful man in the Commonwealth. If he could make the prime minister and then boss him around, then he was the big boss. It was as simple as that.'

And bossing politicians around is exactly what he tried to do or at least imagined he was capable of doing. He is reported to have said of Joseph Lyons, a popular former Labour minister who was supported by the Herald group in his successful bid to be prime minister, 'I put him there and I'll pull him out.' Lyons was elected as PM in January 1932 and Keith Murdoch received a knighthood the following year. But sometime later Sir Keith, as he now was, became disillusioned with Lyons' policies and wanted to get rid of him. In 1972, Rupert successfully backed Labour MP Gough Whitlam as prime minister and then played a key role with the Australian governor general Sir John Kerr in getting rid of Whitlam just three years later.

Sir Keith had prudently bought sufficient shares in the *Adelaide News* and Brisbane newspaper the *Courier-Mail* as a legacy for his family, particularly for his son Rupert. As majority shareholder, he savoured being able to dictate editorial policy in these newspapers. Ideally, he would have loved to own the *Herald* but he was not wealthy enough. Meanwhile, Rupert was a pupil at Geelong Grammar from where he was sent to England to read politics, philosophy, and economics at Worcester College, Oxford.

Sir James Darling, Murdoch's headmaster at Geelong, was as unimpressed with Rupert as the boy was with the headmaster and his school, which he hated. He would occasionally miss lessons and avoided sport. His rebellion was against authority in general. As a school army cadet he and his mates would play havoc with the officers. He saw little sense in marching around with rifles and his group considered themselves pacifists. His rebellious behaviour extended to the school prefects, another pet hate, and he was particularly offended at being caned by them.

Some of the children from more established families than the Murdochs tended to consider themselves socially superior to the son of a newspaper executive and, in their terms, his family might have been considered as nouveau riche. That in itself would not have worried Murdoch although it may have made him a bit of a loner. Murdoch's spirit worried his parents to the extent that his father was not sure that Geelong was the right school for him. But both Dame Elisabeth and his father were strict, proper, and conservative in outlook and thought the school would be character building.

Rupert's gambling instinct evolved while he was still at school. He would slip away on Saturday afternoons for an occasional bet at the Melbourne races. He attended Oxford at the same time as school friend Michael Searby, who later offered an insight into the mogul. He said Rupert had a clever and fast mind but was imbued with an overdose of energy. He described Rupert as a total fidget who liked everything to be nice and orderly. Inefficiency would annoy him and he got bored very quickly. He was a hopeless student who simply could not settle down with a book for more than an hour at a time. Searby said Murdoch's dealings in politics were typical examples of his lifestyle. He loved the game and the feeling that he was getting the story behind the story, but he had little concept of political theory.

In spite of his lack of interest in most subjects at school, Murdoch showed an early aptitude for publishing and debating. He would rarely miss a debate where he would expound his left-leaning views as 'Red Rupert'. Mostly his views would involve an attack on privilege or support for the underdog and they were not extreme. Shortly after I joined the *Daily Mirror* in Sydney in 1966, a general strike by the Australian Journalists Association took place and to my surprise Murdoch reacted favourably. He was said to be pleased that his journalists, unlike those on the conservative Sydney *Morning Herald*, had not defied the strike call. That must have been a one-off as his views have changed drastically since then. Perhaps the remnants of anti-establishment feelings he engendered as a young man are reflected today by his admiration for favoured larrikins.

Murdoch was given hands-on experience in newspapers while at school, as well as receiving constant briefings from his father. Between leaving Geelong Grammar and attending Worcester College, Oxford where he spent three years (1950–52), he was employed as a reporter at his father's newspaper. His contacts opened doors to the *Birmingham Gazette* and the *Daily Express*. Two of his father's London correspondents befriended Rupert and were to have a continuing involvement with News Limited back in Australia. Rohan Rivett later became editor of the *News*, an Adelaide paper, before being sacked by Rupert and Doug Brass became Rupert's editor-in-chief in Sydney.

Oxford proved a happier experience for Murdoch than Geelong. He had the best rooms at Worcester College, his own car and a generous allowance from his father. Murdoch engaged with bright contemporaries and honed his skill as a debater. He took a keen interest in politics and joined the Labour club, creating a mini-scandal when he defied convention to organise an open campaign – Rooting for Rupert – to be elected secretary of the club. His contemporaries included Gerald Kaufman, a future Labour MP who would become principal private secretary to Harold Wilson as prime minister, and Dr Shirley Summerskill, MP, who became a junior minister in the Home Office in the mid-1970s.

Murdoch's college tutor was Asa Briggs, a brilliant academic who became a personal friend and guided Murdoch throughout his studies. His graduation was in no small part due to his efforts and those of Michael Searby's brother, Richard, who became a prominent lawyer. Both helped Rupert prepare and revise. Even he was doubtful he would have passed without their help.

Although Rupert Murdoch enjoyed Britain, he was not

without criticism of English values and sentiment and of Australians who did not share his patriotism. Even then he displayed a contempt for English institutions and the class system. Curiously, it did not prevent him from enjoying to the full a similar lifestyle to the one he criticised. Few 21-year-olds were in a position to blag a new Rolls Royce for a weekend to visit the general manager of Reuters, Sir Christopher Chancellor, a family friend. Or, while still a student, to drive a new car around Europe, wreck it, and then send it home to his father. Or to be able to stay at best hotels in Deauville, lose money at the gaming tables and then cable the family bank for more funds. At one stage, Sir Keith Murdoch was so worried about his son that he wanted to bring him home after his second year at Oxford but was persuaded otherwise by Dame Elisabeth.

By 1952, Sir Keith had consolidated his majority holdings in the Adelaide *News* and would have liked to expand his interests further by buying the Melbourne *Argus* but was unable to get the backing of London's *Daily Mirror* boss Cecil King as a partner. Murdoch's health was failing and there was little more he could do. Sir Keith died in his sleep on 5 October 1952. Yet his legacy to Rupert, then just 21, was worth far more than the capital value of the Adelaide *News* and its building opposite the main Adelaide railway station. He had taught his son the newspaper trade and introduced him to prime ministers, presidents and media moguls around the world. Most importantly, Rupert learned the importance of securing control in any partnership agreement, be it with shareholders or a single partner. That was a lesson that would stay with him for life. Rupert Murdoch would have to be the boss: anything less was not negotiable.

Murdoch's rise to power might have happened more quickly had there not been burdensome death duties levied against Sir Keith's estate. To his dismay, his father's trustees sold the shares in Sir Keith's Brisbane interests to pay off the estate debts. Rupert had wanted to keep the *Courier-Mail* and could have paid the debts from operating profits but the trustees considered he was too young and inexperienced. Worst of all, the chairman of the trust was also chairman of the Melbourne *Herald* which acquired the shares. The decision deprived Rupert of an important earner in Queensland and the synergy that owning several newspapers brings. But that was not the only obstacle he faced when arriving in Adelaide to run his newspapers. A former friend of his father's, Sir Lloyd Dumas, tried to persuade Dame Elisabeth to sell the Adelaide *News* and *Sunday Mail* to the Herald group with an unsubtle warning that they would start their own Sunday paper in Adelaide and put the Murdochs out of business. Rupert was furious and printed their threat on the front page of the *News*, declaring war on the *Herald*. Eventually both parties agreed to a 50 per cent share each of the *Sunday Mail* and gave Murdoch executive control and benefit of the print contract. The newspapers quickly became a cash cow for Murdoch and with bank backing, he soon embarked on an Australia-wide buying spree. Much later in his career, he would take revenge on the group that had thwarted him by taking it over, lock, stock, and barrel.

As part of his expansion strategy, Murdoch bought the Perth *Sunday Times*. The purchase was merely down to Murdoch's gut feeling that he needed to expand and the Sunday paper in Western Australia was the first thing that came along. In geographical terms, it was quite a commitment. Because of the vast distances separating the two cities Murdoch would fly to Perth each week on an old DC4 to oversee publication until it became profitable. While there he would stay with his uncle, Walter Murdoch, and at weekends he would drive with his mates to Shark Bay some 700 miles north of Perth for snapper fishing.

Ron Boland, one of my previous editors and a close confidant of Murdoch, told me that the Perth newspaper was in a mess until Rupert came along. He said Murdoch literally transformed the paper, brought it downmarket, and made a complete success of it. He had done a similar thing with the Adelaide *News*. He had cut back on staff, costs and ran the business as a tight ship. Unlike in London, where journalists in the 1970s and 1980s were able to virtually live off their expenses, his Australian staff were rarely able to charge back.

While he was sorting out his Adelaide base he also bought Melbourne's Southdown Press, which published an assortment of magazines, and the *New Idea*, a woman's weekly magazine that competed with Kerry Packer's *Australian Woman's Weekly*. Murdoch's most successful start-up venture in Adelaide was the Southern Television Corporation, which won the licence to run Channel 9. Murdoch appealed to the Australian Broadcasting Control Board to allow him a monopoly because Adelaide had a smaller population than Sydney and Melbourne but the request was rejected. A licence was also granted to the Advertiser group who were given Channel 7. Murdoch blamed the rejection on Sir Robert Menzies, then prime minister, and later campaigned against him.

Murdoch next flew to Los Angeles and New York with Ron Boland to buy TV programmes and make contacts with other studios. Initially, everything had to be done on a shoestring as Murdoch's initial investment in Channel 9 was a mere £250,000. Even so, he beat his competitors, becoming the first to get on air with the new channel. Before long his investment had paid off and the channel proved to be another cash cow, enabling him to expand into the major states of Australia.

On 1 March 1956, while still in Adelaide, Murdoch married Patricia Booker, a former airline hostess and part-time model. Their daughter, Prudence, was born two years later. The couple separated in 1960 and Patricia later remarried. Prudence was brought up by her father and his second wife Anna Torv, who he married in Sydney in 1967. Anna had been a cadet reporter on Murdoch's Sydney *Daily Mirror* and was noticed for her beauty and ambition by the executives at the newspaper who introduced her to Murdoch. Soon after I joined the newspaper, I became friendly with one of its star feature writers, Bob Gordon. I told him that I had married a great-looking girl whose father was Estonian. Bob said that was a coincidence because he was going out with a lovely girl whose father was also Estonian but she had recently broken off their friendship, saying she had met someone else who was much more important than him, alas. Bob was not invited to Rupert and Anna's wedding.

Curiously, I watched the Queen's silver jubilee celebrations in 1997 with Anna and children Elisabeth, Lachlan, and James from the second floor of News International's offices in Fleet Street. We crammed together at window overlooking the street as the royal couple passed by in their horse-drawn golden state coach on its way from the Palace to St Paul's Cathedral.

In 1960 Murdoch entered the Sydney newspaper market by

stealth. It was the only means by which he could overcome resistance from the established newspaper barons who were rich, ruthless and aggressively territorial. The Fairfax group, whose flagship publication was the Sydney *Morning Herald*, was the most prestigious. Rather than allow the Melbourne *Herald* to enter the Sydney market in 1958, Fairfax had bought the Mirror Group from Ezra Norton. Norton had been one of the more colourful proprietors in Sydney and had inherited the *Daily Mirror*, an evening newspaper, and its sister *Sunday Mirror*, the Brisbane *Sunday Truth* and the Melbourne *Truth*, a mini-version of the UK's *News of the World*. Next most powerful among the Sydney proprietors were the Packer family with their Consolidated Press whose interests included, the *Daily Telegraph*, *Sunday Telegraph* and the best-selling *Australian Woman's Weekly*.

Murdoch used an intermediary to purchase Sydney's Cumberland Newspapers, a group that distributed nearly half-a-million suburban newspapers each week. Only then did he announce that he was the purchaser. That immediately put him in competition with the two most powerful groups who had carved up their territory between them. Murdoch was invited to a meeting with them so they could spell out their plans. Those were put succinctly to him: they said they were prepared to lose £10,000 each week until he was driven out of Sydney. Lesser men might have succumbed to such threats but Murdoch's aim was to buy a major newspaper in town. He had tried several times to purchase the Mirror group from Ezra Norton before muscling in on Sydney. But this time fortune smiled on him.

Fairfax's managing director, Rupert Henderson, wanted to get rid of the Mirror group. He considered it was a drain on resources, especially as the Mirror was competing against stablemate the *Sun*. Further, he considered it was too downmarket to be associated with a newspaper like the Sydney *Morning Herald* and, against the advice of his shareholders, particularly Sir Warwick Fairfax, Henderson sold the Mirror group to Murdoch, thinking its losses would sink the young interloper. Murdoch was ecstatic at the opportunities the purchase gave him for further expansion. The newly purchased group had printing plants in Australia's main capital cities as well as distribution networks and editorial representation. The battle lines would now be drawn and Murdoch was prepared to enter the fray.

There was a comic side to the first skirmish between Murdoch's Cumberland newspapers and the unholy alliance of Packer and Henderson at the Anglican Press headquarters. When Murdoch bought the Mirror group, he also acquired its plant near Sydney's central railway station. This meant that Packer and Henderson needed to find another printing plant for their suburban newspapers. Frank Packer's son Clyde made an offer for Anglican Press, a religious printer that had fallen into receivership. Murdoch was personally approached by Francis James, a director of the near-bankrupt company, with two bishops in tow. The bishops asked Murdoch for help, explaining that the official receiver had given them a 5pm deadline to pay outstanding dues or face a Packer takeover. It was two hours before the deadline expired. Packer's team were intent on entering the Anglican building, taking charge of all the printing presses in the heart of Murdoch's suburban centre. Murdoch immediately agreed a deal with the bishops to buy the building and gave them £30,000 for the receiver. However, by the time they returned to Queen Street, Packer was there with his cohorts and had taken possession of the building. Francis James countered with his own body of men. James marched in with his gang. A battle ensued in which Clyde had some ribs broken and men on both sides were severely battered with fists and tools.

Murdoch surrounded the building with *Mirror* photographers and was given a running commentary by telephone on the progress of the battle. The following day the *Daily Mirror* had a front-page splash with the headline KNIGHT'S SON IN CITY BRAWL. The main page picture was of 20-stone Clyde Packer evicting a one-legged Anglican clergyman from the building. The Sydney *Sun* carried a report describing how 'Monkey wrenches and mallets were wielded, a door was bashed in and windows smashed. In the disturbance the printing house of the Anglican Press changed hands three times within two hours. Punches were thrown, blood was spilt.' The episode, costly as it was, served a purpose in keeping Packer out of Murdoch's territory.

The battles that followed involved mainly circulation wars. Murdoch hired respected journalist Doug Brass to oversee matters in Sydney as editor-in-chief of Mirror Group. Brass, who had wide experience as Murdoch's London editor, raised the profile of the *Daily Mirror* by improving its content and hiring the best journalists and columnists. But while appreciating the superior product, Murdoch was unhappy with the *Mirror*'s circulation and took it downmarket with bold headlines and sensational reporting to increase circulation. One of the old *Mirror* reporters, Steve Dunleavy, became a Murdoch favourite for his talent in getting a story against all odds and sensationalising stories to such a degree that his exclusives became the most talked-about in town.

Dunleavy's father was a *Sun* photographer and, despite the closeness of father and son, each battled furiously to outdo the other. Dunleavy once slashed the tyres of his father's car to stop him on a story both were covering. On a later story, his father took revenge on Steve by locking him in a shed.

Dunleavy then went to the US, first as New York correspondent for the Sydney *Mirror* and then at the *New York Post* in the 1970s. He became the talk of the town and was eventually given a slot on Fox television. While on the *Post*, Dunleavy covered the 'Son of Sam' murders and it was partly down to his masterful exploitation and sensationalism that it attracted global headlines and became one of the stories of the decade.

Dunleavy would do anything for a story. In Sydney he would pose as a policeman, priest or public servant if need be and he was not beyond carrying a Bible or Star of David if it helped secure an interview. I met Dunleavy in the early 1970s in New York when he was holding court at Costello's bar on East 44th Street, then a favourite watering hole of Fleet Street's finest New York correspondents and assorted international hacks. Dunleavy told me, 'When I first came to New York, Rupert gave me the following instructions: "Go nowhere. Cover everything. Pay nothing."' As amusing as it was, that philosophy of getting something for nothing gelled with my own experience working on Murdoch's Australian newspapers, though he made an exception for major news stories,

While at the Adelaide *News* in 1968 I interviewed Sir Donald Bradman, undoubtedly one of the world's most famous cricketers, and suggested to the news chief on the paper, one John Kroeger, that we should follow it up by signing the world's greatest batsman to an exclusive two-part story as I had got on so well with him. Kroeger agreed, 'Great idea, John. Offer him two dollars!'

In March 1969, I was asked by Kroeger to fly to Melbourne from Adelaide and cover the wedding of Prime Minister Harold Holt's widow. Holt had disappeared in December 1967, presumed drowned while diving at Portsea, Victoria. My instructions were to obtain an exclusive interview with Dame Zara Holt on the eve of her wedding to MP Jeff Bate. It was a story every major newspaper in Australia wanted to cover. When I suggested that I should present Dame Zara with an expensive bouquet of flowers, I was told not to spend more than ten dollars on my entire interstate trip! Despite obtaining an exclusive, front-page splash and beating the Melbourne and Sydney papers using my only weapon – youth and gentle persuasion, Kroeger refused to extend his budget by even one cent. Such were Rupert's penny-pinching ways in Adelaide.

Murdoch's *Sunday Mirror* and *Truth* newspapers were brash and sensational with often lurid headlines. They were papers one could never bring home to meet one's mother, particularly if, like Dame Elisabeth, she held an esteemed position in Melbourne society. Later, Murdoch would be able to remind his mother that he started Australia's only respectable national newspaper, not that its status was his reason for the launch. But even so, Dame Elisabeth would never have approved of the Sydney newspapers or the tactics employed by the hardmen who owned them. The 1960s battleground had few rules. Proprietors fought a dirty and costly battle for supremacy. Murdoch hired the best journalists and the best promotions people to produce sensational newspapers that appealed to red-blooded

Australian males. The primary aim was survival and healthy monetary return. Popularisation spoke volumes for survival and remains an entrenched feature of Murdoch's global business plan.

Another feature of Murdoch's operation that has proved virtually infallible over the years has been applying old formulae to new territories with just a few subtle changes to take account of cultural differences. He did this using a core team of people he knew well and could trust. Liverpool-born Les Hinton was Murdoch's chief lieutenant and had been close to the mogul for over 50 years, having started work as a copy boy with the Adelaide *News*, bringing sandwiches and tea to Murdoch. He rapidly climbed the News Limited ladder and was sent to the *Sun* in the UK as a reporter before being transferred to America, eventually becoming chairman of News International and chief executive at the *Wall Street Journal*. He acted as the mogul's eyes and ears and would visit the group's offices around the world where he could make discreet inquiries and assessments of executive staff as well as supervise the health of the various media organisations. Hinton didn't behave like a hatchet man. He was both charismatic and charming and tended to win the trust and confidence of most of his colleagues. But his friendly manner and total discretion may have belied more steely qualities because Les was a committed Murdoch man, dedicated to serving the interests of the firm. He resigned in 2011 at the height of the phone hacking scandal – part of which had taken place under his stewardship of the company. His departure was a great loss to Rupert and News Corporation.

Another Adelaide appointee was Graham King, a marketing wizard who became Murdoch's chief promotions director. He was the brains behind countless TV and newspaper campaigns throughout Murdoch's battles with Packer and Fairfax in Sydney. His services were again sought in London when Murdoch bought the *Sun*. King introduced games and competitions until the *Sun* became Britain's top-selling daily tabloid. He also worked his magic on the *Sunday Times* in 1986, remodelling it into a multi-section newspaper. When Murdoch launched the American *Star* magazine, it was King who was asked to spearhead promotions. I knew Graham and admired his many talents. He was more than just a promotions man. He was an award-winning author, poet and painter who could adapt his many talents to any multi-media enterprise on a global stage.

Cartoonist Paul Rigby was another Australian who Murdoch relied on when expanding his empire. Paul had worked in Western Australia as political cartoonist on the Perth *Daily News* before working for the Sydney *Mirror*. He was also recruited to the UK for the *Sun*, *News of the World* and to the US for the *New York Post*. Most of Rupert Murdoch's Australian journalists were equally at home whether they were in the England, America or Hong Kong. If a newspaper needed relaunching he would send in global trouble-shooters like Arnold Earnshaw to revamp it.

Murdoch kept a tight grip on his leading newspapers through his editors. They would constantly be on their toes, knowing that a telephone call from Rupert inquiring about content or criticising a story was always on the cards. There was constant the fear that the next call from Rupert might be the last. Although well paid, editors in the Murdoch camp had tenures linked to the success of their newspaper or the whim of the proprietor. Murdoch would also invite certain editors to

America to spend some time with him, which of course gave him a much better opportunity for evaluating their strengths and weaknesses. They were also assessed when attending News Corporation conferences in luxury resorts like Cancun, Mexico or Aspen, Colorado.

On one occasion, Sir Nicholas Lloyd, a former London editor, had been invited for lunch with Murdoch's family in New York. Nick was a top Murdoch executive in London and was accompanied by his wife Eve and their four-year-old son, Oliver. After lunch, Murdoch and Oliver had a race down the street during which Rupert grabbed the boy, lifting him high off the ground. Young Oliver gave vent to his feelings with cool disregard to his generous host by biting the mogul's hand. Some time later, Lloyd resigned from News International when he accepted the editorship of the *Daily Express*. Murdoch was sorry to see him go but wrote a 'sweet' farewell letter, referring to the incident when Oliver bit his hand by saying he now understood why Lloyd had left him.

Murdoch's executives tended to idolise their chief for his knowledge of newspapers and his business acumen. To be praised by him was the ultimate accolade, although adulation one week could just as easily be followed by dismissal the next if Murdoch considered they were no longer useful. Phil Wrack, a deputy editor on the *News of the World*, had served on the paper for many years. He was over the moon to have been invited to Rupert's office on his retirement. He related with pride how during their brief conversation Rupert had known everything about him, even the fact that Phil had been given the perk of a Mercedes car which he would be allowed to keep. I had no wish to disillusion Phil, but as a newspaper veteran he should have been aware that up-to-date files were kept on every executive and that Rupert would have acquainted himself with background material minutes before Phil was seated before the great man. How else would Rupert know minor details of his many executives?

Murdoch's battles in Sydney extended to television ownership. His two main rivals had their own TV stations and his aim was for News Limited to have its own channel and achieve synergy with the newspapers. Each would promote the other and maximise advertising. When a third Sydney TV channel, Channel 10, came up for grabs in 1962, Murdoch pulled out all stops in an unsuccessful bid for it. He suspected that the prime minister of the day, Sir Robert Menzies, who he did not like, was instrumental in his defeat. He had been warned earlier by Doug Brass, who had spoken to Menzies, that News Limited was unlikely to be successful. But as a lateral thinker, Murdoch had other plans for entering the Sydney TV market.

Murdoch's offer to Packer and Henderson to buy a share of the existing TV channels was rebuffed. There was no way they would allow Rupert to get a toehold in a medium that at the time was a licence to print money. But then Murdoch learned about a small TV station that was in trouble. Packer and Henderson had monopolised most of the American programmes sold in Australia and told film companies in the US that they would no longer buy from them if they sold to minor outlets. Advertising had slumped and the channel was on its uppers.

Graham King told the story: 'There was a small television station [WIN-4] in Wollongong, which is a small town about 40 miles south of Sydney, and it went broke. It went bankrupt and Rupert negotiated to take it over. But it wasn't the station itself that interested him because it had a small rural audience, which was never going to make a huge amount of money. What he did was to point the transmitter towards Sydney and threaten the big Sydney operators. If a door was closed to him, he kicked it in or found a key somewhere or other.'

Murdoch's idea might have been to capture a large audience in the Sydney outer suburbs but after some thought, he found an even better way to enter the market. A new channel had been started in Melbourne by local businessman Sir Reg Ansett, a self-made millionaire who owned Ansett ANA, a major domestic airline. Murdoch knew that if he could buy up every film made that year in America it would give him great bargaining power with TV stations in Sydney. But he needed sufficient funds to do this. Ansett agreed to match Murdoch's contribution and Murdoch immediately flew to the States with £4 million in his pocket and engaged in a massive buying spree.

Packer got to hear about the plan too late and was left with no other alternative but to agree to Murdoch purchasing 25 per cent of shares in his Sydney TV station. Had Packer not agreed, he would have been in the same situation as WIN-4 before Murdoch's takeover. On this occasion, Murdoch had outsmarted Packer, but he took his revenge some time later when Murdoch was away visiting the US. Packer organised a reverse takeover of Channel 9, reducing Murdoch's share to less than 10 per cent.

Murdoch continued his purchase of newspapers and magazines with the full backing of the Commonwealth Bank. In July 1964 he launched Australia's first national newspaper, *The Australian*, in Canberra. It was a brave venture that ran up huge losses over many years and faced tremendous logistical problems. Canberra, as Murdoch later came to realise, was not ideal as the newspaper's headquarters. Firstly there was a problem concerning the *Canberra Times*, which Murdoch had tried to buy. When his offer was refused he bought a local paper instead and a site very close to the *Times*. Curiously, his father had also tried to buy the newspaper but without success. Murdoch reckoned that if he started the new national newspaper he would be able to get a large slice of advertising revenue from the *Times*, which he considered was rundown and not very interesting. Unfortunately, he scored an own goal through a certain exuberance of youth. He met the owner of the *Times* at a Christmas party and when asked his intentions, effectively told the proprietor that he would drive him out of business. His injudicious remark prompted an earlier than intended takeover of the *Canberra Times* by Fairfax, which had a prior agreement, and in May 1964 it announced that the *Times* would go national. Henderson then relaunched the newspaper as an upmarket broadsheet against which Murdoch would be hard pushed to compete at a local level. It also forced Murdoch into launching *The Australian* two years earlier than he had intended.

Another problem with Canberra was its geographical position. Winter conditions would often delay flights or make take-off virtually impossible after midnight. For a national morning newspaper it was essential to fly material to interstate printing presses from where local distribution would take place. Adrian Deamer, appointed editor in 1966, described the paper's early years: 'It was exciting and entertaining. Real frontier newspaper stuff right out of an old B movie – with Murdoch in the early days, standing on the tarmac in his pyjamas egging the pilots on, convincing them and the DCA officials that the fog was really only a light mist. But it was not the most reliable way to produce a newspaper and reliability, however dull it sounds, is the first requirement of a newspaper.'

Deamer, a serious-minded journalist respected by Murdoch, was later sacked over a divergence of their views. He said in a lecture after his sacking in 1972, 'The gist of his [Murdoch's] complaint, wherever it came from, was that *The Australian* had become too intellectual and too political. It was anti-Australian, it preferred black people to white people, it wanted to flood the country with Asians. He complained it took up every "bleeding heart" cause that was fashionable among the long-haired left. It was not interested in the development and progress of Australia, it was a knocking paper and it stood for everything he opposed and opposed everything he stood for.'

Murdoch later countered that he was not against bleeding heart causes but that the paper was concentrating too much on those matters. 'Deamer would listen to every little gripe, however insignificant,' he said. 'It just wasn't my idea of what Australia's only national paper should be.'

But Deamer maintained that Murdoch's interest at the time was not in Australia but rather with the *Sun*, *News of the World* and London Weekend Television in England. He accused Murdoch of being 'an absentee landlord visiting Australia for short periods three or four times a year and making snap decisions while he is here, often based on incorrect, incomplete or misleading data.' That assessment was not entirely correct because Murdoch's interest in Australia and its political future had in no way diminished as would be seen with subsequent elections and further acquisitions in

Australia. He would go on to get into pay TV and mount a takeover of the Melbourne Herald group – of which his father had been a key executive.

Murdoch's launch of *The Australian* gave him far greater influence with federal and state governments than his local state newspapers could ever provide. He now controlled a serious national newspaper read by politicians and decision-makers in every state of Australia. On a personal level, his ownership of a broadsheet also pleased his mother, who had been unimpressed with his stable of popular newspapers, although he denied that the launch had anything to do with seeking respectability from Dame Elisabeth. But creating *The Australian* was something that might have been high on his father's wish list. Most importantly, the newspaper was well received by a wide spectrum of Australian society and won over a large number of professional readers and students who had in the past shown little appetite for Murdoch's popular newspapers and their obsession with sensational headlines highlighting trivial issues. But however large his Australian interests had become, Murdoch felt the need for further expansion. He had begun making tentative inquiries about buying a Fleet Street newspaper, even though at that stage News Limited would not have sufficient funds to buy one.

4

'AS BRITISH
AS ROAST BEEF
AND YORKSHIRE
PUDDING'

Murdoch's once in a lifetime opportunity to buy Britain's largest-selling newspaper at a knockdown price came unexpectedly in the winter of 1968. He was 37 years old and still referred to in his home country as the 'boy publisher'.

His London editor, Peter Gladwyn, heard rumours that Robert Maxwell, the Slovakian-born publisher, war hero and larger-than-life socialist MP, had put in a bid for the six million-selling *News of the World*. Maxwell's most powerful personal asset was that he had won the military cross fighting Germans in the Second World War. His other attributes were less savoury. He had inexplicably come by lots of previously unpublished scientific papers in post-war occupied Germany and had been making vast profits from selling them at inflated prices to universities around the world. He had also profited handsomely when one of his companies went bust, owing substantial funds that were never repaid and, finally, he was a foreigner (born Jan Ludwig Hoch) and a Labour MP which aroused considerable anxiety among established conservative British families.

The Carr family were particularly disturbed. Sir William Carr had been chairman of the News of the World Group since 1952. The firm's subsidiaries included a book publisher, print works and regional newspapers. Sir William's father had been editor of the NoW for 50 years and the Carr family owned 27 per cent of its voting shares. A cousin, professor Derek Jackson, who lived in Paris, owned 25 per cent of the shares and had asked his bankers to find a buyer. Maxwell jumped in and was promised Jackson's 25 per cent holding. He then raised the stakes by offering to increase his offer with shares in Pergamon Press, his print and publishing firm, bumping up his offer to around £30 million.

On paper, this was a huge sum that Murdoch would be unable to match. Enter Lord Catto, a director of Morgan Grenfell investment bank and its associate Australian United Corporation. Acting on Murdoch's behalf, Catto had already been buying shares in IPC, the company that owned London's Daily Mirror. Now Catto could see a better opportunity for Murdoch to acquire an interest in a major British publication. Meanwhile, an ailing Sir William Carr, horrified at the prospect of a Maxwell takeover, desperately needed an ally to join forces against the former Czech. Catto proposed that Murdoch, whose family was known to the Carrs, should be that ally. Murdoch's friend and advertising supremo, Graham King, was the first to hear about the plan.

Exchanging views on Australian radio, King said, 'There was nobody about on Saturday morning except I bumped into

Rupert wandering along the corridor and he said, "Hey, come here." So we went into the board room and he said, "I think we're going to buy a newspaper in England," and, of course, when he said the *News of the World*, I nearly fell on the floor. You're talking about the biggest-selling newspaper in the world – it was then selling over six million copies a Sunday – unassailable, corporately, safe in the hands of a family. What was he talking about?

'They'd had a bid in from Robert Maxwell, at the time, which they didn't like and didn't want and rejected. But the pressure was to find some kind of white knight to come and rescue the *News of the World* from the hands of the evil Robert Maxwell.'

On 15 October 1968, the Press Association announced Maxwell's proposed takeover. Murdoch and his financial adviser Mervyn Rich immediately began crunching figures to see how much they could offer. Maxwell increased his offer and Hambros panicked into calling Murdoch to fly to London without delay before it was too late.

Murdoch arrived five days later. One of his associates commented, 'Murdoch flew to London to meet at this restaurant with members of the Carr family. With the charm he can turn on and off like a light switch, he seduced them, telling the family, "I'll help you beat Robert Maxwell. We'll run the company together. Sir William can stay on as chairman. All I want is 40 per cent of the stock and the job of managing director."

The *News of the World* published a front-page editorial written by former editor Stafford Somerfield and Sir William berating Maxwell and declaring that the *News of the World* was 'as British as roast beef and Yorkshire pudding' and should not fall into the hands of a foreigner like Maxwell. Sir William, after some misgivings, accepted Murdoch's involvement, never thinking that he would himself be ousted by the young Australian who boldly declared that if he didn't have control of the company he would leave it to Maxwell. It was a daring move, considering Murdoch depended on Carr's input. But Carr was unwell and he would do anything to stop Maxwell. The price he would pay would be very high indeed. Murdoch was promised shares in exchange for some minor News Limited titles like the *Melbourne Truth*, a scandal-mongering weekly whose small circulation depended on sex, scandal, sensational headlines and the odd exposé. In its heyday it had broken many major stories but in the late 1960s its commercial value was negligible by comparison to the fish Murdoch was trying to hook.

With no other assistance coming to the Carr family, Murdoch was convinced he would win the battle and flew back to Australia for a few weeks to plan his next move in the takeover and to visit his bankers. Nobody in the UK knew anything about Murdoch at the time but everyone was familiar with the *News of the World*. As soon as it became apparent that a young Australian millionaire was interested in the title, Rupert and his family attracted wide interest in the national press and on television. Murdoch returned to London in December and photographers must have been alerted to his arrival because he was photographed at the airport with his attractive blonde wife Anna and daughter Elisabeth, then only a few months old. His timing was superb. Murdoch's arrival was just days before the shareholders meeting when the takeover would be put to the vote. Stafford Somerfield, *NoW*'s superb editor, who was to fall out with Murdoch, noted that the press baron didn't miss a trick. 'Everyone will fall for the baby.' It was an excellent stratagem, one employed by public figures to gain sympathy for their cause and one that Murdoch would use again in the future.

Maxwell lost the battle for *News of the World* on 2 January 1969 when the shareholders meeting to decide the issue was 'flooded' with *News of the World* employees 'lent' shares to attend and vote for Carr and Murdoch on the undertaking they would afterwards return the shares to the company. At the meeting, Maxwell denounced Murdoch as an upstart colonial boy while Murdoch spoke only briefly without attacking his opponent. Maxwell later accused Murdoch of being dishonest and resorting to 'any kind of knavery to get his own way' and claimed 'he broke every rule in the book'. From a commercial aspect it was a case of the pot calling the kettle black and coming from Maxwell it was entirely over the top. Nevertheless, he did accurately summarise Murdoch's coup when he said, 'Never has a bigger whale been caught by a smaller fish.'

Murdoch wasted no time in settling in as the new boss and ousting the old brigade. The *NoW* organisation had been run down and profits had suffered. Murdoch's financial input for the purchase was a pittance but it bought him a goldmine. And to give him credit, he put the operation on a strong footing, streamlined its operations and as a direct result made progress with a forward-thinking plan which led to an unprecedented series of takeovers, starting with the *Sun* and very soon extending to America. How ironic, then, that the newspaper that funded his global ambitions would much later be responsible for undermining their very foundations.

During the battle for the *NoW*, Maxwell and Murdoch each

did their best to berate the other. The top floor of the Cheshire Cheese pub in Wine Office Court, Fleet Street, opposite the newspaper, had an executive dining suite used almost exclusively by *NoW* personnel. During the battle for the paper, disillusioned Maxwell executives would be invited for long lunches to discuss their previous employer's business methods. Stories about Maxwell would then appear in the financial pages of various newspapers. Similar tactics were used against Murdoch, who was criticised for bringing his newspapers downmarket to increase sales.

By sheer coincidence I played a part in providing some of the ammunition used against Maxwell. During a gap year away from my legal studies, I hitchhiked to Sydney from Adelaide and got a temporary job marketing encyclopaedias. My immediate boss was Graham Pratt, a Sydney businessman and man-about-town who married 1960s American singing star Leslie Uggams. Five of us, including a Yorkshireman who liked sniffing bicycle seats and Mary, Graham's busty mistress, were bundled into his Ford Falcon estate and driven 1,500 miles to outback towns in northern Queensland and New South Wales. There our victims were conned into buying encyclopaedias, having been told they were specially selected for this dubious honour. Fresh out of university at the time, I had also been conned – initially. I had answered an advert in Sydney to market Funk and Wagnall's encyclopaedia. Many of the prospective buyers could hardly read but believed in education for their children and were overwhelmed to be chosen for a 'free' set of F&W's. The catch (or the con) was they had to pay for future yearbooks which more than covered the free encyclopaedia. The Mr Big behind this scheme was Robert

Maxwell through his company Pergamon Press and associate International Learning Systems Corporation.

My story exposing Maxwell was printed in the Melbourne *Truth* and the Sydney *Mirror* in November and December 1968: 'WE USED LIES, FALSE PRETENCES... I WAS ASHAMED SAYS BOOK SALESMAN'. Maxwell reacted quickly. He sued me and News Limited, demanding £1 million in damages. It was not my only experience of being faced with substantial costs. Eleven years later, I would be sued for $250 million by another conman known to Rupert Murdoch, only this time it would be Rupert's friend, but more of that in a later chapter.

Issuing a writ for libel was Maxwell's preferred method of stifling criticism, but the damage had already been done. Interestingly, exactly 16 years later, I sat in Maxwell's office at the *Daily Mirror* headquarters in Holborn Circus, London, to receive the publisher's congratulations on having led, together with John Merrit, a friend and colleague, an investigation into the 'scourge of heroin' in Britain. Fortunately, Maxwell did not remember he had sued me all those years earlier.

I came to realise how naive and innocent I had been in relation to the world of publishing. By exposing the Maxwell selling scam, I thought their business would collapse and the two owners would never again show their faces in public. How wrong I was. The other half of the company later set up a new publishing enterprise under a different name. His partner in this enterprise was Rupert Murdoch's News Limited and the new company developed a profitable line producing upmarket books that were heavily promoted in *The Australian*. They became a star performer within the News Group and highly praised by the chairman!

The battle between Maxwell and Murdoch was not entirely

over. Murdoch was in the market to buy a daily to keep the presses rolling on a seven-day basis at Bouverie Street. Having examined alternatives, he targeted the *Sun*, then owned by IPC, who also owned the *Daily Mirror*. Their chairman was Hugh Cudlipp, who was well acquainted with the Murdoch family. The *Sun* was a left-wing newspaper previously published as the *Daily Herald* and was 50 per cent owned by unions in the form of the Trades Union Congress, the TUC. Whereas it had previously enjoyed record sales of over 1.5 million it was now selling below a million and falling further. Cudlipp's ambition to go upmarket, with a blue collar readership, as he had tried to do with the *Mirror*, did not work. IPC wanted to close the paper or to sell it. Maxwell expressed an interest in taking it off their hands but he wanted to lay off a large part of the workforce. The union would not hear of it and Murdoch then offered to take it on the same terms as had been offered to Maxwell but undertook not to make the wholesale cuts proposed by Maxwell. The unions trusted Murdoch more than they did Maxwell the socialist MP.

Murdoch's *Sun* was launched in tabloid format as a daily version of the *NoW* on 17 November 1969. IPC had made an expensive commercial error in selling the *Sun* to Murdoch. Cudlipp should have known better than most that the budding Australian newspaper mogul would pull out all the stops to compete. He had known the Murdoch family for some years and had been aware of News Limited's fast growth. However, there was speculation at the time that Murdoch had bitten off more than he could chew as it was only 11 months since he had acquired the *NoW*.

Graham King later commented, 'They sold it to Murdoch in

the belief that it would wreck him, that it would lose him an awful lot of money. The best brains, the best newspaper brains in Fleet Street, had not made a success of it. They couldn't see why an Australian who knew nothing about Fleet Street could make it a success.'

Cudlipp's bitter comment on the *Sun* overtaking the *Mirror*'s readership was that Murdoch was catering to a readership of 'the mentally underprivileged'.

Once again King stepped in to promote the tabloid. 'We used television a lot. Page by page, with goody after goody after goody. Giveaways, competitions, special features, supplements. You name it, we threw it at them. The key to the success of the *Sun* was the realisation that a newspaper isn't or need not be all about news... In our attempt to be continuously outrageous, we were always in hot water with the regulatory body. And we had "pussy week", for example, which caused them a lot of hand-wringing but, in the end, it genuinely was about cats and so that had to be allowed.'

Murdoch's wife Anna was invited to launch the paper and the family set up home at Coopersale, a mansion with farmland in Epping, north-east of London. For a time Murdoch commuted by helicopter to central London, but it was just as fast to drive. And once the *Sun* was established he took great pleasure in commuting by train just to watch his fellow passengers reading his newspaper.

While the *NoW* was a total success in sales, Murdoch was not happy with its independently minded editor, Stafford Somerfield, who insisted who insisted on doing things his way. That was anathema to Murdoch. He would have liked to sack him immediately but there was a problem. Somerfield had been astute enough to negotiate a long-term contract before the takeover that Sir William had been happy to grant him. It would cost the new boss many thousands to pay him off. Murdoch thought he had found an answer to his problem after meeting Lord Goodman, considered one of the most influential lawyers in London. Goodman was a friend and adviser to governments and newspaper publishers. Although he'd not discussed his Somerfield problem with Goodman, Murdoch was in bouncy mood following a lunchtime session with the lawyer. He returned to Bouverie Street and told Somerfield, 'I've just had lunch with Lord Goodman and he's someone who could break that contract of yours.'

Somerfield replied: 'I don't think so, Rupert. Lord Goodman prepared my contract!'

One of the first major serialisations in the *NoW* after Murdoch's takeover was an updated version of the Christine Keeler story published in the paper some years earlier. She was paid another small fortune – £21,000 – because Somerfield was convinced it would increase circulation. He was right. The paper put on an extra 150,000. Keeler's affair with the secretary of state for war John Profumo and a Russian naval attaché had nearly brought down Harold Macmillan's Conservative government in 1962. The Press Council had criticised the newspaper for paying Keeler the first time round and now condemned the newspaper for a second time. Soon after publication, Murdoch inadvisedly agreed to be interviewed by David Frost on London Weekend Television (LWT) to discuss the controversial publication. It was a disaster for Murdoch. He was accused of sensationalising an old story purely for sexual titillation and came off second-best after a ferocious grilling by Frost. Murdoch was furious. He felt conned and that the whole interview was set up to make him look bad. Some years later, however, he invested heavily in LWT but was not permitted to take control of the TV station. The widespread criticism over sensationalism and the *NoW* also resulted in the magazine *Private Eye* labelling Rupert Murdoch the 'Dirty Digger'.

When Somerfield was eventually replaced as editor at the *NoW* it was by Cyril 'Tiny' Lear, the paper's deputy editor and a former subeditor at the *Daily Telegraph*. Tiny had been a colonel in the British army and was tall and authoritative, if lacking in the colour and flourish of the previous editor. But by January 1970, Murdoch was more interested in someone who would be a safe pair of hands and do exactly as he was told.

Murdoch put most of his efforts into the *Sun*. The *NoW* had a tried and tested formula: vicars, knickers, sex, buying up those involved in human interest stories and a good sports section. He kept a watch on *NoW*'s content but by 1970 he had six million sales and success was assured. The *Sun*, on the other hand, was his special purchase. This was a newspaper he would mould into a bestseller and make the highest circulation daily in Britain. There was some stiff competition around at that time. Apart from the *Mirror*, the *Daily Express* was still selling well and getting scoops as was Harmsworth's *Daily Mail*. It was a time when proprietors were not afraid of investing in their product to keep them ahead.

Murdoch chose as the *Sun*'s editor a talented northerner from a humble background. Yorkshireman Larry Lamb had been a rising star at the *Daily Mirror*. His deputy, Bernard Shrimsley, had also been in the running for the job and had worked for the *Liverpool Echo* as well as the Mirror Group. Both Shrimsley and Lamb were intensely interested in politics and were hard task masters. Lamb was later made editorial director of both the *Sun* and the *NoW* and Shrimsley was to edit both newspapers at different times.

Lamb enjoyed the lifestyle his position afforded him. He drove the company Mercedes sports bearing the number plate SUN 1 and, shed his left-wing leanings, became a fan of Margaret Thatcher and accepted a knighthood from her in 1980. (Murdoch himself was against the honours system and had a general aversion to class separation despite the status of his parents, each of whom had been honoured by the monarchy.) An all-round journalist and editor, Lamb was responsible for publishing Page 3 pin-ups in the *Sun* and for creating a winning team that eventually beat the *Mirror* in a hard-fought circulation battle. He was understandably extremely upset when Murdoch eventually sacked him and shared a bottle of champagne with me at El Vino's wine bar in Fleet Street, bad-mouthing his former boss.

Bernard Shrimsley was a master technician and perfectionist who would often change his mind about layout and headlines. The downside was when editions ran late – Murdoch would have preferred more sales to a perfect product. Neither Lamb nor Shrimsley were happy with proprietor interference but put up with it, knowing they were mainly in the driving seat, though they also knew there were few untouchables with Murdoch. But Shrimsley and Lamb were class acts. Both men were dedicated and ambitious and head and shoulders above some of Murdoch's later appointments.

Over at *NoW*, Tiny Lear might have seemed a less likely candidate for editor, but he was a thorough professional. On an assignment to Holland, my task had been to visit Jimmy Humphreys, a London pornographer arrested in Amsterdam.

It was winter and I was rather shaken up when the plane made a bad landing on the icy runway at the Hague airport. Humphreys' stripper wife Rusty and their lawyer accompanied me and urged me to have drinks with them in the evening. The following morning I woke in a somewhat parlous state on top of my bed, fully dressed and still wearing my overcoat from the night before. However, I made it to the prison and was led to Humphreys' cell suffering from a bad hangover. The heat inside the prison made me feel ill. Embarrassingly, I was sick as a dog in the passageway of the prison but returned to interview Humphreys about his diary which revealed dates on which he had gone on holidays with a bent Scotland Yard commander, Kenneth Drury.

In my rush that morning, I had forgotten to bring my notebook and a curious Humphreys asked why I was not taking notes. I explained that I had an excellent memory and did not want notes snatched by warders. He accepted my explanation and I returned to London on Saturday morning. My first call was from the editor, sounding like a colonel reprimanding his batman. 'Where are you, Lisners? You're supposed to have come in with the copy.' I wrote up the few salient facts I remembered and caught a taxi into the office.

Lear was waiting for me with the newspaper's lawyer, John Hinchcliffe, who had begun his career as a journalist. Both read the copy and Hinchcliffe commented rather grandly, 'That doesn't say very much!'

'It doesn't matter,' Tiny responded matter-of-factly. 'It looks good.'

The headline splash looked even better. It read in bold capitals, WE SEE HUMPHREYS' DIARIES, and recapped on the number of police being investigated for corruption and consorting with known criminals. The story was hated by the Yard and loved by the public. Lear knew how to project a factually correct story that lacked detail into a winning package.

The most talented executive during Lear's three-year editorship was assistant editor Michael Gabbert. He had been acclaimed as a *Sunday People* journalist for exposing league footballers fixing games. Gabbert could write a front-page splash while discussing other editorial matters. He was an absolute whizzkid, albeit with personality flaws which prevented him from becoming *NoW* editor. He had been hired by Somerfield, which immediately lessened his chances of further promotion with Murdoch, though some years on he was briefly editor of the *Star*.

Gabbert was responsible for organising major series and features and wrote promotional blurbs. But among his failings was his habit of insulting the editor, deputy editor and news editors if they were unable to grasp some of his more elaborate plans or concepts. Not that he was a loose cannon. Far from it, but rather that he thought a lot of himself and failed to endear himself to those less talented. Gabbert's mind was always thinking up schemes or planning story coups or mischief against his staff when bored. At one point he sent a reporter on an impossible mission overseas and told him to remain there until he got a story. The reason, he confided, was that he fancied the reporter's wife and wooed her whenever the reporter was away.

Gabbert organised a small but interesting team of reporters in the features department on the second floor of Bouverie Street. The two main players were Trevor Kempson and Scotsman Bill Rankine. Kempson was the chief investigative reporter and one of the hardest nuts in Fleet Street, but at the same time he was also easily conned. He was an old-style Sunday reporter: immaculately turned out, flash with expenses money (one could live on them at the time) and highly excitable. He had been a military policeman in the army and believed in keeping his word – even to a crook who would take advantage of the fact. Over long lunches at the Cheshire Cheese pub in Fleet Street, where we were always given the directors' dining room, Gabbert would relate tales of how Kempson was taken in by a 'weeping crucifix' which fellow reporters would expose. The owner of the crucifix regularly rang Trevor asking to be exposed again as it was good for business.

Bill Rankine, who became and remains one of my best friends, was hired by Sir William Carr and had been a Fulbright scholar teaching history at American universities before joining. Bill's father had been a sports editor in Glasgow and Bill was hired to write editorials, features and deputise for Gabbert. He also had to run the Hilton bureau, a helpline for readers. I always thought Bill would have been better suited to the *Guardian* or *Observer* but he was a great asset to the paper and scrupulously honest. When I first began working with the features team I'd ask Bill to taste my copy. Whenever he'd say, 'Och nae, John, you'll never get this published,' I knew I was on a winner.

I was one of a number of freelance journalists invited to work with the features team. Among these freelances were people I considered unsavoury but useful in bringing in information worth investigating. A room had been set aside for them that came to be known as the Animals Room. Newspapers have always attracted people from a wide spectrum of backgrounds and while news was a necessary part of the paper, it was mainly features led, even though the features department was much smaller than the news department.

At the *NoW*, the newsroom was always treated as a separate entity and there was a great rivalry between the features and news staff that continued throughout the paper's history. Under Lear, Gabbert was given authority to commit the newspaper to purchasing or pursuing major stories. He rarely told the editor exactly what he was doing until the story was written, although he had to give some idea of the projects he was planning. Otherwise, his department was autonomous, which gave us all great freedom of action.

Gabbert and Rankine made a good team in that they had the background and foresight to discuss the danger points of any project that was undertaken. If a drug dealer was to be exposed and a reporter could not get out of purchasing a sample, great precautions had to be taken to avoid prosecution for a criminal offence. Affidavits would be sworn in advance, detailing who we were investigating, the basis on which the investigation was undertaken and what actions would be taken. We also sought legal advice and lined up experts to analyse any substances purchased. We also had to be sure that the story could be justified as responsible and for the benefit of the public and that we had not just set out on a fishing expedition but were acting on a proper tip-off.

Many years later I found that few such precautions were taken any longer by the newspaper and that it was left to the individual journalist as to his or her modus operandi. That resulted in the removal of an important safety net and exposed reporters and the newspaper to unnecessary risks. Fleet Street news editors were not always caring souls when it came to fellow journalists. A news reporter was often treated like a foot soldier on the frontline: expendable and easily replaceable.

While 1969 and 1970 were golden years for Murdoch, they were also two of the most tragic years for a close family friend and deputy chairman of the *NoW*. Alick McKay, the son of an Adelaide sea captain who had worked for Sir Keith Murdoch and was then working for IPC in London, met Murdoch by chance when he was negotiating the purchase of the *NoW*. The following year Murdoch invited Alick to be a director of the *News of the World* organisation. Alick had been a popular and admired figure in both England and Australia and Kerry Packer had also been a close friend. McKay who was 60 at the time, lived happily with his wife Muriel in Wimbledon and was pleased with his appointment. It was a bit like rejoining an old family for him, only now he was with Sir Keith's son Rupert and his family. But the connection was to prove fatal for the McKay family.

By this time Rupert Murdoch had become a public figure. He was regularly featured in newspaper articles and on TV programmes, particularly with the controversy surrounding the re-run of the Christine Keeler story. He and Anna were a glamorous couple: young, rich, and powerful, living in luxury in Epping and driving a Rolls-Royce.

To the north of Epping, in Hertfordshire, aspiring commuters sought smallholdings and farmhouses in the pretty countryside. Among them was Arthur Hosein, a tailor from Trinidad, and his German-born wife Else. They were a hard-working couple who had purchased a farm in a village called Stocking Pelham. Hosein had a workshop at the farmhouse making suits for London outlets. It was a seven-day job but he was his own boss and making good money. His wife would help him with tailoring as well as looking after the farm animals.

Hosein was particularly impressed by the news of Rupert Murdoch's purchase of London newspapers. Else, whose exclusive story I later secured, recalled their conversation: 'Each night, no matter how hard he had been working, he watched the late news. We sat there watching Mr Murdoch and Arthur would turn to me and say, "You know, darling, there must be easier ways of making money than this."

'I said, "What are you talking about? You sit at your machine and look out on the beautiful countryside. You are your own governor."' Referring to recent kidnappings, her husband commented that Murdoch would be worth a lot of money if he was held captive. Else thought nothing about the conversation and said her husband became a real fan of Murdoch, but 'Arthur said that with all this publicity, Murdoch ought to be more careful. "You can never tell what might happen to him."'

Hosein was not satisfied with being an ordinary tailor. He wanted respect and wealth. He'd had a few run-ins with people who considered he was 'not good enough' and he called them white racists. Money would bring him respect and power, so he thought that he would kidnap Anna Murdoch and demand a £1 million ransom. Then he could live the life of a country gentleman. He would not ask his wife to help because she would refuse. She was ten years older than him and believed in working hard for what they had.

The accomplice Arthur set on was his younger brother from Trinidad, who already had convictions for violence. Nizamodeen came to stay with them in September 1969, his arrival sudden and unannounced to Else. In early December, Arthur suggested Else take their children to her native Germany and stay with relatives over Christmas and into the new year. To her disappointment, Arthur would remain in the UK and make sure Nizamodeen fed the animals and help him fulfil orders. In fact Nizamodeen had already gone to London to obtain details of Murdoch's Rolls-Royce. This fact was later discovered by chance when Murdoch applied to change the car's number plate, following all the publicity he had been given on television.

Before Else left for Germany on 13 December, Arthur's pattern of behaviour changed. He was secretive and went to London more often than usual, taking Nizamodeen with him rather than leaving him to do chores around the farm. But there was a flaw in their plan. Hosein had no idea that Murdoch was not going to be in London that Christmas. He had been asked to return to Australia for meetings and had offered to lend his Rolls to Alick McKay while he was away.

With Else out of the way, the Hosein brothers set about their plan. They followed Murdoch's car to Wimbledon, believing it was where Rupert and Anna lived. On 29 December, they returned to the house late in the afternoon, assuming Anna Murdoch was home alone. Checking that the Rolls had not returned, they smashed their way into the house and after a violent confrontation in which Mrs McKay fought for her life, they overpowered and gagged her. Bundled into Hosein's car, she was driven to the farm.

Before the kidnapping the two men had purchased a shotgun from a local builder and Nizamodeen had sawn off both barrels. From Else Hosein's account – never before published – it would appear that Mrs McKay was held prisoner in a spare bedroom at the farm. By Else's reckoning, at some time between the night of 29 December 1969 and 2 January 1970, Mrs McKay was callously murdered. Either she was strangled by Nizamodeen or shot with the sawn-off shotgun and her body disposed of. Police believe she was fed to pigs Hosein kept on the farm.

When the Hosein brothers discovered they had kidnapped the wrong person, they continued with their ransom demands. But instead of negotiating with Rupert Murdoch, they cruelly made their demands to Mr McKay's family. Nizamodeen pretended on the telephone that they were part of a gang. The police recorded the following chilling exchange between Nizamodeen (calling himself M3) and Ian McKay, Muriel's son:

M3: 'I'm asking you for the last time, I'm asking you and that's if you intend to co-operate, yes or no?'

Ian: 'Of course we intend to co-operate. We want proof first, we want proof first, we want proof first, we want proof first, we want proof first.'

M3:'Well, look, you are not going to get...'

Ian: 'Because you haven't got it. You've got a corpse, you've got a corpse, you've got a corpse, you've got a corpse.'

M3: 'We've got her.'

Ian: 'You've got a dead person, you haven't got her at all. You know she's not alive so you are just trying to trick us, you're trying to trick us, you're trying to trick us.'

Else Hosein returned from Germany on 3 January and was annoyed at the shambolic state of her home. 'Upstairs curtains in our bedroom had been ripped off railings. It looked as if there had been a fight. I tried to speak to Arthur about it but he went berserk. Something had gone on here.' Was it a party? Had strangers stayed while she was away? Her sister-in-law Haffiza sometimes used the spare room and her bed had been slept in – but not by her. To her disgust Else found a flimsy, blue-green woman's vest in the bed.

Haffiza said, 'See, sis, I told you somebody's been sleeping in my bed.'

Else studied the vest. There was no brand name, nothing to show who it belonged to and it was far too big to belong to her daughter Fareeda. She took it to the sitting room and, angrily, tossed it onto the log fire and watched it burst into flames. At that time she did not realise she had burnt probably the most damaging piece of evidence against the Hosein brothers.

Within days of Else's return, Hosein's behaviour became increasingly erratic. It began to deteriorate after his car was stopped by police while collecting her from Liverpool Street station. He was furious and called his solicitor to demand why police were searching his car. Later, he attacked Else when she challenged him about women present at the farm during her absence.

When Arthur ordered her to leave the property with the children 'or something will happen to you all', Nizamodeen became a bundle of nerves. He begged Else not to go. He held up his hands. They were shaking and he said, 'You see these hands, sis? They can kill. Please, for goodness sake don't leave me here. These hands are able to kill.'

Else later said, 'The way the boy was acting that night... he was guilty of something terrible. Without a shadow of doubt it was Nizamodeen who killed Mrs McKay. Arthur could be violent but he could not kill. He could not stand the sight of blood.'

Things returned to normal for a while but the two men would go out together at odd times and stay away for hours. At home they would whisper to one another and kept close company. Else found strange paper flowers in the car. She would later learn that similar objects, made by Nizamodeen's girlfriend, had been left at prearranged roadside locations to indicate ransom drops.

The brothers were arrested on 7 February. Some 20 policemen descended on their farm to search for Muriel McKay. Else was interrogated over a three-day period until they were satisfied of her innocence. At last all the unusual events that Else had witnessed slowly began to make sense and the remaining questions in her mind would be answered at the trial that October. Why had Arthur pushed her to go to Germany alone with the children? Normally, he was insanely jealous of her going anywhere without him. Why had he suddenly bought the shotgun? He paid £150 in cash for it and did not have a licence. What was Nizamodeen trying to tell her when he said, 'These hands can kill'?

On 6 October, the brothers were found guilty of murder, kidnapping and blackmail and were given life sentences. The judge described their actions as cold-blooded and abominable. Nizamodeen returned to Trinidad after serving 20 years but Arthur Hosein died in prison. Following the conviction, a policeman told Mrs Hosein that evidence of the clothing could have shortened the case by many weeks. The vest she had burnt was the same colour as the suit Mrs McKay was wearing at the time of her disappearance.

Reviewing the case, Scotland Yard was furious at press leaks, which they considered had hampered their investigation. While the kidnappers demanded money from the McKay family, police tipsters were selling information to newspapers, which printed sensitive information about the case at crucial periods. Even the *Sun*, which Murdoch had only recently purchased, printed sensitive information that Scotland Yard considered unwise. In fact, there were remarkable similarities between the behaviour of the press and police then as would be heard by the Leveson inquiry 42 years later. Even more unbelievable was the fact that the kidnappers themselves had called the *NoW* to complain they could not get through on the telephone to Alick McKay!

On 11 October, the *Sunday Times* asked, DID PUBLICITY HELP TO KILL MRS MCKAY? and suggested that leaks to the press were prejudicial to the case. The *Times* might well have asked the question in a more straightforward manner: did newspaper reports help kill Mrs McKay? Some senior officers were convinced the answer was yes.

The detective in charge of the McKay kidnapping and murder, Detective Chief Superintendent Bill Smith, did not want a letter written by Mrs McKay about the kidnapper's demands to be released to the press. When told it was being printed in the *Sun* he told the McKay family how dismayed he was. It was also discovered that a leak to the press by a police source outside London had spoiled an opportunity to catch the kidnappers at a suggested rendezvous spot. Another newspaper report about police tactics further jeopardised later arrangements to trap the kidnappers, according to senior police officers. The Yard's Commander Guiver said one of the lessons to have been learned was that, in future, all publicity must be kept to an absolute minimum in a kidnapping case.

A further complication arose when Dutch clairvoyant Gerard Croiset made a remarkable prediction that two black men in an old farmhouse were involved and a woman was concerned but not involved directly. He also thought Mrs McKay was already dead and he correctly indicated the area she may have been taken as via Epping and close to Stocking Pelham. Releasing that information resulted in hundreds of crank calls and blocked telephone lines which seriously hampered the search.

After the trial, Mr McKay wrote to the brothers in prison and offered a reward for details of what had happened to the body of his wife. He wanted to give her a decent burial but received no answer. I went with Mrs Hosein to visit Nizamodeen at Winson Green prison in Birmingham. Else wanted him to reveal what had happened to the body so she could pass on information to the McKay family. Hosein spoke to her about the abduction. He said that in the early part of the evening of 29 December, he and Arthur went to the Victoria Sporting club in London and Arthur and got quite drunk.

'Yes, sis,' he admitted, 'we had her.' Else asked her brother-in-law if he had shot Mrs McKay. 'No, sis.' How did she die? Nizamodeen was silent for a moment, then he looked at Else and trembling with emotion, said, 'Do you remember that night you were going to leave us? Do you remember that night, sis?' But he would not reveal what the brothers had done with Mrs McKay's body. He said the prison governor had advised him not to do so for his own sake. Mrs McKay's body was never found.

Else Hosein received many racist letters through the post following Hosein's conviction. Attitudes have changed in that regard since then, yet the behaviour of police and press remains the same. The similarities between the Millie Dowler case and the antics of some reporters in the McKay case bore witness to that.

above: James Murdoch cartoon, captioned 'Letter? What letter?': in a letter of 2 March, 2007, former royal correspondent Clive Goodman wrote to the *News of the World* human resources director alleging 'other members of staff were carrying out the same illegal procedures' and he could not be dismissed for alleged gross misconduct.

© *Dave Brown/The Independent 2011*

below: James and Rupert Murdoch before the Commons culture, media and sport select committee on 19 July 2011. 'The most humble day of my life,' said Rupert Murdoch.

© *PA Photos*

Above: Murdoch with third wife Wendi.

© *PA Photos*

Right: Sir William Carr and Murdoch shake hands in early 1969 as they shut Robert Maxwell out of a *News of the World* takeover.

© *PA Photos*

Above: *News of the World* reporter Rob Kellaway wielding a replica machine gun in the Wapping office which he was able to smuggle on board an aircraft to expose lack of airport security.

Right: Former *News of the World* and *Sun* showbiz reporter Sean Hoare who confessed to whistleblowing to the *New York Times*. He died in July 2011.

Above: Murdoch with Rebekah Brooks in London on 10 July 2011. Five days later she resigned as News International's chief.   © PA Pho

Below: Murdoch's former favourite editor Kelvin Mackenzie examining first copy of the *Sun* at Wapping after the move from Fleet Street.

© PA Arch

Author John Lisners
investigating gangsters
Soho.

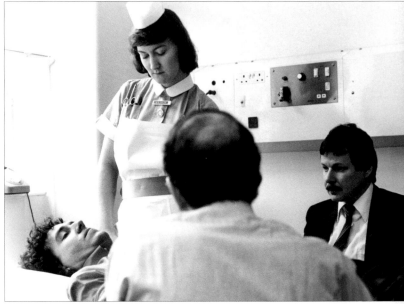

Above: John Lisners partying with Lord Bath and friends.

Below: John Lisners questions the future Labour cabinet minister Peter Hain who submitted himself to a truth drug test in an article for the newspaper.

Above: In Iran John Lisners investigated the child slavery phenomenon.

Left: John Lisners gets thrown in a TV advert for his wrestling fix investigation.

Above: Murdoch in 2005 with, behind, *News of the World* editor Andy Coulson and *Sun* editor Rebekah Brooks (then Wade). © PA Pho

Below: Australian prime minister, Liberal John Howard, with Rupert Murdoch at the US Chamber of Commerce in 2005. © PA Pho

Inset: Rupert's father, Sir Keith Murdoch. © PA Pho

5

FRONT PAGE

I found that the best way to get noticed by editors in Fleet Street was to bring in exclusive stories and negotiate a tidy sum – these were called 'buy-ups'. Sooner or later they would ask you to act on their behalf.

My first modest buy-up involved the ninth Duke of Newcastle's daughter, Lady Kathleen Pelham-Clinton-Hope, in November 1970. There had been an earl in her family since 1572 and combined with the fact that the former debutante had shamed the family name, her story would be snapped up by any of the popular newspapers. Kate thought little of her illustrious forbears: 'That lot? They were all freaky. I used to come across them in the history books,' she quipped.

Kate had been busted for drugs, which she said she had taken since the age of 14. After being kicked out of university in Perugia, Italy, she returned to London but soon appeared at the Old Bailey accused of taking part in an 11-day orgy of dishonesty with a labourer. A series of court appearances for minor drug offences followed. One of her hippy friends then advised her she might do better if she got married before her next court appearance. With that, she married a Tube railway guard named Eddie Reynolds. Her mother was terribly disappointed. 'Mummy said the least she would have expected was for me to marry a Coldstream guard, not one from the underground.' Interviewing Kate was great fun. She had a tremendous sense of humour and led me to many more interviews with eccentric bluebloods. She was totally co-operative, even to the extent of smoking a spliff with her hippy friends, which was published large in the NoW.

But beating NoW news reporters at their own game did not endear me to the tough Liverpudlian news editor Charlie Markus. His deputy Bob Warren was even less impressed. Both hated the features department and its boss Mike Gabbert.

Successive editors were keen to encourage the division between the news and features departments because it created competition among executives and resulted in a type of Chinese wall between the two. So much so that while on one sensitive investigation at the Cumberland hotel I saw someone who looked vaguely familiar. He was wearing a smart suit and drinking double whiskies. I went up to him and politely excused my approach and suggested we may have met one another. He turned to me with slightly glazed eyes and rasped: 'My name is Peter Earle. I'm a News of the World reporter, now fuck off!' I saw the funny side and said I worked for the same organ, at which he became terribly apologetic. He had worked in Fleet Street for many years, had excellent contacts and was in no mood to have his space invaded. Nevertheless, I thought it odd that he should reveal himself in this manner.

I was soon getting frequent bylines and front-page splashes. Whenever I was in the office, the features team would relocate to the Cheshire Cheese and consume vast amounts of wine over a three-course meal. The most vulnerable or short-fused member of the team (usually Trevor Kempson) would then become the object of ridicule or be goaded by Gabbert. In the evening, there would be more drinking at the City Golf club, next to St Bride's church. There Fleet Street's village atmosphere took hold and journalists from other newspapers would swap stories, exchange information or get blind drunk. Somehow, at a young age, one got away with an awful amount of drink while still being able to produce the goods. Journalists from other newspapers could be extremely helpful with tip-offs about stories their own newspaper refused to print. Murdoch's eventual push to Wapping – technology made such a move inevitable – sadly spelled the end of the village. In its prime Fleet Street was so full of wondrous characters and stories that all human life was to be found there without the need for chasing around the world.

On the evening of 29 July 1971, Gabbert called me into his office for a chat. 'I have a question for you,' he said. 'Can you parachute?' This needed some quick thinking. What did he have in mind? I knew that about that time Prince Charles had been involved in various naval air exercises, which included parachuting into the sea. I had no fear of water or heights and gave a positive response. I don't know if he believed me but he didn't question me. All he said was, 'Good. You're going to South America with a few army guys from Oxford. The plan is to parachute into the Amazon jungle and search for Conan Doyle's lost world.'

Gabbert was a master at keeping a poker face but it soon

dawned on me that he was serious. Further, I noticed that he was already sketching posters of prehistoric monsters on his pad and writing a blurb for promoting the story of our intrepid reporter about to enter the 'Gateway to hell' in search of this lost world.

Flying to South America was right up my street. I had always had a taste for adventure but the only thing that concerned me was that I had never parachuted, although I had no fear of the jump itself. Gabbert then dropped another bombshell – I would have to leave in two days. Fortunately, I had interviewed Stewart Brown, a former paratrooper, and I asked him for advice. We practised falling off his lounge suite and forming the star position, a necessary procedure when leaving an aircraft.

Trevor Kempson was sent to Netheravon airfield to borrow a static line chute, reserve chute and helmet for me, but told the sergeant major arranging this that a spare chute was not necessary. Trevor was the chief investigative reporter and a former military policeman so one could not expect everything. Colonel John Blashford Snell, explorer, ex-Sandhurst officer, army engineer, author and a great adventurer, asked me to meet him at Moss Bros in the Strand so he could outfit me. He'd left a top hat and tails off his list but otherwise everything that a gentleman should take with him before joining the natives had been purchased. It remained unused in my valise throughout this adventure. He also supplied me with a superb army dagger. The pterodactyls could do their worst.

On 31 July, recovering from a series of injections administered to prevent every disease known to mankind, I boarded my VC10 bound for Georgetown, Guyana, minus my spare chute. The newspaper was now a joint sponsor of a

Scientific Exploration Society research expedition partly made up of SAS soldiers and scientists. Other worthies funding the expedition included the Mount Everest Foundation, the Royal Society, and the Winston Churchill memorial fund. The plan was to parachute into one of the most politically sensitive areas of South America. Our object was to climb, research and explore Mount Roraima (9,094 feet) and its sister peak Mount Kukenam (8,500 feet) where the borders of Brazil, Venezuela and Guyana converge. My part was to tag along and report this great adventure to our readers. There was no forward planning. No rescue arrangements if we got stuck on mountains or drowned in rivers. No means of getting copy to the *NoW* from the deepest Amazon jungle. Nothing. The paper covered itself by taking out £100,000 insurance on my life. Burnham Forbes, the left-wing PM of Guyana, was convinced we were spies and Venezuela had already put the boot in by denying us permission to enter their territory. Trespassers would be shot. This was really going to be exciting.

On arrival in Guyana, I was about to hitchhike to Georgetown (a more dangerous activity than jumping into the jungle) when the high commissioner's Rolls-Royce drew up. Blashers had pull in high circles. Of course when I was later arrested, it seemed they no longer wanted to know me and Gabbert would be too busy having a long lunch at the Cheshire Cheese ribbing Kempson for having forgotten the spare chute. Expedition leader Adrian Warren, a zoologist, had interesting tasks ahead. One was to find a partner for a unique and possibly lonely and homesick male toad he'd found near our intended area a year or two earlier and had taken back to London.

Our second-in-command was Captain Roger Chapman, a scholar and brave soldier who in 1968 had dived into the white waters of the Blue Nile in Africa, risking crocodiles and savage currents to save another soldier's life. Roger won my eternal respect for giving me his spare chute, accepting a greater risk to his own life. Whether by design or incompetence, probably both, the British high commission had arranged a permit for me to enter the interior (mandatory) for only three days (insane). They knew we would parachute into the jungle and had been advised the expedition could take two or three months yet the maximum permit they could get for me was three days in the jungle. In fairness, I could see that I would have been excess baggage so perhaps it was by design, in which case I would congratulate them for appearing as inept as they did.

Nevertheless, I immediately organised a private aircraft to fly me to Pipilipai, a small Amerindian jungle outpost lying next to the Kako river 200 miles inland from Georgetown and 50 miles from Roraima. The rest of the party would join us, making their way in canoes up river. My pilot for the flight to Pipilipai was big George Grandsoult, a gentle giant who'd been a 'pork knocker' (dived for diamonds in jungle waterholes) and survived a light aircraft crash into the side of a mountain. George was game to land his Islander aircraft where no other pilot would dare. His clients had included government ministers, pork knockers and soon enough, prisoners.

The jungle at Pipilipai did not disappoint. It was anaconda country. The river was infested with alligators, snakes and venomous turtles. At night a thousand eyes, reflected by the light of a torch, watched us. I had use of an uncomfortable hammock and a vampire bat descended on my big toe, preparing for a Duchess of York-style feast. Within a day we had adopted a pet banana bird called Fred. On the second day, Monday, we were notified that the Venezuelans had refused permission for us to parachute into their territory, which would have been the preferred drop. That evening, an American missionary came to dinner to tell all about the local Halleluha religion and how local polygamous tribes slept with wives and daughters and when there was a shortage of women, brothers would share wives. With my three-day permit running out I called George to collect me and take me back to the capital.

I spent all Wednesday trying to get the permit extended and tried to arrange a helicopter to take us to the summit. That night we stayed at the army officer quarters at the airport waiting for word of my permit. My last gambit was to call the prime minister's press secretary, Frank Pilgrim, who had worked as a journalist in Britain and was a top civil servant. He promised to talk to the minister for home affairs, Oscar Clarke, but was unable to make contact. He said he would try again the next morning before we were due to leave for Kamarang. He told me to proceed to Kamarang and said he would see the minister in the meantime. The arrangement was that I was to proceed unless I heard to the contrary. I did not hear back and I proceeded.

The jump from an Islander at 2,000 feet was breathtaking. I had forgotten most of what I had learned in the paratrooper's sitting room and landed on my feet inches from a tree trunk and a few feet from a river. The only problem was not knowing how to access the toggles from the straps, but I discovered just in time before hitting the ground. Floating down from the sky alongside the vertical cliffs of Roraima with its waterfalls and lush vegetation and giant creepers hundreds of feet long was possibly the most enthralling few moments of my life.

The next day I was told there had been a radio message that I was to be arrested for going into the jungle without a permit. My fellow travellers watched as a narrow, long boat with an outboard motor chugged down the Kako river towards us in Makurupai, carrying a policeman toting a sub-machine gun. All fingers pointed to me and the policeman had no doubt who he was arresting. 'Mr Lisners. I am taking you to Kamarang.'

My jungle prison was a small, two-storey wooden police station with an upstairs cell. Wide-eyed children watched as I was marched to my new quarters, an L-shaped room painted blue. My bags were searched and my name entered into a police book. I noticed the last entry was five months earlier. A Portuguese-speaking policeman saw I had chigger mites (also known as jiggers) in my feet from swimming in the river. He dug out 40 of them with a large needle. The rest would have to wait until London. I was well looked after and the next day George Grandsoult's Islander aircraft arrived to take me back to Georgetown. This time it was at government expense and I was George's first prisoner.

At CID headquarters I was told I had not been arrested, simply detained, and that I was not a prisoner. A curious distinction, but one that I put down to diplomacy. However, they wanted to be sure I left the country and gave me an option: a flight immediately to New York or a smaller plane that would stop at all the Caribbean islands and then on to London. I chose the latter. The High Commission were polite but I did not find them helpful. The expedition had proved a headache for them, particularly with the Venezuelans. One of the Guyana ministers applied questionable logic to the situation. He admitted I had done my best to get permission and that I had been advised by the PM's secretary to go unless I heard otherwise. But he said the presumption was that I would have gone anyway, whether or not I had heard and therefore I was to be kicked out of the country. I couldn't argue with that.

Gabbert got his story the first week and made the adventure sound exciting. By the following week, the *Sunday People* carried a spoiler, THE (LOST) NEWS OF THE WORLD and claimed the Roraima summit could be reached on foot from Venezuela and the only thing that was missing was a Wimpy bar at the peak. That story, exaggerated as it was, scored equal marks with Gabbert's for misleading their readers but, as entertainment, both newspapers did well. The story also marked the end of my association with Tommy 'Fagin' Bryant. While I was away, Fagin kept calling my home number at all hours of the day and night to complain to my wife that I was not making him money and that I would return diseased and incapable of further work. He was incandescent that his biggest earner was leaving him for the national newspapers.

Sex was a staple diet for the *NoW* but then it was also of great interest to the *Daily Telegraph*. The important difference was presentation. The *Telegraph* would present its sex stories more discreetly and hang them on a more acceptable peg, like a court case in which every sordid detail could be meticulously reported and depravity soundly condemned. Despite the *NoW*'s preoccupation with sex and shock-horror, it continued to print many human interest stories and features that would still appeal to middle-class readers of the *Mail* and *Express* today.

As a freelance I was able to present an eclectic mix of features and series. In September 1971 I suggested a series called the 'The British Way of Loving' and interviewed housewives in council houses about their hidden desires. Another series was labelled 'The Baby Snatchers'. There had been a spate of the crime around the country and I proposed that we run a two-part series with stories of women who had snatched babies and their reason for it. I drove all around the country speaking to as many of those women as I could and then consulted the resident psychiatrist at Holloway women's prison, London. He saw that my investigation revealed a strong pattern of behaviour in women who had taken babies not belonging to them. A number had suffered a miscarriage or been abandoned by a boyfriend or husband and had no child of their own. The psychiatrist was honest enough in his assessment: 'You bastard,' he said. 'You've stolen my thunder.'

Through getting out into the field and talking to people it was amazing how many stories could arouse interest and further discussion among readers. JUNKIE BABES was another front-page splash in the *NoW*. It featured children of mothers living in close quarters in newly built council houses. These young children were fed sleeping drugs every night to stop their crying and shouting which could be heard by other tenants in the badly constructed public housing.

In November of that year a member of the band Marmalade approached the *NoW* to sell an exclusive story of womanising and other capers while performing overseas. I was sent to Sweden to check it out and interview the girls who had been groupies. That resulted in the story being far more interesting than was originally suggested by the musician who spilled the beans. It also ensured the story would be legally safe. My early legal training came in useful here as I was able to prepare affidavits for the women involved.

After the mid-1980s, it seemed there was far less pressure on journalists to check stories they had been given, with the result that a number of people invented or set up stories which they sold to the *NoW* about liaisons with stars. This was an unfortunate departure from the 1970s, when strong competition meant greater care was taken to check before publication. Editors were also ready to pay more money for stories that would sell their newspapers. If the newspaper was sued it settled quietly and quickly if the matter was not worth disputing. For major stories, though, much more care was taken, particularly where the potentially libelled person was well funded.

In November 1971 over drinks at the City Golf Club, Jimmy Nicholson, a doyen among crime reporters, approached me and a fellow freelance. Jimmy's stock phrase was, 'Hi, big noise – your shout'. He suggested we look at the coming court case of the Beast of Jersey. Nicholson was a mine of information about crime, although some of his information needed careful deciphering. But his present tip was gold. We flew to Jersey in the Channel Islands for the trial of Edward Paisnel, Beast of Jersey, and signed up members of the Paisnel family and other innocent parties involved in the saga. We managed to sell the various stories to each of the popular Sunday newspapers and were splashed on their front pages.

Paisnel had terrorised the island for some 12 years, assaulting girls and boys while wearing a hideous mask. He was finally trapped driving through red traffic lights. Up to that time he had been able to get away with his activities by refusing to allow police onto his property. Paisnel seemed to know every inch of Jersey, which helped him to evade arrest for so long. He was also a man of the land. He could catch trout by tickling them and had been a builder and was able to hide evidence in a variety of places. Once he was nearly caught but had managed to get to the safety of his house.

The police had tried to arrest him but Jersey law worked in his favour. There, a man's house truly is his castle and he could refuse them entry, giving him time to hide the evidence. Paisnel was related to an old Jersey family and to the Black Baron of France, Giles de Rais, who was executed for crimes against children. Paisnel's wife Joan was an English rose, a ballet teacher who knew nothing of his activities and the contrast between this beauty and the beast was extraordinary. The *Sunday Mirror* paid us handsomely for Joan Paisnel's story, which they had first refused to purchase on the advice of their own staff reporter. We sold the daughter's story to the *News of the World*. She claimed to be a witch. The mistress's story was sold to the *Sunday People*. She had slept with Paisnel in a coffin and provided intimate details of their affair. For us it was a great coup to be on the front page of the three largest selling Sundays on the same day.

Crime, sex, rock'n'roll and showbiz flourished in abundance in 1970s London and newspapers mined it for all it was worth, particularly the *News of the World* and the *Sun*. A Maltese crime syndicate had amassed huge wealth as landlords of brothels and apartments in Mayfair and West End. Some of their members were in partnership with crime lords such as Bernie Silver, who came from a more violent era. Prostitution was a safer bet than robbery and enabled vast profits to be made through rentals and property purchases. At the same time, pornography was in its heyday and one of its main exponents, Jimmy Humphreys – who I had interviewed in Amsterdam – prospered as a maker and importer of blue films, creating a vast network of distribution points in the UK.

A fringe group of pornographers had also entered the market, either as filmmakers or as small-time concerns importing porn from Holland, Denmark and Sweden where laws were less restrictive than in the UK. Some of the smarter operators managed to keep within the law and went on to create mini-empires based on 'acceptable' pornographic material after the rules were relaxed.

Violent crime had lessened with the jailing of major London gangsters such as the Krays and their cohorts, although bullion and bank robberies were still a regular headache for Scotland Yard. Both the *Sun* and *NoW* regularly featured these criminals and were accused of selling sex and sensation to increase readership. Of course, it was a fair criticism. Sexy features sold well, as did pretty ladies who were prepared to remove their clothes for the newspaper.

Tales of fallen vicars and their sexual peccadilloes were also staple fodder, as were the antics regularly undertaken by pop musicians living on the wild side. All made good copy, greedily consumed by a readership always hungry for more. Anyone who had gained a level of notoriety was eagerly sought and pursued with open cheque-books. Editors would have only to answer three basic questions: would their budget stretch to the buy-up? Would the proprietor criticise them for the purchase? And would they get away with it? The last point involved consideration of public and press council reaction and whether, legally, there could be a problem.

Campaigners who were opposed to sexual content in newspapers, such as Mary Whitehouse, were generally ignored or alternatively encouraged in their opposition which provided useful free publicity.

In its struggle to uphold the moral probity of its millions of readers, the *NoW* was prepared to spend vast sums on uncovering personal and public vice. Investigations lasting months were encouraged and funded by a succession of features editors at the newspaper. Expenses were generous but required the approval of the particular commissioning editor, although it was not always necessary to give an accurate description. Payment of a specified sum to an unnamed 'contact' covered a multitude of sins. A commissioning editor could also put through a payment under a different heading if it appeared that too much money had been paid for a particular story. Strict accountability was rarely enforced in commissioning editors and the overriding criterion was producing a successful product.

Over a three-year period in the early- to mid-1970s, I was involved in a series of exposés while working with features staff at the *NoW* which eventually led to the jailing of a group of Maltese vice kings in Soho. During this time we worked closely with Scotland Yard officers based at Limehouse, near Canary Wharf. These police were part of the Serious Crimes Squad under the leadership of Commander Bert Wickstead, known to criminals as the Grey Fox, a nickname that he carried proudly. Bert was a copper from the old school: tough, uncompromising and down to earth. He had no qualms about talking to us or helping us with information about villains, providing it was a two-way dialogue and we could be useful to him. He loved getting his photograph in the newspaper and did not mince words. 'I've been so busy, I've not had time to shit,' he would often complain.

As far as I was aware, our relationship with him was totally above board and led to a mutual exchange of information for the common good. We had similar relationships with members of his team, but more than anyone else, Bert was held in good esteem and on retirement from the Met was given the job as head of security at the *NoW*.

POLICE AND THE PRESS

Throughout my association with News International there had always been a good working relationship with both the City of London police, in charge of London's financial centre, and the Metropolitan police (generally meant to refer to Scotland Yard). The fact that we were prepared to expose bent coppers did not alter that relationship although it might have strained it at different times. I had also taken part in a *Sunday People* exposé of West End Central police station in which we named high ranking police officers who were on the take, colluding with London gangsters. Laurie Manifold, who at the time was assistant editor of the *Sunday People*, headed the investigation and amassed irrefutable evidence of wrongdoing which resulted in hefty prison sentences for the culprits. It led Sir Robert Mark, Scotland Yard's tough commissioner, to take immediate and strong action to eradicate corruption. However, among a huge workforce in any organisation, there is always likely to be a small percentage of employees who are crooked, just as in newspapers.

Within any law enforcement organisation or agency, employees are lectured about the standards expected of them and the heavy penalties for when these are not met. For that reason, Former assistant commissioner Robert Quick, head of anti-corruption at the Yard between 1999 and 2001, addressed this when he accused journalists of corrupting police. In his statement to the Leveson inquiry, Quick said, 'Around 2000, I wrote a short report highlighting the role of journalists in promoting corrupt relationships with and making corrupt payments to officers for stories about famous people and high-profile investigations in the MPS [Metropolitan police service]. I proposed an investigation of these newspapers and officers on the basis that I believed that journalists were not paying bribes out of their own pockets but were either falsely accounting for their expenses and therefore defrauding their employers or that the organisations were aware of the reasons for the payments and were themselves complicit in making corrupt payments to police officers.' During an investigation called Operation Nigeria, he said, it became clear that officers were receiving between £500 and £2,000 for stories about celebrities, politicians, and the Royal family as well as reports of police investigations. These were leaked by officers already suspected of corruption.

The fact that payments were made to police officers cannot be doubted and, indeed, was admitted by Rebekah Brooks to a parliamentary inquiry, but it is highly unlikely that journalists set out to corrupt officers. For an officer to accept a bribe or incentive he or she must already be corrupt. Apart from constituting a criminal offence, it would also be insulting to suggest a financial incentive to an honest police officer as that would be tantamount to inferring corruption on the part of that person.

The more likely scenario is that a policeman or law enforcement officer will have made an anonymous approach to a newspaper, offering information in exchange for payment. It is perfectly acceptable for a journalist to negotiate a payment for a member of the general public. Sometimes a whistleblower may be exposing something important for the greater good but otherwise public officials should be treated with caution and further advice should be sought to avoid breaking the law. There is, however, a threat to the independence of a newspaper where too cosy a relationship exists between its top executives and the heads of a public bodies or large organisations.

Scotland Yard, led by Sue Akers, is currently investigating press malpractices under three headings, some of which may take years to complete. Operation Weeting is a continuing investigation into allegations of phone hacking by the *NoW*. Operation Elveden, supervised by the Independent Police Complaints Commission, is looking into emails received from News International that allegedly show payments made to police by the *NoW*. Operation Tuleta is investigating hacking in general terms, which includes examining evidence contained on hard drives and in other documentation seized from earlier operations.

When Parliament's culture, media and sport select committee inquired into hacking, its chairman John Whittingdale commented, 'The only reason that I can think that the hacking enquiry was not fully pursued was that it was a story that the police did not wish to uncover. They did not want to damage their relationships with News International. It was appalling negligence if not corruption. I fear that the damage to public confidence in the police as a result of the hacking scandal will be colossal and am concerned that there may be worse to come when these matters go to trial.'

Past commissioners of the Met have been questioned about their relationship with the press in general and News International newspapers in particular by parliamentary committees and the Leveson inquiry. The evidence that emerged has been surprising and points to unhealthy association between police and NI executives and journalists, such as commissioner Sir Paul Stephenson's hiring of *NoW*'s Neil Wallis. His stay at Champneys was also criticised. There was no suggestion of wrongdoing, but he resigned out of a sense of duty and honour and because he had 'become the story', which he considered would detract from his work, apart from any health considerations.

Sir Paul said he had no reason to doubt Mr Wallis's integrity and no reason to associate his name with hacking until January 2011, when he first saw Wallis's name in the public domain. Conservative committee member Nicola Blackwood MP asked, 'I wonder whether I could take you back to your resignation statement, where you stated that you had no reason to suspect "the alleged involvement of Mr Wallis in phone hacking", and that you had "no knowledge of the extent of this disgraceful practice, or the repugnant nature of the selection of victims", or its "reach into senior levels". However, in the year you met – or have been reported to have met – Mr Wallis, 2006, the ICO [Information Commissioner's Office] produced a report that said: "Investigations by the ICO and the police have uncovered evidence of a widespread and organised undercover market in confidential police information. Among the 'buyers' are many journalists looking for a story. In one major case investigated by the ICO ... evidence included records of information supplied to 305 named journalists working for a range of newspapers." In its follow-up report, it listed the *News of the World* as one of those newspapers, 228 transactions of positively identified phone hacking and 23 journalists. Do you not think that that might have alerted you to the fact that Mr Wallis might have been involved in phone hacking at that time?' Sir Paul replied that he did not think that.

Labour committee member Steve McCabe MP pressed the point. 'In the case of Mr Wallis, in your own words, he is an acquaintance of yours and someone with whom you have had a relationship for professional purposes for over five years. He was a personal friend of Assistant Commissioner Yates and Mr Fedorcio [director of the department of public affairs at Scotland Yard] says that you and Mr Yates were both consulted on letting the contract at the Met to Mr Wallis. Is it not strange that when you accepted the hospitality at Champneys, you did not know that Mr Wallis also had a business contract with it and that no one at the Met sought to provide you with that information?'

Sir Paul Stephenson: 'First, I am completely baffled as to how anyone in the Met would have the information that he had a relationship with Champneys.'

Steve McCabe: 'In pure business terms... let's forget about what happened to Mr Wallis subsequently. The commissioner of police is having free hospitality at this establishment; there is a business connection between the Met and Mr Wallis and Mr Wallis also has a clear business connection with Champneys. Isn't it strange? I think you said in your resignation statement that you are "dependent to a great extent on others providing the right information and assurances". Would you not have thought that someone should have at least taken the trouble to point out to you that in accepting this hospitality, you were accepting hospitality at an establishment where there was a business connection between an individual who was already under contract to the organisation that you run?'

Conservative committee member James Clappison, MP: 'One thing that strikes me, looking at this in the round, if I can take it that way, is the extent of the connection between yourself and other Met officers and News International and particularly the amount of times you met them and had lunches or dinners with them. I understand from the Metropolitan Police Authority that you had 18 lunches or dinners with the *News of the World*, and seven or eight dinners with Mr Wallis himself over about a five-year period. Can you explain to us why it was necessary to have that amount of lunching and dining with the *News of the World* and News International? Did the same thing happen with other newspaper groups?'

Sir Paul Stephenson: There is a reason why the Metropolitan police commissioner must meet with the media to try to promote and enhance the reputation of the Met, talk about the context of policing and, if you will, make sure there is a relationship there... Between 2005 and 2010, 17 per cent of my contacts with the press involved *News of the World*. That is 17 per cent of all my contacts. I understand that *News of the World* represents some 16 per cent of press readership. In the same period, 30 per cent of my contacts with the press involved News International. That sounds like an extraordinary percentage, but I am told News International represents 42 per cent of press readership...'

Asked by Mr Clappison about his meetings with other newspapers Sir Paul said he had met twice with the *Guardian*.

Mr Clappison replied, 'Yes, twice. The *Guardian* carried a report a day or two ago that you had a meeting with them to try to persuade them that the coverage of phone hacking was exaggerated and incorrect and that you had a meeting to that effect in December 2009. Is that right?'

Sir Paul Stephenson said, 'Yes.'

Chairman Keith Vaz, Labour MP, said, 'Does it not seem a little odd – you are a very distinguished police officer – that the *News of the World* seemed to have an ex-employee working for the leader of the opposition [David Cameron] and that the *News of the World* had an ex-employee working for you? Did it not strike you as a little bit odd that whether by coincidence or deliberately the former editor of the *News of the World* ends up with the leader of the opposition and the deputy editor of the *News of the World* ends up with the Met police commissioner? ... At some stage you would have met the leader of the opposition, before he became prime minister and Mr Coulson would have been with him and Mr Coulson would have known, would he not, that Mr Wallis was working for you? It is inconceivable that Mr Coulson would not have known that Mr Wallis had a contract with the Met.'

Sir Paul said: 'My recollection is – I think that I am right in saying this – that I do not think I ever met Mr Coulson at all before Mr Cameron became prime minister.'

Vaz asked if Sir Paul was consulted before Wallis was appointed. Sir Paul replied, 'Yes, I was. Just let me say with the benefit of what we know now, I am quite happy to put it on the record that I regret that we went into that contract. I quite clearly regret it because it is embarrassing.' In his witness statement to the Leveson inquiry, Sir Paul stated, 'Having played no part in engaging Mr Wallis, I was aware of no issues that could reasonably raise any level of suspicion or concern.' Had he played any part in securing a job for Neil Wallis's daughter at the MPS? No, he had not. Did he know whether or not it was true that Neil Wallis sold crime stories to the media while engaged by the MPS? 'I do not know if it is true – I am only aware of what has been alleged in the media. This is a most disturbing allegation, and if it true, would be both disappointing and embarrassing for the MPS.'

Sir Paul said he had met James Murdoch twice – when he was at a meeting with Rebekah Brooks in her office and again at a News International drinks party also attended by senior members of Government including Prime Minister David Cameron. He met Rupert Murdoch at the same function. He had met Andy Coulson when the Met hosted a dinner at New Scotland Yard after Coulson had been appointed to Number 10. Neil Wallis also attended this function. 'The purpose of the function was to enable us to get to know Mr Coulson and his assistant Ed Llewellyn, both of whom were important figures at the heart of government, to tell them what we regarded as important and to get a sense of how they saw policing in London.' Neil Wallis was also said to have had a 12-year friendship with assistant commissioner John Yates, who was conducting an investigation into the NoW.

Sir Paul's predecessor, Sir Ian Blair, had been appointed commissioner in February 2005 and resigned at the end of 2008. On his watch, Rebekah Brooks was lent Raisa, a retired police horse, to ride at her Oxfordshire home. She was later criticised for returning the horse in poor condition, a claim denied by her racing horse trainer husband Charlie Brooks in 2010. When this was revealed, Rupert Murdoch is reported to have jumped to Brooks' defence on Twitter: 'Now they are complaining about R Brooks saving an old horse from the glue factory!' In addition, Lord Blair's son had once been given a week's work experience at the *Sun*, arranged by Dick Fedorcio. His own son had also done work experience at the paper, as had the son of former commissioner Lord Condon.

The commissioner from 1 February 2000 to 2005 was Lord John Stevens. He had been a copper for 43 years and was considered to be a larger-than-life figure. He said that the Met's relationship with the media was based on mistrust before he was appointed. He agreed a more open relationship with Home Secretary Jack Straw. 'I tried to follow a policy of being open and transparent with the media to give answers to proper questions without going into confidential areas,' said Stevens. 'I had a variety of personal contacts with the media when I was commissioner ... I helped organise the Millennium Convoy to Romania ... to assist terminally ill children.' He said the convoy was supported by Ross Kemp, the actor and first husband of Rebekah Brooks.

After retiring from the Met, Lord Stevens wrote a number of articles for the *NoW*. 'This was part of a package which was negotiated around my autobiography, *Not for the Faint Hearted*, which was serialised in the *Times* and the *News of the World* ... The financial package was negotiated by the publishers ... I was paid what I was told was the going rate. I was contracted exclusively to do seven articles a year. The articles went under the title "The Chief". They were edited by Neil Wallis and based on major policing issues that arose during 2005–2006, such as the 7/7 bombings ... I was aware that countless politicians had done the same thing ... I terminated the contract with *News of the World* in October 2007. I have had no further dealings with Neil Wallis or the paper since then.' Lord Stevens found that since the phone hacking scandal broke, 'my perception is that the MPS and other police forces are highly sensitive and feel that any contact or relationship with the press is likely to be adversely construed and lead to criticism.'

That perception by Lord Stevens was hardly surprising given the evidence to Leveson by Sue Akers, deputy assistant commissioner at Scotland Yard, charged with supervising Operation Elveden. She revealed that News International had disclosed material to the MPS indicating that police officers had been receiving cash payments from *NoW* for providing confidential information. As a result of the NI disclosures, there had been 22 arrests including journalists, police officers, armed forces, a member of the Ministry of Defence, and a person acting as a conduit. She said, 'There is a recognition by the journalists that this behaviour is illegal, reference being made to staff "risking losing their pension or job", to the need for "care" and to the need for "cash payments". There is also an indication of "tradecraft", ie, hiding cash payments to "sources" by making them to a friend or relative of the source. The evidence further suggests that the authority level for such payments to be made is provided at a senior level within the newspaper.'

Akers said the practice was widespread. 'The evidence suggests that such payments were being made to public officials across all areas of public life.' These included not only the police, but the military, health, government and the prison service. 'It reveals a network of corrupted officials. There appears to have been a culture at the *Sun* of illegal payments and systems have been created to facilitate such payments whilst hiding the identity of the officials receiving the money.'

Email searches identified a police officer from the MPS Specialist Operations (SO) directorate who was seeking payments from journalists with the *News of the World*. The officer was arrested in December 2011.

The cases did not merely involve the odd drink or meal. Akers said, 'These are cases in which arrests have been made involving the delivery of regular, frequent and sometimes significant sums of money to a small number of public officials by journalists.' Multiple payments involving thousands of pounds had been made. In one case 'the figure over several years is in excess of £80,000. There is also mention in some emails of public officials being placed on retainers ... One of the arrested journalists has, over several years, received over £150,000 in cash to pay his sources, a number of whom were public officials.' According to Akers, the vast majority of disclosures were not in the public interest but could best be described as salacious gossip.

Historically there have been plenty of examples of corruption that police lecturers at Bramston and Hendon police colleges could have used to warn new recruits. Operation Countryman was a 1970s investigation that took six years to investigate rotten apples in the Met. Around 400 police officers left the force either during or after the investigation. Recommendations made were that 300 police officers should face criminal charges, but nobody was brought before the court. However, high-ranking officers were sent down in 1977, each getting between 10 to 14 years. They included Flying Squad commander Kenneth Drury and Chief Superintendent Bill Moody from C1 (Obscene Publications Squad) and commander Wally Virgo whose corruption I helped expose.

Before he was sent down, I interviewed Drury at length for the *NoW*. I already had information that he was in cahoots with Britain's biggest pornographer, Jimmy Humphreys – who I interviewed on my trip to Amsterdam with his wife and lawyer – and that he had been on the take for years as well as accepting considerable hospitality from the pornographer, including trips abroad. At our interview, I told him, 'Reg, I'm at the starting point where I consider you're a bent cop but I'd be very happy to hear your side of the story.'

Surprisingly, Drury did not take umbrage at the accusation. 'Honest, John, I'm not bent. Humphreys was my informant. Look, I ran the Flying Squad. It has been called the cream of the Yard and it consists of 150 of London's best detectives. But without informants it couldn't work. Every copper worth his salt has informants. And I'd wager I'm not the only officer to have socialised with one. There are rules governing a police officer's conduct with informants but, honestly, if you followed them literally you could never catch a single thief. If a detective got into bother every time he bought a quick gin for a tart, there would be no Scotland Yard. And, of course, sometimes you have to spend an evening at a nightclub or even visit their homes. A good snout is worth his weight in gold. Once a detective has got himself a good snout organised, nobody else ever knows the man's identity.

'Meets between the snout and the copper can take place almost anywhere. It depends to a large extent on the social standing of the informant and can range from a tatty working man's club to a plush West End nightclub. The social side comes in and that's why I don't think I was wrong to go to Cyprus [with Jimmy Humphreys]. The social side and work overlap all the time. You don't meet a snout and say, "Look you've got nothing for me. You can get lost." I've had informants that I wouldn't let within a hundred miles of the missus. But Jimmy Humphreys, to hark back to Cyprus again, has always been a perfect gentleman with me.'

Drury explained that the Yard would pay money to informants. He had paid £400 to one villain whose tip led to the recovery of a million pounds of LSD and resulted in a dock full of nasty villains. 'The system works like this. A detective has had a tip from a snout that has helped him to get a case to court. He writes a report to his senior saying that an informant who chooses to be known such-and-such a name – never the real one – should be paid. At the Flying Squad these reports came to me. I wrote on my assessment of what the payment should be. It then went up to my senior who would either endorse my recommendation or vary it up or down. The officer would then draw the sum in cash from the special informants fund at the Yard. He would then contact his informant and very, very carefully pay him out. Usually that's the tricky bit and the most dangerous for your man. I wouldn't trust a cafe or a pub. I'd do it in a car or at his home. No matter how big the sum it is always paid in cash. And the informant has to sign a receipt for it, still using his code name which is taken back to the nick.'

Drury claimed his trip to Cyprus with the pornographer was due to the challenge of finding a Great Train Robber. 'It's all down to Ronnie Biggs, the bloody missing train robber who should have put his hands up and come in to do his bird years ago. He has definitely become a challenge to the Flying Squad. Catch him and you become a flaming hero. Anyway, up comes one of my informants that he's in Cyprus. It was very vague. No name or exact address or anything ... so I took the trouble to check around and one of the people I checked with was Jimmy Humphreys ... but let's face it, there have been tips that Biggs is everywhere from Timbuktu to Eskimo-land and you can't spend the taxpayers' money chasing shadows all over the world ... Jimmy did not pay for my holiday. We split the cost 50-50. Right down the line. It was pricey too. My half came to £450 – about a month's pay. A hell of a lot, but the wife and I hadn't been away for some years and I decided to give her a good holiday ... but as you know, it all went wrong. My superiors at the Yard decided I may have overstepped the line.'

Ronnie Biggs faced prison only in 2001 after he had returned voluntarily to the UK. But after my Drury story was published and because of my interest in West End Central police station, I was summoned to Scotland Yard by assistant commissioner Gilbert Kelland. He was unhappy with my inquiries as there was some overlap with ones he was making himself in a drive to clean up the Met. I was warned off although I insisted on pursuing my inquiries regardless.

PEERS AND PSYCHOPATHS

Between bent coppers and investigating pornographers throughout Europe, I secured the publishing rights to Winifred Shannon's story of her brother Graham Young, Britain's most notorious poisoner. Young was 14 when arrested for poisoning his family. His mother died but Winifred and his father survived. Young was sent to Broadmoor hospital and released at 23. His parole officers omitted to tell his new employers, a photographic plant in Bovingdon, Hertfordshire, that they should lock up their chemicals given Young's past interest in pharmaceutical endeavours. This had meant experimenting with creating different forms of poison and administering them to his nearest and dearest while taking a clinical interest in their agonising journey to death. Shortly after his release, this is exactly what happened to two fellow workers at the Bovingdon workplace. Luckily, another four intended victims survived his wicked attack.

Young fashioned himself after the notorious Victorian poisoner William Palmer. Young was cold-blooded and showed no remorse for what he had done. His sister had shown him love and kindness but he repaid her friendship with a cocktail of death as he had begun to do with his mother when only 11. At Broadmoor he had been able to convince psychiatrists of his sanity by reading their books and modelling his behaviour on reformed patients. He was fascinated by cruelty and the macabre. He drew swastikas and other evil symbols. Before his mother died, he had drawn a cartoon of her lying in a grave. His trial attracted wide attention and kicked off a bidding war in the tabloid press.

Editors don't normally take kindly to freelance journalists suggesting a headline they should use for a splash – a major story. Just before the two-part feature on Young was due to be printed, I called Bernard Shrimsley, then editing the *Sun*, and told him that the poisoner had virtually written his own headline. Bernard was hesitant until I told him what it was. I had just been given a letter written by Young to his sister shortly before his release from Broadmoor. It began, 'Dear Win... Just think. Another few months and your friendly neighbourhood Frankenstein will be at liberty again.' The headline inspired by Young was splashed on the front page: YOUR FRIENDLY NEIGHBOURHOOD FRANKENSTEIN. Beneath it was a photograph of the poisoner as an innocent 10-year-old.

After he was jailed for a second time, never to be released, it was revealed by prison authorities that a fellow prisoner working with Young in the kitchens had mysteriously died and others had fallen ill.

The question of how I, a freelance journalist, came to get these stories against fierce competition with the national press has often been asked. A number of factors were involved. I was freelance and the urge to be successful was a strong motivator, as was the financial reward for selling major stories and features. I was also an early riser and had planned well ahead for these events by following them closely in all the daily newspapers, tabloid and quality, which meant quite a large yearly investment.

I would often sell features to the very paper that had been in competition with me for the story, particularly the *NoW*. More often than not, I would be competing with their news journalists while the features department maintained a neutral position. I was both an enemy and a friend to the organisation involved. Understandably, I was not very popular with a succession of news editors.

When a major buy-up involved many thousands of pounds the newspaper was in a much stronger position than me as it had far deeper pockets. The only way I could get around that was by getting in first. The serious newspapers, the heavies, were always a good source for stories. They would often assist my forward planning by covering seemingly minor events that I could see might develop into major news items. I would work on those stories and keep in touch with the parties involved or secure rights to what they had to say at an early stage. By the time the story blew up I would be in a key position to handle it, both on a personal and professional level.

Rupert Murdoch's disregard for the upper echelons of British society did not diminish his newspapers' interest in them in any way. Curiously, as already mentioned, they contributed to the downfall of the *NoW*. Considering Murdoch's own privileged upbringing it was difficult to fathom his attitude to the British class system although various theories have been suggested. In the 1950s, when he attended Oxford, class distinction was far more prevalent than it is today and Australians, even rich ones with titled parents, may not have been as welcome or acceptable as children of old British families.

Further, Murdoch's three wives had come from ordinary families and would certainly not have fitted in the upper class circles as easily as someone from his own background. His first wife had been a model and air hostess. Anna, his second wife and mother of Elisabeth, Lachlan and James, was from a working class background in Scotland and her Estonian father had been a merchant sailor. She, like Rupert, was far happier living in America than in Britain, particularly because of the constant criticism levelled against his work in the early 1970s. Rupert's Chinese third wife, as accomplished as she was, did not belong to a dynasty. And until he gave up his Australian citizenship to become an American, Murdoch was always proud to be an Aussie and all that that involved: a free spirit – independent, suspicious of authority and egalitarian at heart.

My own experience with blue bloods was a happy one from the start and one that helped in an understanding of classes in the UK. I came to hear of one of the more colourful members of the gentry through a BBC radio programme in 1972. Alexander Thynn, Lord Weymouth, was the eccentric seventh

Marquess of Bath whose family home was Longleat. He was interviewed about a book he had written called *The Carry Cot*, in which it was revealed that his wife, Anna Gael, a Hungarian actress and journalist who he had met as a schoolgirl, was living in Paris. The programme discreetly attempted to delve into Alexander's unusual marital set-up without actually spelling out all the details. He was interested in more than one sexual liaison and quite prepared to bring up children fathered by him with a series of what he called 'wifelets' who could live on the family estate. To Alexander, a wifelet's background and colour were of no consequence but intelligence and sexual liberation were a must and if she was beautiful, then all the better. At the very minimum she would need to be attractive.

I drove to Longleat House, Wiltshire, in my Aston and was waved through the gates of the 16th-century Elizabethan house, one of Britain's most stunning estates. A tall, imposing figure in his sixties dressed in a tweed jacket and slacks approached me. He was attempting to restrain two very large ridgeback dogs from eating me. The man was obviously not the gamekeeper so I ventured a guess that he was the Marquess of Bath and told him I had come to interview his eldest son, Alexander, Lord Weymouth. I had never seen a ridgeback dog before and asked the Marquess where they were from. 'Africa, I think,' replied the aristocrat. I admired the two powerfully built canines eyeing me warily and inquired of his lordship what purpose these dogs served. 'Oh,' he said, 'I don't know. Killing niggers in the bush I suppose.' I was later told that he was a rather eccentric man whose dinner guests had to make do with silver cutlery tied to the table with string in case they took off with it.

Alexander was a total contrast to his father. He was a writer, painter, philosopher and musician and had already achieved some fame with his book. His background could not have been more privileged or traditional – from Eton school, where he was a prefect and member of the top rowing eight, he served in the Life Guards as an officer and was a welterweight boxing champ. He studied philosophy at Oxford and went to art school in Paris where he met Anna as a schoolgirl. He had decided to follow his every whim, which birth and good fortune had made it possible for him to do without taking on a 9-to-5 job.

Surprisingly, he was totally open about his desires and the lifestyle hinted at on the radio programme that led to our interview and now he was willing to provide the details I sought. The walls of his 30-room apartment at Longleat were adorned with thickly applied oil paintings depicting *Kama Sutra* figures engaging in Kama Sutra antics and he told me of his plans to install wifelets on cottages surrounding his 900-acre estate. We drank lots of cider (his favourite) and got on famously and played chess, which stimulated Alexander's interest in me, at least while I was able to win against him (this did not last).

Alexander talked about a polymorphous society meaning, in his case, that if ten women he greatly fancied wanted to have children by him and allowed him to bring them up, then he would be very happy, 'but I don't expect it to happen'. The one thing he asked me not to do was to print that he wanted to be a prize stud. I promised I would not do that. The following Sunday, the *NoW* published my story under the headline LORD STUD. I had made it quite plain to the features editor that this was not to be and I had given a written undertaking to this effect. I felt deeply unhappy for Alexander who had been a generous host. I figured this would be the end of a brief but productive relationship. In fact, it turned out to be the opposite. Alexander complained to me that it was not the done thing to publish against his wishes but after my explanation he relented and said, 'You'd better come down and stay for the weekend.' There followed many years of lively weekends spent at Longleat with a host who was colourful and funny and who was surrounded by clever people, including the occasional wifelet.

The variety of NoW stories I was involved in producing was never-ending. Graham King organised a series of TV adverts featuring me as a wrestler to promote my exposé of the highly popular ITV's World of Sport wrestling matches on telly. A professional wrestler from the north of England, Don Branch, said he was willing to expose this entertaining sport as the great scam it was but would need to get me in the ring to illustrate the moves. To get finer details of the scam, he visited wrestlers in their changing rooms backstage wearing a hidden microphone and spoke to them about the fight.

Meanwhile, we had already filmed me at London's famous Fisher amateur boxing club, throwing Branch around the ring. The first fight we reported on was between a former policeman from Gambia, Masambula, and Tony Charles, billed as the mid-heavyweight champion of Wales. Our secret microphones caught the two men discussing their moves and fixing the fight. Wrestler after wrestler followed a similar path, secretly discussing moves from body slams to Boston crabs to Irish whips, via back-breakers and double-leg Nelsons, and deciding in which round they would fall. Their moves were as choreographed as professional dance routines and equally entertaining. Our headline urged readers to wager £1,000 to prove us wrong and told readers: SECRET DRESSING ROOM MICS REVEAL HOW WRESTLING IS FAKED (AND BY FAKED, WE MEAN EVERY MOVE). Nobody came forward, despite the millions of TV fans thrilled by the twice-weekly matches. But while our two-part series exposing the sport was heavily promoted it did not win the general approval of readers. Hundreds of them complained the newspaper had spoiled their fun and they didn't care if it had been a fix.

But sales of the *News of the World* continued to be healthy and together with its sister paper Murdoch's UK investment was fast becoming the jewel in News Limited's crown. It was time to expand in the USA but first the mogul flew back to Australia to take an active part in backing the election of Gough Whitlam as Labour prime minister.

6

POLITICS AND POWER

The image of Murdoch as an outsider and Robin Hood figure, defending the underdog and upholding democracy through the medium of his newspapers, may well have been true in the early stages of his rise to power. But if so, it did not last long. He learned the meaning of power from his father and soon came to benefit from it through his father's contacts and the influence his newspapers gave him and his enormous wealth. If he fought with governments, the battle was more likely to be over regulation and fiscal controls than upholding human rights. Murdoch has waged a continuous battle for more than 30 years against Brussels and the euro, presumably to avoid regulation. I once asked his right-hand man Les Hinton why he was doing it. Les, affable as ever, would only say, 'I'm not going there...'

Throughout his life Murdoch has sought the company or maintained contact with global power brokers and people of influence. He was barely 30 when photographs of him appeared in the press standing beside US president Jack Kennedy. Dialogue with a succession of American presidents and prime ministers in England and Australia would follow. He met, exchanged views, and dined with Nixon, Carter, Reagan, Clinton, and George W Bush. He was particularly impressed with Nixon and highly supportive of Reagan and Bush whose Middle East wars he backed without question. In England he became a great admirer of prime ministers Margaret Thatcher and Tony Blair, the latter being godfather to his daughter Grace. He was made equally welcome by Blair's successors, Gordon Brown and David Cameron. He was one of the privileged few given access to the back door of Number 10.

But the love affair with British politicians underwent a tremendous change in 2011 and 2012. Murdoch claimed at the Leveson inquiry in April 2012 that Brown had declared 'war' on his empire. David Cameron who called for the inquiry now wanted to keep a distance from the Murdochs after the revelations involving News Corporation newspapers. Prior to the proposed takeover of BSkyB, James Murdoch revealed to the inquiry, he had discussed the matter with Cameron. Rupert Murdoch admitted his failures as head of the organisation but said his executives and lawyers had let him down. He distanced himself from the *NoW* saying he had never taken much interest in the paper and wished he had got rid of it years earlier. He said his main concern was the *Sun* which reflected his views and political leanings.

Socially, Murdoch had met most Australian politicians of note as a young man and later he would hold great sway with the leaders as the most powerful media baron in Australia.

As a boy, his father had taken him fishing with Malcolm Fraser, a future prime minister. Fraser's father was a friend of Sir Keith and Lady Murdoch. Another powerful Murdoch ally was the leader of the Country party, John McEwen, who helped the newspaper boss in his search for a property close to Canberra where he could hold soirees and entertain government grandees.

As long as they were leaders in their field, preferably recognised internationally, Murdoch was also keen to meet non-political figures. In the 1980s, he became an admirer of Christian evangelist Billy Graham and spread the gospel among his faithful newspaper readers. Graham was a hugely influential figure who travelled the world preaching and was also an adviser to US presidents. Murdoch's admiration for him continued into the next decade. During Billy Graham's Puerto Rico crusade in March 1995, Murdoch telephoned its headquarters. Asked to leave a message, he said, 'Please tell him that I am praying for his crusade.' By coincidence, David Frost, who at the time was on a Caribbean cruise, had also called from his ship with a similar message. It was the same David Frost who had berated Murdoch on television all those years earlier for publishing call girl Christine Keeler's memoirs. Both men had by now become fully fledged members of the global glitterati set.

In 1998, the press magnate took part in a further religious event, this time involving no less a figure than the global head of the Catholic church – Pope John Paul II. Murdoch was honoured by receiving the papal appointment of knight commander of St Gregory. Murdoch instructed his editors in the UK not to report the event. But in Ireland, where it was reported, his appointment aroused angry protests as Murdoch was a Protestant (although his wife Anna was a Catholic). But Murdoch had also been indirectly responsible for spreading the Christian message through his book publishing company HarperCollins. One of its subsidiaries is the evangelical Zondervan imprint which also prints the Bible.

Murdoch's abiding interest in politics and his involvement in its machinations may not have been apparent to some of his employees, even those at the *Times*. A report in the paper in 2010 under the headline, REPUBLIC IS BACK ON THE AUSTRALIAN AGENDA, quoted the Labour prime minister, Julia Gillard: 'Australia should become a republic when the Queen dies or if she abdicates.' That in itself was nothing new, as the question of becoming a republic had been debated over many years. Of greater interest was the commentary piece under the headline, THE QUEEN KNOWS THE SCORE... BUT LET THEM TAKE THEIR TIME. It remarked on the affection held towards the Queen by Australians, even among committed republicans and the Queen's own affection for Australia: 'But that kind of response could not weather the changing shape of Australian society. The sacking in 1975 of the prime minister, Gough Whitlam, by Sir John Kerr, the governor general – her [the Queen's] representative, even if she had nothing to do with it – has coloured many Australians' view of the monarchy. For them it is a puzzle that her face is still on their money...'

Australians were hardly puzzled. They were far more interested in the machinations behind the sacking of Whitlam and the part played by Rupert Murdoch and his old friend Malcolm Fraser, who succeeded Whitlam as prime minister of Australia and had canvassed Murdoch's support in getting rid of the Labour government. Australians were well aware that the action by Sir John Kerr, essentially the British monarch's representative in the country, had nothing to do with the Queen and an awful lot to do with Murdoch, whose newspapers were guilty of gross bias. Journalists on his flagship *The Australian*, outraged at numerous slanted reports, had gone on strike and 75 of them wrote to accuse Murdoch of turning the newspaper into a 'propaganda sheet'. They created substantial losses for News Limited but Murdoch neither denied nor regretted his action. He considered that, without his support, the sacking of the Whitlam government would not have taken place and the new conservative coalition would not have been elected. If it was the case that Rupert won it for Malcolm, then it heralded a similar action played in London 17 years later.

The *Sun*'s reporting of the British general election of 1992 was similarly biased against Labour and its leadership. As electors prepared to vote, editor Kelvin Mackenzie struck a blow against the Labour leader Neil Kinnock with the devastating headline, IF KINNOCK WINS TODAY, WILL THE LAST PERSON TO LEAVE BRITAIN PLEASE TURN OUT THE LIGHTS. Whether or not the headline and picture – of Kinnock's head in a light bulb – swayed the public sufficiently to claim victory is not known, but John Major's Conservatives won and the *Sun* claimed victory with a boastful headline: IT'S THE SUN WOT WON IT.

Back in Australia in 1972, however, it was quite a different matter. Murdoch had returned to engage in politics and after years of Conservative government rule in his country of birth, he decided it was time for a change. Over dinner with Whitlam, he discussed proposals for defeating the government and pledged the support of his newspapers to help elect him as the first Labour prime minister in 23 years. Adapting a variation of the favoured political slogan suggesting 'time for a change', the proprietor rolled up his sleeves and became a Labour party propagandist, urging electors to vote for Gough and contributing handsomely to the party's election coffers.

But most politicians, including prime ministers, have a limited shelf life, much the same as Murdoch's editors. In Murdoch's opinion, Gough Whitlam did not come up to scratch and his fiscal policies were proving disastrous. He had to go. With the same fervour and single-mindedness that Murdoch had adopted in helping Whitlam become prime minister, he now planned a similar campaign to oust him just two years after he was elected.

A gardener at Murdoch's country estate in New South Wales was convinced his boss was involved in a plot with Sir John and the leader of the Australian Liberal party, Malcolm Fraser, to get rid of Whitlam. Whether this story is apocryphal is not known although Fraser denies any knowledge of it. But according to the gardener, Fraser, Murdoch and Kerr had met on the veranda of Murdoch's property discussing ways they could oust Whitlam as prime minister. The gardener's story was related in 1981 on a visit to Murdoch's property by the general manager of the Adelaide *News*, John Fisher, and the local Commonwealth Bank manager, Gerald Speck. Mr Speck was manager of the Hindley Street branch and had looked after News Limited business. Murdoch was one of the bank's best customers and the Commonwealth Bank had backed many of his ventures. Murdoch had invited Fisher and Speck to spend a few days at his country estate.

Before Fisher joined News Limited, he had been an aircraft

engineer in Perth and later inherited his father's business and garage adjoining the Adelaide *News* from where they delivered the paper. Murdoch had been impressed with Fisher and offered him the job of circulation manager and then general manager.

During their visit, Fisher and Speck were relaxing on the veranda when they were approached by the gardener. 'You're sitting in Sir John Kerr's chair,' Speck was told. The gardener added, 'That's where Mr Murdoch, Sir John, Malcolm Fraser and a few others plotted to get rid of Gough Whitlam!'

During my own interview with former Prime Minister Fraser in Melbourne, he denied the three men had ever plotted against Whitlam but admitted that he and Murdoch had wanted to get rid of the Labour leader and had discussed the matter. Even if Fraser had not been at Murdoch's estate at the same time as Sir John, independent reports certainly confirmed that Sir John visited the homestead and held talks with Murdoch over a financial crisis centring on Whitlam prior to Sir John sacking him. Sir John was reported to have discussed the various options he would consider, as it appeared that the Australian senate (the upper house) might reject the government budget, without which it could not function. The only way out would be for the prime minister to call a general election, which Whitlam had refused to do.

Whitlam had been told of the visits and was furious that Sir John was discussing matters of state with the opposition leader and Murdoch. The constitutional convention was that the governor general takes the advice of the prime minister and not that of a newspaper boss or opposition leader. But Sir John had also sought the advice of the attorney general and felt justified in the action he took against Whitlam because a stalemate had been reached and the country was in crisis. Added to this, previous scandals involving government figures had seriously affected the Labour party and Whitlam's fiscal policies were not working.

Fraser wanted a general election in the knowledge that Labour's popularity had decreased to the point where he would have an easy victory. The Liberals held the majority votes in the senate by a thin margin, which Whitlam was hoping to dilute further. As long as Fraser could keep the senate majority the stalemate would be preserved. But there were senators who were unhappy with the situation. Holding a government to ransom through the senate rejecting the budget went against convention and fair play yet Fraser was determined not to lose that advantage.

Whitlam, on the other hand, wanted to call a senate election, knowing that if he lost he would still have a majority in the house of representatives. Fraser refused the offer and insisted Whitlam call a general election. That is where Sir John had to step in to stop the impasse. Although Whitlam had appointed Sir John, a former judge, as governor general, they were now at loggerheads. Had Whitlam removed Sir John from office, which he was empowered to do, he could have avoided being sacked but he never thought Sir John would dismiss him. Fraser says he telephoned Murdoch and asked his support. Murdoch agreed, providing Fraser could keep the senate on track in rejecting the budget.

The situation deteriorated with the government desperately needing cash to pay the wages of public servants. This led Labour to throw caution to the wind and seek private loans. These were not forthcoming but wreaked further havoc with the government's credibility. It could not have come at a worse time for the party but was a godsend to the Liberals and Murdoch press, which thrived on the political intrigue, continuous scandals and sacking of government ministers. The Labour party had left itself wide open to a devastatingly one-sided newspaper campaign, which in itself led to the journalists' strike on *The Australian*.

Malcolm Fraser was appointed caretaker prime minister by Sir John Kerr in the afternoon of 11 November 1975, following the sacking of Gough Whitlam. This fact was not generally announced so that Fraser could herd together the senate to vote for the budget. As a result, Labour senators voted with the Liberals and the budget was immediately passed. Only afterwards did the senate realise they were doing Fraser a great service as he could now conduct government with funding that had been denied to Labour. The proclamation dissolving both houses of parliament was read out on the steps of old Parliament House. Whitlam's response struck a chord with the huge crowd gathered to hear him. His short but brilliant speech brought him admiration and sympathy from around the country. 'Ladies and gentlemen, well may we say "God save the Queen", because nothing will save the governor general. The proclamation which you have just heard read by the governor general's official secretary was countersigned "Malcolm Fraser", who will undoubtedly go down in Australian history from Remembrance Day 1975 as Kerr's cur.'

One of Fraser's first tasks was to set the date for a general election, which, with Murdoch's backing, he won in a landslide victory with a 55-seat majority over Whitlam. He served as prime minister until he was defeated by Labour's Bob Hawke some eight years later in 1983. In the run up to that election, Murdoch switched sides, having decided Fraser was history, and supported Hawke.

While Murdoch's own politics have veered sharply to the right of the political spectrum, Fraser maintained he had always been a conservative with a small 'c'. He backed Australian human rights legislation, a more open immigration policy and steered clear of the present Liberal party of Australia led by right winger Tony Abbot, a former priest. Even today he remains critical of the right wing policies followed by his old party and of the UK's Gordon Brown staying as prime minister when it was obvious he did not have the backing of his party. Brown's predecessor, Tony Blair, came in for even greater flak. However, Fraser's old alliances with the Murdoch family made it difficult for him to criticise the neo-con beliefs of his old friend Rupert.

From Fraser's eyrie on the 32nd floor of a prestigious block in Collins Street, Melbourne, where he today occupies a vast office with picture windows overlooking the central business district, he recalled the Whitlam sacking and spoke of the press mogul he has known for 70 years. 'I'm nearly a year older than Rupert. My parents knew Sir Keith quite well and my mother was always close to Dame Elisabeth, who is highly respected and has done much for good causes. The family holidayed with the Murdochs and Sir Keith took us fishing. My grandfather was Canadian and came to Australia in the late 1840s. The Frasers were from Scotland but left for Nova Scotia in 1746 otherwise they would have had their heads chopped off. Lord Lovat of Fraser was the last to lose his at the Tower of London although he delayed his execution by pleading to cure his leg of gout first. He didn't want to be dragged off to the block by the sassenachs.'

Like Murdoch, Fraser had a privileged upbringing, on a pastoral property in the Riverina district of New South Wales. He graduated in modern greats at Magdalene College, Oxford and at 23 was elected to parliament. To the surprise of many, he and Gough Whitlam reconciled their differences and Fraser agreed to deliver a lecture in the second annual series organised by his former adversary, the Whitlam Oration, in June 2012. He says of Whitlam, 'Gough was not a good man-manager. He had no idea of economics and maybe no idea of due processes once he went beyond the law, but it is just as important in government. But he had an idea of Australia and Australian independence and of respect and equality of all people and equal opportunity.'

After his own time as prime minister, Fraser joined Whitlam in the debate over media ownership regulation and was against the Hawke government's changes to regulation that allowed Murdoch to buy the Herald and Weekly Times group of newspapers when he already dominated newspaper publishing in Australia. Media, he said, needed government regulation to protect diversity. Where media ownership became too concentrated there was a danger of it rivalling the power of parliament. 'I still hold the view about ownership of newspapers [not being in the hands of one person] and so did Menzies [Sir Robert, Australia's longest-serving prime minister]. He stopped a British company from buying four radio stations. He said people who do not belong to this country should not have such a strong instrument of public propaganda. When I was in office there were seven or eight proprietors. Now there's only one and a half.'

The 'half' owner he was referring to was Australia's richest billionaire, Gina Rinehart, who invested heavily in the media and is the biggest shareholder in Fairfax Media. She inherited her fortune from her father, Lang Hancock the mining magnate, and owned vast iron ore resources in the Pilbara region of Western Australia. Fraser continued, 'Gina Rinehart wanted control of the *Age* newspaper. Luckily, she loses interest in things. She's got enough money to buy the *Age* and then you'd have two powerful people [Murdoch and Rinehart] owning the news in Australia. Rupert's view is that market forces should determine it.'

While insisting that Murdoch never asked him for favours, despite the support he gave to his election campaign, Fraser unashamedly agreed that he had approached Australian media owners to canvass their support in forcing the 1975 election. 'There was one conversation with Rupert, a very brief one initiated by him [Murdoch]. Alan Missen [Liberal senator for Victoria] had come to me and said, "Prime Minister, you know I spoke against the decision [to block the budget] but the issue is so important and the government [Labour] is so terrible I will support the decision. The press will write that I am about to cross the floor of the senate. But I won't."

'Rupert said to me. "Now, I just want to hear it from you. Is the senate going to stick?" I told him they would. "Right," he said. "I'll stay with you as long they stick."

'There was no argument, no discussion about tactics, no conversation of how we could get them [Whitlam's government] down. * Any suggestion that I got together

---

* Murdoch was to ask for similar assurances from Margaret Thatcher in June 1986 at the time of the Wapping pickets when he sacked printers and moved to the Wapping plant to print his newspapers. Some Conservative ministers began getting cold feet and Murdoch wanted a personal assurance from Thatcher to stick by him. She agreed to do so.

with Murdoch, Doug Anthony [National party leader and deputy prime minister under Fraser], and Kerr to devise a plan to get rid of Gough is absolute crap. [Though Fraser did have a number of private conversations with the governor general]. Everyone wanted to get rid of Whitlam. I read a story about a drunk getting on to a Melbourne tram when Whitlam was sacked and holding up a newspaper displaying big headlines about the sacking. Everyone on the tram cheered. There were a load of scandals involving the Whitlam government at the time. We had said if there were no further scandals we'd let the budget get through. But one scandal followed another.'

When Fraser asked Kerry Packer for his support it was not as forthcoming as Murdoch's. Packer was in two minds about the wisdom of blocking supply and suggested the Liberals change their mind. Fraser accused him of having 'wobbly knees' and asked Tony Eggleton, federal director of the Liberal party, to contact Murdoch and get him to talk to Packer. Murdoch solved the problem. Fraser also contacted Fairfax newspapers but realised they would not impose their views on reporters. That was not the case with Packer and Murdoch, said Fraser. 'We did not believe the fiction that media barons do not control the policies of their papers.' Fraser still insists it was this realisation that later led him to campaign for the greatest possible diversity of media ownership to stop media bosses from bullying governments.

But was he not helpful to Murdoch when as prime minister in 1981 he amended the law in the mogul's favour? Fraser's administration was criticised when it removed the requirement that Australian owners of TV stations had to be resident in the country. Murdoch was then able to increase his stake in media ownership in Australia while resident in New York. They also removed the requirement that the Australian broadcasting tribunal grant prior approval for a sale of a TV station. In future, approval could be sought after a sale and tribunals could no longer deny a TV licence on public interest grounds.

Fraser said he changed the law because its original intention was not to limit ownership on grounds of residency but only on citizenship: 'The broadcasting control board was thinking of changing rules on ownership. The law as it passed said you have to be an Australian citizen. Then we learnt that it was having talks among itself to say it implied citizen and residency. At the time Rupert was in New York. The board, contrary to the wishes of the country and the law, were going to apply the law differently. We put in a small amendment. I went through all the original debates and what had been said by both parties. The word "resident" had never been mentioned so we amended it. Some of the press named it the "Murdoch Amendment" but he'd never spoken to me about it or I to him. I simply thought the board was going to do him an injustice and followed the intention of the original legislation to ensure the control board would follow it. Yes, it would have been helpful to Rupert but contrary to some media owners he only wanted to be treated as anyone else wanted to be treated. He never asked for anything.'

Mungo MacCallum, a political reporter and broadcaster, commented, 'I think Malcolm Fraser passed this legislation not so much out of gratitude for past favours from Rupert, but out of fear of what Rupert might do if he didn't get it, because Malcolm Fraser had seen how viciously the Murdoch press could operate in trying to tear down governments in the past and he didn't want it to happen to him.'

In 1975, Fraser also offered a former Murdoch employee named John Menadue the post of ambassador to Japan. Political journalist Peter Bowers claimed that the gesture represented more than the fulfilment of a long-time interest in Japan. To Menadue, the offer was 'the clincher', the proof that his old boss Rupert Murdoch, 'had played an inside political role in the dismissal of the Whitlam government in 1975'. Bowers would quote Menadue as saying, 'Dangerous then, more dangerous now. America and Britain may be able to accommodate him but our country is too small to live comfortably with an interventionist the size of Rupert Murdoch.'

Fraser observed Murdoch's brutal treatment of Whitlam from the frontline, never more so than when Whitlam was wrongly accused of having received substantial loans from Iraq. The story had been a 'scoop' obtained by Murdoch and splashed in *The Australian* on 25 February 1976, reporting that a man named Dr Henri Fischer claimed he had been approached by the Labour party to raise funds for Whitlam's election campaign. Fraser, according to recently released documents held in Australia's national archives, had exchanged information with Murdoch concerning Fischer. But Whitlam denied seeking or obtaining Iraqi funds and is reported to have won damages for libel from *The Australian*.

Despite Fischer's claim that a donation of US$500,000 would be forthcoming, nothing was paid. Nevertheless, the story achieved the desired result of creating further question marks over the suitability of Whitlam as leader. Apparently, the Foreign Affairs department and the Australian Security

Intelligence Organisation were asked to make inquiries confirming Fischer's story. The director general of security was none too pleased that information was passed to Murdoch and warned that public disclosure of intelligence information could jeopardise investigations.

I myself was witness to the close ties that had been built between Murdoch's newspaper and the Liberal government of 1977 after I returned to Australia. I was employed as group investigations editor at the Murdoch press, with an office in *The Australian*. Some months later editor Les Hollings offered me the post of political writer in Canberra. I asked Les what would be expected of me. He replied, 'To write whatever the prime minister tells you.' I thanked him for his offer and went back to England.

By a strange coincidence, seven years after the Dr Fischer/ Iraqi funds story, Murdoch offered several million dollars for another dubious story that would make world headlines when it was claimed that the diaries of Hitler had been found. They turned out to be a hoax and the man behind them was also called Dr Fischer! That knowledge alone may have sounded alarm bells for Murdoch when he offered to pay a king's ransom for the serialisation of the diaries but he was so keen he threw caution to the wind.

Academic and Hitler authority Hugh Trevor Roper – who had the title Baron Dacre – initially confirmed the documents' authenticity but then wavered. Told of the historian's change of mind, Murdoch is reported to have said: 'Fuck Dacre. Publish.' The first instalment was duly published but the hoax was then revealed and Murdoch did not have to pay for the forgeries. But the *Times* and *Sunday Times* in the UK received worldwide publicity. The *Sunday*

Times particularly went from strength to strength as the top-selling Sunday broadsheet.

Ever keen to expand his growing list of influential friends, Murdoch saw an opportunity to speak to New York mayor Ed Koch soon after purchasing the *New York Post*. On a programme in the Frontline documentary series broadcast in the US, Koch was reported as saying, 'When the phone rang, the voice on the other end said something like, "Congressman Koch, please." I said, "Speaking." He said, "Congressman, this is Rupert" and I guess I was still a little sleepy maybe. I said to myself, "Rupert? Rupert? Rupert's not a Jewish name. Who could be calling me at seven o'clock in the morning named Rupert?" And then suddenly, because he was speaking, I realised it was Rupert, the Australian. I mean, the voice came through. And I said, "Yes, Rupert?" He said, "Congressman, we're going to endorse you today on the front page of the *New York Post* and I hope it helps." I said, "Rupert, you've elected me."'

A former Murdoch editor, Bruce Guthrie, recalled how Murdoch could also inspire fear in politicians. When John Howard was opposition leader in Australia in the late 1980s, he was due to have a meeting with Murdoch. Staff who saw him waiting commented on how nervous the deputy looked. Guthrie said, 'The water in his glass splashed everywhere.'

But it wasn't just Murdoch who wanted to meet those in power. Politicians of all persuasions were just as intent on meeting him to seek his patronage or arrive at an understanding. The losers, as ever, were likely to be members of the public who unquestioningly believed any ensuing propaganda in Murdoch's newspapers.

Such was the acceptance of his baronial power that even where Murdoch's newspapers had given a politician a bad press or attacked their party, they would appear suppliant to his greater power. A perfect, if disappointing, example of this was Australia's first woman prime minister, Labour's Julia Gillard. She came to power in 2010 and Murdoch's right-hand man in Australia, John Hartigan, made no bones about giving the PM and her party a hard time in the press, particularly in *The Australian* and the Sydney *Telegraph*. However, this did not inhibit Murdoch from visiting Gillard at Parliament House in Canberra nor, indeed, did it put her off lunching with Murdoch on a trip to New York.

In the run up to her election both her party and the Greens who supported Labour received considerable criticism. Yet within two or three days following Murdoch's visit to Gillard, she agreed to the publication of a full-page article in the *Sun* in the UK under her own name. AUSTRALIAN PM WRITES FOR THE *SUN* was the headline. The article began, 'Why we all must stay the course in Afghanistan' and went on to support Murdoch's backing of the USA and its involvement in the Middle East. 'Nations and their leaders can make no graver decision than go to war. When this happens our citizens deserve to know exactly why we take up arms. Right now, soldiers from 47 nations, including the UK, are serving under a United Nations mandate to stabilise Afghanistan. Australian forces are deployed in Afghanistan to serve two vital interests. First, to ensure Afghanistan never becomes a training ground for terrorists who attack Australians and the citizens of our allies. Second, to uphold our commitment to our alliance with the US which was triggered following the terrorist attacks of September 11,

2001. Australia's contribution in Afghanistan is also an expression of the common interest we share – not just with the US and the UK but with the other 44 countries of NATO and the International Security Assistance Force in countering international terrorism...'

In political terms, the article gave international exposure to Gillard and acted as a further reminder to Republicans in the USA and Conservatives in the UK of Murdoch's global political influence. Murdoch had previously given a lecture broadcast by the Australian Broadcasting Corporation (ABC) that carried exactly the same message: 'Our world remains a dangerous place. In this promising new century we are still seeing naked, heartless aggression, whether it comes from a terrorist bombing in Islamabad or a Russian invasion of Georgia. At the same time, our traditional allies in Europe sometimes seem to have lost the will to confront aggression, even on their own doorstep. We can lament these developments, but we cannot hide from them. The fact is that, throughout our past, Australian lives have always been affected by events in distant and unfamiliar places. That will remain true for the future as well. We need to be prepared to respond to these threats, as we have done in Iraq and are doing in Afghanistan.

'But we need to be more than a reliable partner that the US can call on. Australia needs to be part of a reform of the institutions most responsible for maintaining peace and stability. I'm thinking especially of NATO. Though NATO was designed to prevent a land war in Europe, it is now fighting well beyond its borders. As we see in Afghanistan, not everyone is doing their share and that is a problem too many people want to ignore. The only path to reform

NATO is to expand it to include nations like Australia. That way NATO will become a community based less on geography and more on common values. That is the only way NATO will be effective. And Australian leadership is critical to these efforts.'

Murdoch's speech was delivered as the 2008 entry in a prestigious annual Australian tradition, the Boyer Lectures. ABC, who had broadcast the event every year since its inception in 1959, overlooked the fact that Murdoch was not Australian, as did Murdoch himself. After all, in 1985 when he took American citizenship he swore an oath to 'entirely renounce and abjure all allegiance and fidelity to any foreign prince, potentate, state or sovereignty...' But in this lecture he showed that at heart he was still an Australian, although his wallet had crossed the oceans to become well and truly American. However, through the vast influence of his majority ownership of the media, he has not stopped meddling in Australia's affairs. His sphere of influence was further widened recently with his takeover of more Australian pay TV stations. Urging fellow Australians to consider independence, he said (the italics are the present author's), 'The establishment of a republic of Australia will not slight the Queen, nor will it deny the British traditions, values and structures that served *us* so well. But *we* are no longer a dependency, and *we* should be independent.'

With a personal contact book that reads more like a global *Who's Who* and a bank account exceeding the wealth of a small country, one could be forgiven for thinking that no door or access to political leaders could be barred to this most powerful of newspaper moguls. Murdoch's major expansion until the 1990s had been in Europe and the US. These were markets he understood well and the culture, language, and business models were already familiar to him or could be readily understood. Early on in the development of his empire he made small inroads into the east with Singapore and Hong Kong – the latter while it was still a British colony, although already almost on the point of ceding sovereignty to China, a country with potential riches beyond imagination. India would also prove a rich resource and politicians there were keen on business and approachable, but China represented a real challenge and a worthy prize. Murdoch's presence near China's borders, however, was no more than that of a mouse that roared while the massive Chinese dragon was a jealous custodian guarding its colossal treasures.

It was not a language barrier blocking Murdoch's pathway to Chinese presidents or their treasures. There was simply an impassable barrier erected by the wise burghers of Beijing. They knew exactly what he wanted and they barricaded their walls. Murdoch, the great opponent of socialism and communism, defender of democracy and free trade, had arrived bearing dollar gifts for a ruthless dictatorship with no regard for human rights. As far as they were concerned, he was the barbarian waiting at the city gates to win over their leaders and plunder their riches. They would not let him do this. Even before he had drawn up his battle lines, their files on his business empire and documentation of his influence had been catalogued and absorbed. In short, they had his measure.

But they were willing to play a cat-and-mouse game, one that cost him millions but eventually won him some favours.

He first visited China in 1985 with Anna and their children and invested in a hotel complex that he later sold. In 1987 he bought the Hong Kong *South China Morning Post*, which was a cash cow, although its editorial line was not pleasing to the mainland Chinese and it was sold by the mogul. By 1993, Sky TV was making huge profits and Murdoch again ventured to the east, buying the controlling interest in Hong Kong's STAR TV. By now he already owned the expanding Fox network and controlling share in BSkyB in Britain. STAR TV broadcast to mainland China and Murdoch wanted a meeting with Chinese leaders Deng Xiaoping and president Jiang Zemin to arrive at an accommodation, but without success.

On 1 September 1993 the mogul made a speech in London on the advances of technology and telecommunications. The speech ricocheted with the destructive force of an Exocet missile. He told an audience of advertising and TV executives that 'advances in the technology of telecommunications have proved an unambiguous threat to totalitarian regimes everywhere... Fax machines enable dissidents to bypass state-controlled print media. Direct-dial telephony makes it difficult for a state to control interpersonal voice communications. And satellite broadcasting makes it possible for information-hungry residents of many closed societies to bypass state-controlled television channels.' Within a month of his speech, the Chinese premier, Li Peng, had banned all private satellite dishes in the country.

Murdoch's own goal set him back four years, but he continued to work with China. He withdrew BBC programming from the STAR TV transponder that covered the country, he made donations to a foundation run by Deng

Xiaoping's disabled son and paid a reputed $1 million for a book contract for Deng's daughter. He also cancelled a book contract made via HarperCollins, the publisher owned by News Corporation, with the last British governor of Hong Kong, Chris Patten.

Years later Murdoch talked to News Corporation's vice president in China, Bruce Dover, whose excellent book *Rupert's Adventures in China* documented the journey. Murdoch said the line about the 'unambiguous threat to totalitarian regimes' was written by Irwin Stelzer, the American economist, *Sunday Times* columnist and Murdoch confidant. Murdoch said: 'I read through it in the afternoon before the speech and just didn't pick it up – not in the context of China... I was really thinking in terms of all that happened in the Soviet Union, the Berlin Wall coming down. It didn't dawn on me that it would be portrayed as it was.'

As for Chris Patten's book, Dover said HarperCollins editors had failed to listen to Murdoch, who had long thought Patten did not understand China. The editors were also 'blithely unaware that the News Corp investment in China now topped US $1billion and that the business was haemorrhaging financially at the rate of US $100 million a year.' Murdoch's curt response to the editors had been 'kill the fucking book.'

Evidence of a partial rapprochement with China came when its president, Jiang Zemin, was due to visit the US in 1997. Murdoch was invited to meet members of the politburo who wanted to ensure that Fox TV gave the politician a good press. Murdoch was given a new list of contacts in China. He had won their respect with his perseverance and a business style that had similarities to that employed by Chinese tycoons.

Murdoch also persuaded Australian diplomats to arrange a meeting for him with China's vice premier. Zhu Rongji was quick to remark, 'I see you became an American citizen so you could operate a television network in the US. Would you be willing to become a Chinese citizen to get into the television business in China?'

Murdoch would become exasperated with the preferential treatment shown by the Chinese towards Jerry Levin, CEO of Time Warner. Dover was told by Chinese foreign ministry officials, 'Some of the leaders still regard Mr Murdoch with great suspicion. It is like having Genghis Khan at the Palace Gates. He may tell you he is your friend but then he might also rise up and strike at one thousand places... you will need to be more patient.'

Dover recalled introducing Wendi Deng, a Guangzhou factory manager's daughter, to Murdoch at a cocktail party in Hong Kong in 1997. She had been educated in the US and worked as a STAR TV intern. Murdoch was impressed with her looks and intelligence and she was later asked to be his interpreter and guide in China. Dover described how he and Wendi accompanied Murdoch to Shanghai a few months later. There the mogul was nearly killed by a bus. Dover said he had told Wendi that his first thoughts had been, 'Oh, my God, what if he'd been killed? Who do I call first – the News Corp office, the ambulance or my stockbroker?'

But with a change of political leaders in China, there was to be another setback for Murdoch. Deng Xiaoping, according to Dover, stated that opening the country to the West was like opening the windows. 'You have to live with the flies that come inside'. By 2004 they had become a pestilence and Rupert Murdoch was among them. He was pushing too far and too fast. With the arrival of a new leader, Hu Jintao, he lost the protective umbrella he had enjoyed under Jiang Zemin. In 2007 Murdoch realised he would have to wait a long time to access nearly 400 million homes with TV. But he created a legacy that one day may be taken advantage of by his Chinese-speaking children.

7

FLEET
STREET

Village Fleet Street virtually came to an end with News International's exodus to Wapping. Overnight the culture moved a world away from the way things had previously worked in the 'Street of Shame', as it was affectionately known.

Murdoch built what was virtually a newspaper factory along The Highway in Wapping, near Tower Bridge. Compared to Fleet Street it was like suddenly being placed in a wilderness. It had high security fences and guards sufficient to keep striking printers out and the journalists in. Many journalists resisted new technology almost as much as the printers who lost their jobs with its introduction. Constant demonstration outside NI offices during the first year restricted freedom of movement further. Bodyguards escorted executives from the building and reporters tended to stay within the compounds rather than venture out for their stories. This suited the management because it meant a huge cut in expenses. Previously journalists could catch taxis, buses and tubes within minutes. That was not the case with Fortress Wapping.

Sadly, change had to take place. The narrow laneways around Fleet Street were too small to accommodate the large print lorries constantly making deliveries and Bouverie Street was a nightmare. My Aston Martin was constantly driven away by police to the Wood Street pound where I would pick it up in the evenings by taxi and be handed the keys by police who told me how much they enjoyed driving it to the pound. Police respected decent vehicles in those days.

The new changes stuck. The phone became the vehicle for stories rather than journalists meeting contacts outside the office. True, there had been some abuse by journalists who were not supervised and, within the Fleet Street area, one was never more than three minutes away from the nearest pub. But within the Street there had been strong competition and a desire to prove oneself and get exclusive stories that would be talked about with colleagues from other papers. In future the competition would be from within one's own paper where it would be impossible to operate along similar lines. In my opinion, this led to laziness and a certain frustration for journalists who were still expected to produce similar content. I had proved time and again that interaction with the public produced excellent results for a skilful reporter. As amusing as it was, I always remembered journalist Steve Dunleavy's chat with me in New York when he recalled how Murdoch told him to 'pay nothing, go nowhere and cover everything'. That now would become the war cry of the journalists at Wapping. That might also account for the need of some of them to resort to dishonest methods to produce the goods they could not get otherwise, either through laziness or by restrictions placed on them, cooped up in Wapping.

Rich rewards followed if one was prepared to go anywhere and put oneself out to find a decent tale. One of the joys of being a freelance writer was being able to choose your own projects and pursue them wherever they took you. For me, it was a world without borders. Human interest was a highly saleable commodity and once I had established a reputation there was generally little difficulty in getting the newspaper to bankroll me wherever I wanted to go. News International would usually back me, although from time to time a particular editor might not believe I could come up with the goods and would refuse to give an advance, but that was rare, even after the move to Wapping the late 1980s. But it did happen to me with a *News of the World* executive who lacked foresight about how big *Baywatch* and its glamorous star Pamela Anderson would become.

I had been invited by an independent television company to its British launch of *Baywatch* in January 1993. Reporters and photographers from most of the national dailies and Sundays attended. For photographers it was an absolute feast with a bevy of nubile *Baywatch* beauties eager for publicity. Showbiz reporters were also there and represented competition. But I need not have worried as, for whatever their reason, most newspaper representatives regarded the event as a photo opportunity with extremely pretty actresses and little more. I concentrated on obtaining background stories and found them to be amazingly open about personal and family dramas affecting their lives.

Pamela Anderson was particularly forthcoming as she had

little experience of being interviewed. She was natural, friendly and delightfully co-operative with personal details. Her looks had been unaffected by plastic engineering and it was rather a shame she later felt the need for it. Much to the chagrin of the news department at the *NoW*, I sold the story of my interviews with the girls for a handsome sum and it was used across two pages – a double-page spread. I also told the executives that I had phoned Pamela's family in Canada and they agreed to allow me exclusive interviews and access to all her previous photographs. However, in this instance I was not prepared to fly to Canada unless I was sure the newspaper was interested. It turned out to be a lesson for me as well as for the newspaper. I should have followed my instincts, as I usually did in these matters, and not been swayed by the negative opinion of a minor executive because Pamela became a huge star and everyone later fought battles over her.

The editor was, however, keen to back me when I suggested joining Andy Warhol and inmates at his New York studio – the Factory. For three hilarious days I chased Warhol around his Union Square studio, dodging starlets and freaks and socialites all seeking fame. While I was chasing him, I in turn was being chased by Geri Miller, a former topless go-go dancer turned actress with minor parts in two of Warhol's co-productions, *Flesh* and *Trash*. Geri – 'I'm not all tits, you know' – had just been for an audition for another part which she failed to get because 'the producer wanted to sleep with me but I refused. He was annoyed and rang me. "Listen," he said. "Don't you understand – I'm the casting couch?" I told him, "Well, frankly, you look more like a lumpy sofa to me" and hung up.' Geri had caused a stir at the Roundhouse in London during a performance of Warhol's play *Pork* by removing her top and twirling each breast in turn before an astonished audience.

While he did not like face-to-face interviews, Andy was content for me to photograph him and interview a retinue of starlets, actors and hangers-on who arrived daily seeking parts in films. US actors would fall over themselves to speak to an English journalist, hoping they would find fame outside their country. Androgynous Andy was the centre of a fantasy universe. He was the guru of fame and illusion. As an artist, his Polaroid made him millions through the photographs he took of soup cans and other humdrum objects, which he then painted and sold to the real stars of Hollywood. Warhol's fame was largely due to Sam Green, a New York art promoter who was well connected. Sam was at the Factory when I arrived and keen to talk with me. He had been a director of the Institute of Contemporary Art in Philadelphia while in his twenties and cultural adviser to New York's mayor John Lindsay. Warhol very quickly went from being a nobody to being a somebody and Sam organised exhibitions for his sought-after, avant-garde art.

The two men soon became a must-invite duo in New York art circles and fulfilled their social ambitions in meeting the rich and famous and becoming constant name-droppers. Eventually Green became a bag carrier for society photographer Cecil Beaton, who introduced him to Greta Garbo. Green's most famous friends were Yoko Ono and John Lennon – the latter I interviewed in Majorca in 1974. Green's affair with married woman Barbara Baekeland, whose husband was heir to a multi-million dollar fortune, ended in tragedy. She was murdered by her son Tony in Belgravia, London and a film about her life – *Savage Grace* – was released in 2007. In discussing the movie, Green never lost an opportunity for self-aggrandisement in his praise of the actor who played him. 'I will concede that I am brilliantly portrayed by Hugh Dancy. He is stunningly well dressed and looks exactly as I did. It is as if he raided my wardrobe from those days.' Warhol would have been proud.

Warhol himself drew on the talents of film director Paul Morrissey and associated himself with Morrissey's films *Flesh*, *Trash* and *Heat*. But Andy could lay some claim in helping make the band the Velvet Underground famous. At the time of my visit, Green shared his plush Manhattan apartment close to Central Park with sex-change actor Candy Darling. Both were close to Andy but happy to relate anecdotes about him. Green said he had told his 'close friend' Cecil Beaton about Warhol. The photographer replied, 'Oh, I remember him. He's peculiar, my dear. He's such a little urchin character.'

Beaton described how he'd met Andy in Philadelphia. Warhol had said to him, 'Mr Beaton, I'm so pleased to meet you. This is the greatest moment of my life. I hardly know what to say. Oh, if only you would allow me to paint your portrait. I would do anything to get the chance.' Beaton agreed and asked where Warhol would like him to sit. 'Could you go into the bedroom as it is more private? I want it all to be just right.'

Inside the bedroom, Beaton sat on a chair, asking if Warhol wanted a full-face or profile and was told full-face would be just fine. 'But then he asked me to remove my socks and shoes and his portrait was of my two feet with a rose between the toes!'

Green was quite open about his and Warhol's social climbing. 'We were good at it. We'd get invited or gatecrash as many social occasions as possible. Andy used all his connections and work to further his social climbing. But he's so shy when he meets people it's difficult for him to talk to anybody. He says very little to them and just wanders around and looks. He's a genius at making money and being a businessman. He starts off the vogue for collecting art or furniture before anyone else thinks of it and by the time they have, he has the best collection. Andy gets over $75,000 for a portrait and all he does is take a Polaroid camera off to the lab and get a silk screening. And they're all lining up. It's a great honour to be the inspiration of a Warhol portrait.

'He employs young people at the Factory because they have no set ideas and they adjust. He wants everyone to have a brand new approach. Part of his shyness is that he is unable to talk to you unless there's an instrument between you and him. He and I can't talk at dinner parties but he gets on the phone and he's got his tape recorder and it's just talk, talk, talk.'

At that point, Candy Darling, tall, blonde with lily-white skin and bright red lipstick, made an appearance. She was a cross between Jean Harlow, Marilyn Monroe and Danny La Rue, the famous drag artist. 'I'm playing the white whore in *The White Whore and The Bit Player*,' she announced.

Candy's chance of stardom had come through meeting a man at a party who told her he could make her a star. 'He said he liked the way I looked. I needed someone to tell me what to do and he did a lot of things to me against my will but he taught me what to do. This made me known within a few months. I didn't look like another modified Jean Harlow. I looked like the real Jean Harlow. You know that's why Geri Miller will never be a real hit star. She doesn't have blonde hair like I do.' Candy's dog suddenly growled and she snapped at it: 'You'd better simmer down or I'll cut you up!' She continued, 'Andy doesn't need sex. It may sound over-refined but when you get to primitive people it's something to do with propagation and very important to them. It's not at all important for someone with such a high intelligence and consciousness as Andy...'

Sam interrupted, 'Andy thinks sex is disgusting.'

'Well, isn't it?' asked Candy.

By now I had to escape the madhouse of Union Square. But I still needed to speak to Warhol and knew the only way I could do this would be via the telephone. I walked to one of the adjoining rooms and found a pay phone from where I called him. It was crazy. I had been constantly in the same premises as the artist over a period of three days but had to phone him from within his studio. All went well. We spoke for 40 minutes and I got my story. The interview concluded, I left Warhol clutching his comfort blanket and means of communication with the outside world – a tape recorder, microphone and Polaroid camera.

The *News of the World* editor from 1973 to 1975 was Peter Stephens. He had been editor of the Newcastle *Journal* before joining the *Sun*. Like Tiny Lear, his predecessor, Peter was considered a safe pair of hands. Unlike some of his successors at the paper, Stephens was more conservative in his views about naming and shaming but was keen on human-interest stories with a salutary message. As an example, he would not name a lady psychologist who helped her clients with sexual problems by offering her services as a sex therapist. His view, a correct one in my opinion, was that she was giving a genuine service and should not suffer the indignity of exposure. He had no hesitation, though, in naming criminals or less worthy individuals who he considered deserved to be exposed. Stephens was more of an elder statesman at the newspaper than a thrusting, adventurous editor. He left those tasks to the up and coming editors like Nick Lloyd (now Sir Nicholas Lloyd) who became an assistant editor and eventually editor of the *NoW* as well as other titles such as the *Daily Express*.

Stephens was later given a managerial role as editor in chief of both the *Sun* and the *News of the World* and curbed the wilder excesses of the titles. But while he was in the editor's chair I was given tremendous support for my stories.

Trevor Kempson and I were assigned a team to investigate the vice kings of Soho. They consisted of a number of Maltese property owners who lived in Mayfair and Knightsbridge and made their money from prostitution and clubs. In the main they were left alone by those members of the West End police who received constant bribes and would tip them off whenever there was a raid. Trevor and I worked well together. I would plan the investigation, assimilate the evidence and write the story while Trevor, a former military policeman, would front up to the villain with me in tow.

For a period of three months, I rented a flat in Half Moon Street in Mayfair and became part of the 'scene'. We met the villains and liaised with police. I had to take particular care as I was also working with the *People*, exposing bent coppers. Commander Bert Wickstead was chasing the same targets as we were and it became essential that we maintained close relations. Thankfully, as Bert was a straight copper he was quite happy to exchange information. Equally, he was extremely grateful to see his name and photograph in the newspaper as 'gangbuster Wickstead' and 'the old Grey Fox'.

To tease him I would call him the old gay fox and, not quite understanding the nuance of a flippant remark, he would insist, 'Honestly John, I'm not.'

Fleet Street journalists had much in common with the Met. They liked drinking, they enjoyed being part of a clan and they loved free meals and expenses-subsidised drinks. They also enjoyed the occasional liaison with the opposite sex, facilitated by the unsupervised nature of their job. The tribal unity that existed between journalists and policemen led to trust and confidence in exchanging information which suited both sides but would not have been approved by Scotland Yard chiefs. Certainly, I was quite happy to give the police any information regarding those I was investigating, providing they didn't nick the villain before I could get the story in print. In return, the police gave me valuable information that helped with our story. There was never a need to contemplate payment as it was always an exchange and it would have been an insult to offer an inducement.

Trevor Kempson also got on extremely well with Scotland Yard. He could speak their language as it were. I had the feeling that Trevor would very much have wanted to be a police officer. He certainly dressed and acted like one.

I had a particularly good relationship with two inspectors who were generous with assistance. Although there were considerable differences in our make-up, we got on well and I invited them to several functions – though one, unfortunately, led to a demotion. I had been invited to a book launch in Knightsbridge and thought one of my contacts might enjoy some culture. Book launches could become riotous affairs and by about 11pm, one of our party had been sick on the carpet of the posh venue and the hapless inspector crashed his car into several parked vehicles on his way home. He was arrested and convicted on a number of embarrassing charges. Other than that, we had a fun and memorable evening.

Among the villains we exposed were Big Frank Mifsud and Bernie Silver, an old London crime boss who was charged with murder but later acquitted. Big Frank was arrested at his Knightsbridge flat and fled to Switzerland. He was caught by police and jailed, pending extradition to England. I was given information on his whereabouts at a Solothurn mental institution (he was pleading insanity at that time) and, remarkably, he spoke to me there and also on the aeroplane bringing him back to London. Waiting for us on the tarmac at Heathrow was none other than Bert Wickstead, with photographers ready to snap the old Grey Fox arresting the captured villain on home turf. In fact, the whole episode was more like a celebrity photo shoot than a serious arrest and capture of a wanted criminal. The police were just as publicity-minded as showbusiness personalities.

On two or three separate occasions I was told when major villains were to face trial at the Old Bailey. The police van bringing them to court would be escorted from prison by several police outriders, roads would be blocked and red traffic lights ignored. Armed police were stationed on rooftops and sirens blared as the convoy got nearer to the Central Criminal Court. Such a dramatic road to justice would need coverage and reporters would be tipped off by police mates regarding the best position. Justice, or in this case, injustice, was seen to be done. A jury was bound to be influenced by the high criminal status afforded such prisoners.

Providing a journalist did not embarrass the newspaper, we were never instructed on how to conduct our investigations or given advice on limiting our actions. The important thing was to get the story. But then we had sensible editors in charge, like Nick Lloyd, who were different to old school journalists like Kempson. Lloyd was very much a career journalist. While he had worked for the *Daily Mail* and the *Times* as well as the *Sun*, he had the survival instinct of a politician and an ambition to match. He had been to Oxford and Murdoch sent him to the US to attend Harvard. The mogul had high hopes for him within the NI organisation before he was headhunted for the editorship of the *Express*.

With Lloyd at the helm of the *NoW*'s feature department, we had someone who the police could not bully or scare into submission when it became obvious our research into the vice kings was proceeding at a faster rate than theirs. While we co-operated with the Yard, we did not let that inhibit us from printing new evidence as it came to hand. The newspaper made much of our investigation and after each edition, members of the criminal fraternity would come forward with further information.

While I was busy writing another instalment of our vice kings' exposé, the front desk at our Bouverie Street offices called me to say a Colin Levy would like to see me. I was too busy and asked Trevor Kempson to see what the man wanted. Kempson came back after half an hour, excited beyond belief. He obviously had some explosive information but would not share it with me or Nick Lloyd. This was fairly typical of Fleet Street one-upmanship: an older journalist not wanting to be upstaged by a younger man who posed a possible threat. Even so, I felt a little peeved that he was keeping this excitement to himself. After all, I was the person the fellow had asked to see. As it turned out, I was pleased I was not told. We were about to become embroiled in a scandal that did not reflect particularly well on the senior reporter's judgment.

Colin Levy was married to a prostitute who serviced high-profile clients and wanted to sell photographs of his wife Norma in bed with Tory minister Lord Lambton smoking a joint. Publication would damage Edward Heath's Conservative government but, worse still, Lambton was under-secretary of state for defence. It followed that that he would be vulnerable to blackmail attempts and this would have to be considered by both MI5 and MI6. Levy presented a real danger as it appeared this case was not a one-off. He had photographs of other leading figures and Tory grandees with his wife, a much sought-after dominatrix. Levy was a loose cannon, an untrustworthy conman who wanted to extort as much money as he could from his wife's activities. Norma Levy later told police she thought he was connected with security personnel in the US. Initially, Kempson did not reveal all the facts about Norma Levy to the editor, but he was told to make further inquiries.

This proved an exciting time for the newshounds. Levy's story had all the elements of a major front-page splash, tailor-made for the *News of the World*. It had sex with call girls, a high-class madam, toffs, drugs and a government minister involved with an Irish call girl. Only a little imagination would be needed to include the IRA. And at the centre, controlling it all, was Kempson, who thought he was about to clinch his biggest exclusive. He enjoyed the drama and, to keep interest alive, dropped little hints of what the story might involve. We occasionally saw a shadowy character wearing sunglasses slip in and out of the office and accompany him in a taxi to a West End hotel for secret interviews.

By now, editor Peter Stephens was becoming apprehensive about the outcome of an investigation that had echoes of the Christine Keeler scandal which had resulted in damning criticism of Murdoch. Kempson carried on regardless. The photographs Levy had of the prostitute and the government minister were not considered good enough and Kempson wanted further proof. He organised a *News of the World* photographer to hide in the prostitute's wardrobe and take fresh photographs of Lambton in bed with two women. In addition, Kempson insisted on hiding a tape recorder in a giant teddy belonging to Norma Levy. A slit was cut in the toy and the bear was fitted with the *News of the World*'s Nagra reel-to-reel spy tape recorder that could record for five hours. Everything went according to plan except that, unknown to Kempson, Scotland Yard and Commander Wickstead were already aware of Lambton's secrets.

Peter Stephens was anyway unhappy about publishing a photograph of Lambton and I was told he had called Murdoch for advice, particularly as this matter would be of great concern to the government and Edward Heath as prime minister. Murdoch had previously met with Heath but there had been no meeting of minds. Heath was not concerned with Fleet Street or what they thought of him. He did not seek patronage from Murdoch although, like most newspaper proprietors, Rupert was invited for cocktails at Downing Street and Chequers from time to time. Heath probably would not have thought too kindly of the *News of the World* boss because Murdoch had encouraged his readers to vote Labour at the 1970 general election despite the fact that it had previously supported the Tories.

As for giving advice to his editors, Murdoch would

generally not interfere but relied on them to follow his line of thinking. Providing a publication did not conflict with his business interests, Murdoch allowed editors to use their own judgment. Whatever the case, Stephens decided against publishing. A furious Kempson felt let down. He had been sure the paper would publish the story and had given Levy his word (without authorisation) that he could have all his material returned. The reporter had always fought fiercely to uphold his promises to newspaper contacts. That may have been an honourable thing to do to an innocent tipster but it was absurd to do so when that person was an obvious crook who had engaged in virtual blackmail to destroy a third party. But now Kempson felt strongly that he had let down Colin Levy. Foolishly believing he was doing the right thing, he gave all the newspaper's photographs back to the conman. Levy promptly sold the package to *NoW*'s competitors the *Sunday People*.

Meanwhile, Scotland Yard had been raiding Soho pornographers' shops and came across the name Jellicoe in a coded notebook. This had nothing to do with the Lambton case or Lord Jellicoe, the Lord Privy Seal and Tory leader in the House of Lords, but police sought to interview the peer if only to eliminate him from their inquiry. As it turned out, Jellicoe did have his own, unrelated, little secret. He had been visiting a prostitute in Mayfair and thought the police had finally rumbled him. Before they could put any questions to him, he put up his hands and confessed his peccadillo to an amazed Scotland Yard porn squad officer. He then resigned from government.

Kempson received little thanks for his efforts on the Lambton case. The *People* got his story and the *News of the*

World took the flak for the methods used in taking the photograph. But there was an interesting postscript to this episode. Labour opposition leader Harold Wilson took more than a passing interest in the Lambton case. He was also on better terms with Murdoch than Heath had been. Wilson dined with Murdoch and invited him to Chequers and Murdoch was sympathetic to the miners' strike of 1972. Now, at the Labour party's request, Lord Wigg, a retired army colonel and MP close to Harold Wilson, was invited to the *News of the World* offices and given access to all files involving the Lambton investigation.

George Wigg had also been involved with the security services and he now used his contacts to evaluate the Lambton affair and report back to Wilson. He would sit for hours on end with Millie Matthews, the *NoW* features department secretary who was assigned to assist him and do his typing. The pair got on famously. Millie was an attractive south London girl and a dedicated Labour supporter. She enjoyed working with the former MP and provided him with information to pass on to Wilson and the Labour party that may have been useful for the next general election. Wilson scraped in with a majority of three and later served as prime minister for a second time.

While in the army, Wigg had met Arnold – later Lord – Goodman and introduced him to Wilson and other Labour dignitaries. I had come across Goodman's name when researching vice operations in 1975. I found a reference to a Mayfair millionaire who owned many Soho properties used for vice and among the club records and ownership papers of the premises I was surprised to find Lord Goodman's name appeared as co-owner.

Goodman had built a reputation as an advisor to politicians of both parties and to the government. He had also been a personal advisor to Harold Wilson. During his long career he was Master of University College, Oxford, and without doubt he was highly respected as one of the great power brokers in British life. Murdoch met Goodman soon after purchasing the *NoW* and occasionally used him as an advisor. Tony Blair also considered him a special figure when he appointed Labour fundraiser Lord Levy, saying, 'I want you to be my Lord Goodman figure.' But not everyone was enamoured of the good Lord. After his death, former client Lord Portman claimed Goodman stole funds worth £10 million from his family trust.

From my own research into Soho vice it appeared that Goodman and the Mayfair millionaire also owned the freehold of a property in Greek Street, London with two drinking clubs, one a gay club and the other run by a prostitute. I had not known of the connection between Goodman and Murdoch but, on passing my memo to an editorial executive, I was advised to drop the case. I took it to the *People* where assistant editor Laurie Manifold continued the investigation. Within two weeks of his inquiries, he said we could go no further. There had been a fire in the building and the premises were now empty.

In an *Observer* article of 1971, Goodman was praised for his good works. 'He has managed to live at the centre of London life without anyone ever discovering anything in the smallest degree embarrassing about him. Even though some of his clients have been men of notoriety.'

The following year, 1976, the Mayfair millionaire's wife was murdered with a shotgun outside a public house in

Brighton. Two hit men were later convicted but refused to say who had ordered the killing. The millionaire himself was wanted for questioning over the crime but had sailed to Malta with his nanny, who he later married. In 1984 the police said they no longer wanted to interview him about the incident and that he could return to Britain. Though the millionaire had obviously been a client of Goodman's, neither he nor Goodman may have been aware of what use was being made of their joint properties.

8

MURDER, MAYHEM AND MADNESS

Sunday newspaper editors can have a more challenging task filling newspaper columns than their daily counterparts who benefit from a continuous stream of breaking news stories during the week. By the time Saturday comes around, the Sundays have to produce something fresh for their front page to give their paper an up-to-date appeal without regurgitating old stories. That calls for lateral thinking and a pressing need to find a new angle. On the other hand there are benefits. Working for a Sunday paper allows more time for analysis and preparation on articles than dailies can hope to spend and there is greater opportunity for timeless pieces and long-term investigations providing the paper is minded to do so. While successful investigations can bring credit to a newspaper, they can be expensive and time-consuming and for this reason are not always welcomed by budget conscious editors.

The Sunday tabloids have nurtured a more ruthless brand of journalism than exists among their brother dailies and within News Corporation particularly it has resulted in methods bred from fear of missing the exclusive and the desire to succeed. Like their editors, journalists are continually aware that their bosses subscribe to the simple but effective principle of produce or perish. For a high-flying reporter on a big salary and expensive mortgage, survival under this style of regime can lead to taking short cuts or resorting to desperate measures in getting their story that would not normally be taken.

Where questionable tactics have been taken, and succeeded, the journalist is rewarded providing he or she has got away with it and I have seen a number of instances of this with both editors and journalists. While working at Murdoch's *Star* magazine on a visit to New York, I called across the newsroom to an Australian reporter who'd been a long serving News man. I quite openly asked if it would be all right to make a private call to Australia. An experienced Murdoch hack came up to me and whispered, 'John, you can get away with an awful lot of things in life if you don't shout about them. The comment encapsulates the behaviour of a number of journalists within the group. I had an association with the *NoW* until 2006 and, although I never witnessed hacking, or was aware it was taking place, looking back on it once the matter was exposed it certainly reminded me of wondering how some journalists and executives on the paper came by their information on various stories they had undertaken.

News Corporation's big advantage in news gathering is its huge resources. But this has given Murdoch executives an unrealistic sense of their own might and has led to reckless behaviour by some who feel uninhibited about breaking rules and ignoring statutory regulations. Humility on being rumbled is no antidote for wrecked lives. Reputational concerns, it would seem, have been less important than the bottom line and the fear has always been of the go-getting culture spreading to the broadsheets. Murdoch's undertaking over editorial independence given to regulatory bodies and his constant declarations of non-interference in newspapers like the *Times* has been met with incredulity by newspaper observers and some executives.

The major restraining influence on staff, it would seem, is fear of Murdoch himself. I have been in many newspaper offices with editors when Murdoch has telephoned them and the change in their demeanour has been staggering: something akin to a puppy rolling over in submission and whining. I imagine similar scenes have taken place with prime ministers and politicians when the mogul comes to town.

The gung-ho approach by tabloid editors has been reflected in the choice of some Murdoch editors and executives. Kelvin Mackenzie was an amazing editor in his stint at the *Sun* from 1981 to 1994 and, from a distance, I have professional admiration for his success and chutzpah, both of which have been formidable. But I always considered him the bovver boy of Fleet Street editors and Mackenzie confirmed my opinion with his outrageous but hilarious criticism of the Leveson inquiry into the press. It appeared in the *Evening Standard* on 12 October 2011.

'Where is our great prime minister, who ordered this ludicrous inquiry?' Mackenzie asked. 'The only reason we are all here is due to one man's actions – Cameron's obsessive arse-kissing over the years of Rupert Murdoch. Tony Blair was pretty good, as was Brown. But Cameron was the daddy. Such was his obsession with what newspapers said about him ... that as party leader he issued all his senior colleagues, especially Michael Gove, with knee pads in order to protect their blue trousers when they genuflected in front of the special sun ... There was never a party, a breakfast, a lunch, a cuppa or a drink that Cameron and co would not turn up to in force if the Great Man or his handmaiden Rebekah Brooks was there ... Cameron had clearly gone quite potty. And the final proof that he was certifiable was his hiring of my friend Andy Coulson ... And then the phone hacking scandal erupted. Not a scandal of Rupert's making, but the order went out from Cameron: stop the arse-kissing and start the arse kicking ... And the answer is this bloody inquiry chaired by Lord Leveson. God help me that free speech comes down to the thought process of a judge who couldn't win when [he was[prosecuting counsel against Ken Dodd for tax evasion and, more recently, robbing the Christmas Island veterans of a substantial pay-off for being told to simply turn away from nuclear test blasts in the 1950s.'

One of the more interesting items that came from Mackenzie's contribution was the conversation he had with Rupert Murdoch regarding the *Sun* backing Cameron over Gordon Brown for prime minister in the 2010 general election. 'Rupert told me an incredible story. He was in his New York office on that day that the *Sun* decided to endorse Cameron for the next election. That day was important to Brown as his speech to the party faithful at the Labour party conference would have been heavily reported in the papers. Of course, the endorsement blew Brown's speech off the front page. That night a furious Brown called Murdoch and in Rupert's words, "roared at me for 20 minutes". At the end Brown said, "You are trying to destroy me and my party. I will destroy you and your company." That endorsement on that day was a terrible error. I can't believe it was Rupert's idea. Strangely, he is quite a cautious man. Whoever made that decision should hang their head in shame. I point the finger at a management mixture of Rebekah [Brooks] and James Murdoch.'

Mackenzie had attended the Leveson inquiry as a witness. Had he, they asked, as *Sun* editor, known the sources of many of the *Sun*'s stories? His honest but startling reply was, 'To be frank, I didn't bother during my 13 years, with one important exception.' That story involved an allegation about Elton John, which Mackenzie said he checked and decided was true and then published it after taking legal advice. The story was untrue and cost the *Sun* £1 million in libel damages. That did it for Mackenzie. 'So much for checking a story. I never did it again. Basically, my view was that if it sounded right it was probably right and therefore we should lob it in. How will this inquiry change that?'

Mackenzie may be correct in thinking it might have been Rebekah Brooks backing Cameron in preference to Brown, even though she had been friendly with Brown and his wife. In Tom Bower's book *Sweet Revenge: The Intimate Life of Simon Cowell*, the author says, 'In the weeks before the general election, the outcome had become uncertain. Every vote now counted to avoid a hung parliament. Hoping that Cowell could swing a few votes, Brooks asked that he give a few quotes to a *Sun* journalist in support of the Tories ... On the eve of the election, he awoke to find the *Sun*'s front page covered by a long article, supposedly written by him urging *Sun* readers to vote Tory.'

On the idea of introducing a press restraint law, Mackenzie commented, 'If anything, the only recommendation that should be put forward by Leveson is one banning, by law, over-ambitious and under-talented politicians from giving house room to proprietors who are seeking commercial gain from their contacts. In tabloid terms, arse-kissing will be illegal. Should have an interesting passage through Parliament.'

Unlike Mackenzie, I did have to check my stories, even if I did sell them to the *Sun* and *News of the World*. And unlike some reporters at NI, I did not feel the need to invent stories, nor would I have done so, because people would tell me truths that were beyond invention and sometimes beyond comprehension. But that was one of the luxuries of being a freelance journalist. You could invest time and effort into getting it right and that always paid dividends.

The *News of the World* paid a heavy price for invading the privacy of Max Mosley, the former president of the FIA, the Formula 1 motorsport body. He was exposed for taking part in consensual, sadomasochistic sex with several women. The *News of the World* had videos taken of the party at private premises and wrongly stated in the article that it was a Nazi-style orgy. If it had been true the paper could have got away with it but it wasn't and the wrongful allegation was particularly unpleasant for Mosley as he was the son of Oswald Mosley, the British fascist leader. There were many other things awry with the story's presentation and even the court evidence provided by reporters was questionable. Mosley won his case and then embarked on a campaign to help victims of hacking. He had stood his ground against the paper, despite the personal unpleasantness suffered through exposure and the family tragedy that followed. As a lawyer I thought Judge Eady's decision in the High Court was a fair one. As a journalist, I understood the culpable shortcomings in the story and considered a great deal more supervision should have been carried out before publication. At their request I wrote the following comment on the case for the *Independent*:

'So, does Mr Justice Eady's decision last week in favour of Max Mosley's right to privacy really threaten press freedom? Not in my opinion. His judgment was about proportionality, responsibility and the rights of privacy entrenched in the European convention on human rights. In determining these rights, he examined with forensic precision the full shock-horror sex exposé written in the finest tradition of an old-fashioned *News of the World* scoop. He then applied the law, awarding a fairly modest sum of £60,000 to Mr Mosley, which may even have surprised some of the judge's more outraged critics.

'Mr Justice Eady's 54-page judgment is essential reading for all those involved in the media. But on examination, it is clear he was far from convinced that the story headlined F1 BOSS HAS SICK NAZI ORGY WITH FIVE HOOKERS was in the "finest traditions" of the newspaper.

'The *News of the World* has never been shy about courting controversy. Like its sister paper the *Sun*, its budget for stories is the envy of other tabloids on Fleet Street. As a consequence, it usually gets its stories right, but not, as the judge found, in this instance. The problem was the lack of evidence ... linking fascism to the sadomasochistic orgy was the vital ingredient that the story needed to justify the intrusion into Mr Mosley's private deviance, which was practised behind closed doors and among consensual adults. Unfortunately for the newspaper, the main informant identified as "Dominatrix E" was unwilling to corroborate its version of events.

'How different things would have been had the *News of the World* been able to supply evidence of a fascist theme, considering the hurt that such behaviour would have caused the millions who still suffer from the effects of the Holocaust. There would then have been a strong case for exposing Mr Mosley's private actions, and the weight of public opinion would, I venture, have solidly backed the newspaper. But on this occasion the judge found no evidence to support the thrust of the paper's story and was unimpressed by the verbal evidence of its editorial staff. In newspaper terms, they cocked it up and paid the price.

'Further, without the peg of fascism, the judge's hands were, figuratively speaking, tied. Article 8 of the convention allows everyone the right to respect for his private and family life without the interference of public authorities (or newspapers). Like all rights, these are subject to limitations that would also apply to the right of newspapers to publish matters where there is a legitimate reason for doing so. Article 10 gives everyone, including newspapers, the right to freedom of expression and, again, this is subject to reasonable limitations.

'The convention was not introduced by Mr Justice Eady. Parliament enacted it in 1998 and, as Eady said, 'the UK government signed up to the convention more than 50 years ago.' Eady was aware that he would come in for some considerable stick following his judgment. He understands newspapers well and used to advise the red-tops when practising as a barrister. He was therefore careful to emphasise that this was not a landmark decision and he was not prepared to give Mr Mosley aggravated or exemplary damages.

'While he may well have thought that Mosley brought many of his problems on himself (having been warned by friends that he was being investigated), the judge agreed that there had been an infringement of his right to privacy and emphasised the balancing act required between articles 8 and 10. Aside from the distasteful emotional context of Mr Mosley hiring five dominatrices for an S&M orgy, should this attract less protection than say any other type of orgy among consenting adults whose sexual practices might be equally offensive to some people?

'What Mr Justice Eady's decision emphasises is the need for editors to be aware of privacy rights and to be responsible and fair in their reporting. The question of privacy does not arise through this case alone. Recently there have been a number of successful injunctions brought by members of the public, including members of the press, seeking to stop the publication of private matters. The question of intrusion has been one facing the media for a long time, and the tide is turning towards more responsible reporting. In the 1970s, the *Sun* was criticised for its stance towards homosexuals. Eventually it got the message and changed its direction without loss of revenue and without complaining that press freedom had been compromised. There was a period in the 1980s when the *News of the World* was prepared to print a number of kiss-and-tell stories without fully checking their accuracy. Although heavily criticised at the time, the storm soon blew over and the newspaper changed course, having paid out considerable damages.

'The risk of libel has always been there and now there is the additional matter of privacy, which although present through newspaper codes and legislation has not always been taken seriously. But tabloid editors will have to take note following the Mosley case. What they fear most is the rich litigator and an angry proprietor unhappy with the published story. They must now take more care with privacy issues and have the sense to examine how far they can push a story without detriment to the subject – or themselves. Even so, it is unlikely that the present decision will inhibit newspapers from investigating genuine stories or doing the odd kiss-and-tell. All that it requires is proportionality and reasonableness. The two most successful groups, News Group Newspapers and Associated Newspapers, have vast funds at their disposal. As long as they get their story right, they should not feel threatened by the decision.'

CRIME AND CRIMINALS

As a student of law I had always been interested in reasons for crime and had researched psychological profiling of criminals. Crime, sex and human-interest stories were essential reading for the Sunday tabloids and 1975 was full of them.

On 13 July 1975 the *Sunday People*'s exclusive splash was I GOT AWAY WITH MURDER. It was a confession made to me by Victor Spampinato, a hit-man and enforcer for Soho vice bosses. I had interviewed him a year earlier in his native Malta where he had fled after he was acquitted of killing London gangster Tommy 'Scarface' Smithson in a gruesome Chicago-style shooting. Spampinato's accomplice, Philip Ellul, was sentenced to death at the Old Bailey but was later reprieved and released from prison after serving 11 years. The principle that a defendant could not be tried twice for the same crime then meant Spampinato felt safe in revealing his role in the grisly affair.

When I tracked him down to the village of B'kara in Malta in 1974, he was living a hand-to-mouth existence and lodging at his mother's home. Police in the UK had also spoken with him and were anxious he appear as a witness for the prosecution against underworld bosses implicated in the Smithson murder. But they also wanted Philip Ellul, who had already been convicted of the killing.

Bert Wickstead – the Grey Fox – went to a great deal of trouble to find Ellul. He had returned to America after serving his sentence so Wickstead flew to Los Angeles and made television appeals for his whereabouts. Ellul was leading an itinerant life, sleeping on park benches. Police flew him back to the UK and put him up in a flat and paid all his expenses. He agreed to give evidence against Bernie Silver, the Soho crime boss charged with involvement in the murder. Sir Michael Havers QC defended Silver.

The trial had been due to start on 16 September 1974 but the 'witnesses' failed to turn up. Havers attempted to pin the blame on me. He asked the Old Bailey judge permission to have me brought before the court to explain how I came to interview Spampinato. To ensure I attended, two hefty police officers were sent to fetch me from the nearby newspaper office where I was working. By his questioning it was obvious that Sir Michael was in possession of an awful lot of information that could only have come from Spampinato. It quickly dawned on me the man had changed sides and would not be helping the prosecution. I had taped his confession and Havers did not want it read in court. His best strategy was to have the judge condemn me for allegedly interfering in the course of justice. It was a clever ruse to lessen the impact of the evidence I could give. Sir Michael asked if I had taped Spampinato and, of course, he knew. A good barrister rarely asks a question to which he does not know the answer. I was quite candid about the tape, realising he would have got the facts from his client. Scotland Yard requested the tape recording, which yielded 297 pages of manuscript.

Sir Michael next accused me of being in contempt of court for having interviewed a witness in a murder trial. I successfully argued against him but he continued the attack. He accused me of being in cahoots with the police, which was certainly not the case and I denied all his innuendos. After a long session, the defence barrister finally released me. But as I stepped down from the witness box, Sir Michael sidled up to me and, through pursed lips, whispered, 'Well done, son, you're a fucking better liar than I am!'

Some months later I returned to Malta. Spampinato's financial situation had undergone a miraculous change. He was driving a new car and building a magnificent Mediterranean style villa above a five-car integral garage overlooking B'kara and refused to talk to police about his new life. But his confession remains today as a chilling portrait of a calculating killer. Spampinato had been told, 'This punk has got to be exterminated.' He obliged.

The UK Press Gazette considered the impact of the story on the Press Council, which 17 years earlier had castigated IPC newspapers for a similar front page in the Sunday Pictorial (later the Sunday Mirror, a stable mate of the Sunday People). It was headlined, I KILLED SETTY... AND GOT AWAY WITH MURDER. Beneath was a signed note: 'I Donald Hume do hereby confess to the Sunday Pictorial that on the night of 4

October 1949, I murdered Stanley Setty in my flat in Finchley Road, London. I stabbed him to death with a dagger while we were fighting.' Hume's signature was reproduced below the words.

The *Gazette* pondered the question: how might the *Sunday People* defend publishing the confession? Could the editor defend it on the grounds that: (1) The paper described the confession as appalling. (2) The series challenges the public to face the issue of a confessed murderer who cheated a British jury. (3) The fact that justice was not done makes a confession of greater not lesser public importance. (4) The confession completely vindicated the Scotland Yard men who had conducted the inquiry. (5) Had the confession been made in court or otherwise to the press in general, it would have been given the widest publicity, thus (6) The offence was what journalists traditionally consider the acme of enterprise – exclusivity. 'All to no avail,' said the *Gazette*. The Press Council had ruled against criminals giving 'romantic explanation which, never having been tested in court, may or may not be true.'

That year was also the beginning of a series of murders by the Yorkshire Ripper, Peter Sutcliffe from Bingley, West Riding, who went on to kill 13 women and was only arrested in January 1981. The *News of the World* spent thousands buying stories about Sutcliffe. His wife, who had known nothing about her husband's activities, had been entertained by the editor and his top executives in an effort to persuade her to sell her story. Eventually, the paper paid a freelance journalist £80,000 to serialise her book. Certain executives at the *NoW* threw caution to the wind in their frantic attempts to get the story at all costs. Like terriers, they would risk life and limb to get their quarry and, with the weight of the newspaper's resources behind them, there was little they would not do or pay.

Another Yorkshire serial murderer, Donald Nielson, known as the Black Panther, had lived only 20 miles south of Sutcliffe. In 1976 he had been imprisoned for life for the murder of four people, including heiress Lesley Whittle who he had kidnapped and shackled in an underground tunnel with a noose around her neck. Having just stepped off the plane from New York, I was sent to his home address for a chat with his family shortly after his arrest. A man I assumed was Nielsen's father was understandably not best pleased to see a reporter on his doorstep. I told him how sorry I was to hear what had happened and explained I had come all the way from New York to speak with him. 'Well,' he said with a gruff Yorkshire accent, 'you can bloody well get straight back there then,' and slammed the door in my face.

In the same year, I obtained fraudster Ronald Milhench's exclusive story for the NoW before he was sent to jail for forging Labour prime minister Harold Wilson's signature over a land deal. Milhench had wrongly attempted to implicate Wilson in the deal just before a general election and offered to sell his fraudulent tale to the Daily Mail for a considerable sum. His story was splashed across the front page of the NoW because of the many elements it contained. He revealed details of a tawdry love life that included wife swapping and orgies at his Wolverhampton mansion and political intrigue at the highest level.

A number of unfortunate rumours, mostly without any substance, had arisen around Wilson. He had been accused of being sympathetic to the Kremlin and there were rumours of friendship with KGB spies. That was put down to the fact that Lord Kagan, a Lithuanian-born friend of Wilson who had suffered under the Nazis and was a friend of Russia, was also friendly with a KGB spy at the Russian embassy in London. Kagan had run a successful textile firm in Yorkshire and manufactured raincoats worn by Wilson. But in 1980 he was sent to prison for ten months for theft involving his old company.

Curiously, I had an interesting meeting with him and Harold Wilson at the House of Lords around 1993. I was introduced to Kagan by another party who immediately said, 'Come and meet my friend Lord Wilson.' The former PM was sitting with a group of peers drinking gin. He waved for me to join the circle and ordered a large gin and tonic and proceeded to entertain the group.

'When I was MP for Huyton,' he began, 'there was always a problem over the Irish question. Whenever I went on a tour to America, I would tell them there was only one way to solve the Irish problem. What you do is to hire some divers and cut away the Irish roots anchoring the country then shove it out to the middle of the Atlantic Ocean. Problem solved.' Roars of laughter and more gin followed.

Milhench was a nasty piece of work and his presence was somehow unsettling and worrying. It was difficult to judge the truth of anything he said but there was one particularly tragic story that checked out. It involved the untimely death of his wife in questionable circumstances and he spoke about it in a matter-of-fact way, revealing an incredible degree of callousness. Milhench, a keep-fit fanatic and an expert water skier and diver, had been a constant visitor to Chasewater, a large water-ski lake in south Staffordshire. In February 1974 he told police he had taken his wife there for a drive. February is one of the coldest months of the year. Milhench said they were near the water's edge when the hired vehicle suddenly lurched into the lake and sank in deep water. Fortunately for Milhench, he happened to have scuba-diving equipment in the car, which saved his life. However, he was unable to save his wife, Kathleen. Milhench claimed he had pushed her out of the car's window before saving himself. An inquest jury returned a verdict of accidental death.

Some weeks before Kathleen died, Milhench had doubled her life insurance to £40,000. While suspicions were raised about the circumstances, Milhench told me and my assistant journalist that, before he appeared in court over the forgery case, he made a deal with police. He would admit the forgery allegations and firearms offences and would not create difficulties over the Wilson letter or say anything about it in the future. In return, he would be given a three-year prison sentence and police would not pursue their inquiry into his wife's death. Was he suggesting there was more to the death? I never did find out if he was teasing us about this or whether he was fantasising or suffering from some kind of mania.

Milhench accurately predicted the sentence the court would pass on him and I recorded that at the time. After serving his time, he left England for the Philippines and was reported to have become extremely wealthy in a relatively short period of time. Some reports said he owned several yachts and lived in a $12 million apartment. One of his friends was the wayward Lord Moynihan, owner of the Yellow Brick Road and Fountain of Youth brothels in Manila. An Old Bailey judge had described the peer as the 'evil genius behind a series of frauds'. I visited him in the Philippines in the late 1970s on behalf of the *News of the World* when he was on the run from British police. The splash headline in that case was: RUNAWAY PEER IN HIS VICE DEN.

Moynihan boasted, 'John Stonehouse [the Labour MP who faked his own death] has nothing on me ... I've never been straight in my life.' He and Millhench had a lot in common.

Another friend of Milhench was identified as Baron Frederik van Pallandt, one half of the 1960s singing duo Nina and Frederik, whose hits included 'Puff the Magic Dragon'. Pallandt was involved with an Australian drugs trafficking syndicate and had purchased a yacht from Milhench. According to a Sydney court hearing, Pallandt had been owed $20 million for transporting drugs for the syndicate but was found shot dead after a dinner party in Manila in 1994. The Australian syndicate were named as murder suspects.

In May 1995, Milhench was sent to prison for five years in Hong Kong. He had been lured there by police in a sting operation. In the local press he was described as a wealthy Englishman. How police came to raid his safe deposit box was never explained, but it was raided and on discovering its content – a loaded, unlicensed revolver and a false passport – the trap was sprung. Milhench pleaded guilty in court and said he had played silly games like an overgrown schoolboy pretending to be a James Bond. He told the judge that he had teamed up with Lord Moynihan, who had died in 1991, to break up a ring of traffickers in illegal immigrants. A psychiatrist testified that he suffered from mild hypomania – an addiction to risk-taking – and that had an inflated sense of self-importance.

Crooks, conmen and killers made for interesting reading but it could be harrowing for the interviewer. Jimmy Humphreys, the tough pornographer being held in a Dutch jail, was like a caged lion. One word out of place and there would be a sudden mood change. Spampinato confessing to murder was unnerving. He was sitting too close to me on the fifth-floor balcony of my hotel and I did not trust him at that distance. Milhench was a fantasist but a dangerous one. Although sociable, he was not the company one would choose to keep. The answer in these cases was to never show emotion or to express judgement.

The horrific murders committed by Dennis Nilsen, a former policeman and army chef who by day was a mild-mannered civil servant and ghoulishly preyed on lonely young men by night, shocked the UK. Nilsen plied young men with alcohol and then invited them back to his flat where he would murder them and hide their bodies under floorboards or cut them up and dispose of them down the drains. I investigated his background for several months, obtaining material for a book, and wrote about him in the *News of the World*.

I had asked to visit Nilsen in prison but the Attorney General Sir Michael Havers – who had defended Bernie Silvers – refused permission. He said it was not possible for a journalist but allowed access to a writer friend from his club. My book came out first and Sir Michael's friend was flabbergasted that it contained material he thought only Nilsen could have revealed. But I had obtained such a complete profile that when I sat down with Professor John Gunn, forensic psychiatrist and fellow of the Royal College of Psychiatrists in London, we were able to predict his actions.

Nilsen the serial killer was a lonely man. The reason he hid bodies beneath the floorboards was so he could fish them out when he was lonely and sit them in chairs for company while watching television. Nilsen was a man who could show pity for a winged bird or, for that matter, to an injured person like the young man who needed an ambulance outside his north London flat, but not for his victims. When the young man who had taken the ambulance later came back to thank the murderer for saving his life, Nilsen killed him. He was sent to prison for life on 4 November 1983.

John Bindon, the son of a London taxi driver, was a builder and actor and a Jack-the-lad character, highly popular with the ladies but less so with their husbands. His claim to fame was balancing full beer mugs on his manhood at society parties on Mustique in the presence of HRH Princess Margaret. Bindon was everybody's friend and, when not entertaining society ladies, became a part-time gangster who knifed a small time London villain called Johnny Darke. Because of his association with Princess Margaret and his lover Vicki Hodge, a model and baronet's daughter, Bindon's trial for murder at the Old Bailey drew large crowds. The *Daily Mirror* had signed up Hodge in the event that Bindon was found guilty. If acquitted, the paper would be able to use his story so either way they would have a big exclusive.

Whenever the Fleet Street popular newspapers needed to prevent someone whose story they were writing from being 'snatched' they would employ minders. At Bindon's trial, 15 *Mirror* men positioned themselves inside and outside the Old Bailey with chauffeur-driven cars waiting to take their buy-ups back to the *Mirror* where a champagne reception would be waiting. I couldn't match the mega-bucks offered by the *Mirror* but I still had my wits about me. While the jury was considering its verdict, Bindon was taken to the cells beneath the court. I had agreed to work with another freelance journalist, David

Mertens, on this project and I would try and get to Bindon. I asked David to chat with Vicki.

Somehow I managed to talk the authorities into allowing me down to the cells where a warder let me in to see Bindon. I quickly introduced myself and wished him the best and told him to be positive. I had no idea which way the jury would decide but in that moment he appreciated my company. We were very soon taken upstairs to the court in time for the decision. Bindon, to his great surprise, was acquitted but did not say a word. He looked towards me and nodded and we both walked out of court, while the *Mirror* journalists, believing I was part of the welcoming party, kept a respectable distance. Ensuring that no one could take our photographs, they ushered us into the chauffeur-driven car that took us the few hundred yards to the *Mirror* offices. Bindon turned to me in the car and said, 'Fuck me, I don't know how I got away with that!' He was elated.

We walked into the *Mirror* offices and were swept upstairs by an army of security men and journalists. Champagne was put in our hands. Mertens had done the same as me and travelled back with Vicki Hodge. Each of us got our story and then I was spotted by the editor as I poured champagne. His champagne! 'What the **** is he doing here?' he exclaimed to his executives. Security was called and Mertens and I made a quick exit to the *Sun* where we wrote our 'spoiler' – a story that looks like the real thing but has far less detail. The *Standard* reported our little escapade as 'Front Page stuff'. To the credit of the *Mirror* hierarchy they did not carry a grudge but rather admired our chutzpah. But one thing was made absolutely clear to me: Bindon had got away with murder.

Not a man to be crossed, Freddie Foreman was probably

the toughest retired gangster I had ever met. He had been an enforcer and contemporary of the Krays and competed with the mafia in America. Foreman had been involved in a number of London heists over a long period of time, although little was heard of him because he was so successful. Eventually, he was arrested in Spain and brought back to Britain. When writing his story he confessed to the killing of two gangsters, 'mad axeman' Frank Mitchell and Tommy 'Ginger' Marks, the death of neither man arousing great sympathy. Foreman could be as mean as a Miura fighting bull and equally powerful. It took me nearly two weeks to win his confidence because men of his calibre observed silence. He sat looking at me, arms folded and exuding menace, until he decided it was safe to talk. Unlike other criminals I had met, Foreman was a cut above – intelligent, amusing and a great storyteller. Somehow, I got away with publishing it!

Another side to the man was that he could be as charming as a vicar on a Sunday afternoon and he loved showbiz. His son Jamie became an actor, is currently appearing in *EastEnders* and is great friends with actor Ray Winstone.

Northern Ireland was not on every journalist's wish list but the *NoW* asked me to go there for a story on faith healer Finbarr Nolan, a seventh son of a seventh son. Someone told me he was actually the eighth son of the seventh son but I ignored that. Nolan looked like a pop star and had built up a huge following in the Republic as well as in the UK. He was impressive and did not ask for money from those he healed but he was certainly amply rewarded by the many who believed he had special powers. As much as I liked him, I wrote a somewhat cynical piece about his faith healing enterprise. But I was impressed with his new Jaguar and the ease with which he was able to cross into the Irish Republic at a time when most cars were searched by the army in case they contained arms for the IRA. Nolan was no fool. He had ensured ease of passage before we arrived at the border but it was unsettling to pass armed police and roadblocks on the way.

On my return to the UK I was worried he might take offence at my interpretation of his work but I heard nothing from him for some time. Months later, however, I received another invitation to write about him. Good or bad, the publicity had increased demand for his services. The maxim that all publicity is good publicity proved correct in this instance. On reflection I felt he was doing far more good than harm. He was not demanding money and the fact that many believed in his healing power was no worse than a doctor giving placebo drugs to patients.

My next series of visits to Northern Ireland were quite scary but produced a major scoop. On the afternoon of Friday, 2 June 1976, Mary Gilmore was hurrying home along Belfast's Crumlin Road to her small, terraced house in Chatham Street. She was nine months pregnant. Without warning a terrorist opened fire with a machine gun and three bullets ripped into her body. She fell screaming to the ground clutching her body and screaming, 'Oh, my God! My baby!' She was rushed to the Royal Belfast hospital for sick children and baby Catherine was delivered by Caesarean. Doctors found a bullet had pierced the mother's womb and lodged just below the baby's spine. The next day little Catherine bravely fought for her life during a two-hour operation. The family received offers for their exclusive story from all over the world and chose to let me take care of matters. But problems began the moment I stepped off the aeroplane at Belfast.

Three taxis in turn refused to take me into the Catholic stronghold where Mary lived with her husband. The fourth taxi driver agreed but said, 'If we come in from the top end we'll be stoned and if it's the bottom end, we're in danger of being hijacked.' The next time I came I hired a car but was told by the locals to shift it at strategic times otherwise it would be 'borrowed'.

As dangerous as it was, I was glad to have experienced the Ardoyne. I was taken to families where grandfathers talked about the cruelty of the Protestants and described the horrors they had endured. I realised, of course, that a similar story would have been told by the other side. All the families I met were very friendly towards me and I put that down to my being Australian. It was more acceptable to them than being English or Protestant. One family insisted on giving me a keepsake handkerchief designed with motifs by IRA prisoners. I stuffed it down my underpants when returning to London as passengers were being searched by Special Branch and it could have meant many hours of questioning. Cathy's story and picture were syndicated around the world and she grew up to be a healthy child.

CARRY ON COPPER

While the *NoW* was friendly with the police in the late 1970s, they were prepared to publish exposés involving them. But it is extremely doubtful that their exploits would have been written about after the turn of the millennium, considering the close friendship that existed between senior executives of the Met and News International.

Bramshill Police College is a 17th-century mansion on an estate in Hartley Wintney, Hampshire. It sets out to produce the chief constables of the future and takes in bright police from all over the UK who train for a minimum of 11 weeks. The motto 'Authority is strengthened by learning' was appropriate to the intake of 1978. Some of the 236 student police were, according to the female staff, less interested in their courses than in the staff who made their beds.

All was revealed in the newspaper by Jean, a divorcee nicknamed Black Knickers by student cops. Proudly she told the newspaper that she had never made love to a policeman under the rank of inspector. 'They're much more fun,' she insisted. 'I've been out with 30 of them so I should know. There was no oochy-coochy talk with me. It was laid straight on the line – this was for kicks only.' On the night of the monthly staff dance – police called it the grab-a-granny dance or the scrubbers' ball – arrangements were made for 'afters'. These would generally take place in a block – known as the whorehouse – where Black Knickers would invite her one-night-stand to her room.

Jean was still getting over a broken marriage and found she had become attractive to a large number of men. This was an opportunity not to be missed and she, like some of her mates, made the most of it. But they had to take care. Some of the women in the block were quite moral so the policemen had to sneak in. Not that it mattered to Jean. She was open all hours. One of her lovers had an interesting take on authority. 'He would say, "You've sinned", and wanted me to confess that I had made love to other blokes. He'd then wave his baton around, like a headmaster would use a cane, before making love to me. Another policeman would make love to me for a long time and then put his head on my bare chest and cry in a child-like voice, "Mummy, Mummy, Mummy..." Can you imagine it? A huge, muscular, hairy policeman pretending I was his mummy.'

Another housekeeper, a widow, told how she was date-stamped on her bare bottom by six student police after they had been drinking. 'They used a stamp brought specially from the Met offices.'

The first hint of a temptress whose sexual predilection was affecting police in Brixton, south London, surfaced around April 1980. Crime reporters had written nibs ('news in brief' items) suggesting up to six policemen had been transferred from Brixton police station to other areas. Nobody would give a reason other than a woman had been involved. As the weeks went by, more police were moved until their numbers had reached a biblical 12.

Through a *Daily Mail* contact I was given the lady's address. When I knocked on her door, it was opened by an extremely attractive English girl with raven hair and the face and figure of a model. She had unwittingly – and unwillingly – attracted the attention of her 12 disciples, who had formed a not-so-secret fellowship with T-shirts emblazoned 'The 42 Club', after the number of her house. Entitlement to wear the T-shirt was restricted to those who had bedded the Brixton beauty and the queue at her front door was growing longer by the day. A senior inspector sent to question her and report on the police involved also fell for her charms and was removed from the case. The lady had made a number of complaints to the Met about policemen constantly harassing her for sexual favours. Worse still, she had kept a daily diary of events over an 18-month period, one of the reasons Scotland Yard tried to keep a lid on the affair. She told me she would never sleep with another policeman as long as she lived.

'According to their wives I am the Jezebel, a scarlet lady. A tart. My flat was visited by a steady stream of police officers ranging from constables to sergeants and they had one thing on their mind: sex. They all wanted to make it with me. Why me? I was a divorcee with a respectable job and two young children who I love and care for. Not a calculating seductress with a hungry passion for policemen on the beat. I know the record doesn't look good. The whole thing became a game. All wanted to be members of the so-called exclusive 42 club. That meant having a night of sex with me – usually while they should have been on duty. But let me put the record straight. It was not 12 and one inspector [that I slept with]. I made love with four of the Brixton policemen and allowed a fifth one to attempt making love to me because I felt sorry for him because he was impotent.' After an inspector was suspended from duty for inappropriate behaviour, she was finally left alone. 'What started out as a bit of fun turned into a nightmare.'

I was called as a witness to a special disciplinary hearing at which the police involved were represented by a defence lawyer. Through my association with the *News of the World* it was put to me that I had made up the story and that the police were innocent of the accusations made. I replied that the story I had written was like reading about *Snow White and the Seven Dwarfs* compared to what had really taken place and that if they wished we could read from the lady's diary and compare dates of the visits. This was not what the defence wanted to hear and I was quickly dismissed. My story was splashed in the *Sunday People*.

One of the more far-reaching investigations I was involved in was the story of Jeffrey Archer and call girl Monica Coghlan. The *News of the World* asked me to head an investigation into

Archer in 1986, when the multi-millionaire novelist was deputy chairman of the Conservative party and close to the prime minister, Margaret Thatcher. I was to work with investigations editor Eddy Jones and a team of reporters. The story created a great deal of controversy at the time and there were accusations of entrapment.

We were tipped off by a solicitor who claimed to have seen Archer visit a prostitute he had slept with. I wrote the story but gave the politician the benefit of doubt. I did not write that Archer had slept with Monica Coghlan, only that he had paid her to go away some time afterwards. The terrible thing is that Archer could have avoided all the problems if he had threatened to call the police or ask Special Branch to check out the call girl and told them he did not know her.

At the same time as our investigation, Archer was getting advice from his friend Stewart Steven, editor of the *Mail on Sunday*. But he knew most of the Fleet Street editors he had been cultivating, including David Montgomery, the *NoW* editor who had recently lunched with him. The *Sunday Business* published my thoughts on the story:

'In early September 1986 I accepted, with some hesitation, the *News of the World*'s offer to head an investigation into an "unbelievable tip-off" involving a key person in the higher echelons of the Conservative party. Investigative journalism is a high-risk business for the investigator, target, editor and proprietor alike. If successful, the upside is a reputation-enhancing scoop and increased circulation. But when it goes wrong, it can lead to expensive litigation and ruined reputations.

'I had previously witnessed the highs and lows of the investigative journalist's art, having successfully exposed John DeLorean, the American businessman who milked the UK government for millions of pounds with his car factory in Northern Ireland. For a while I was the toast of Fleet Street but when the writs arrived, I suddenly felt very lonely (this story and its fallout is addressed in detail in the following chapter). David Montgomery was then the *News of the World*'s editor. He was an ambitious, tough-minded Ulsterman who later became chief executive of Mirror Group. The paper's investigations editor, Eddy Jones, pushed him to pursue Jeffrey Archer. In my opinion, Montgomery was reluctant to proceed and anyway did not believe Archer had a liaison with a prostitute or that if he did that he would be susceptible to investigation. Most Fleet Street editors, Montgomery included, had either met Archer or dined with him and Montgomery was convinced that the Tory deputy chairman was far too shrewd to admit to anything which might compromise him.

'Friends and acquaintances have always been intrigued by the original *News of the World* story on Archer and the prostitute. Apart from their questions – 'How could you do it?' 'Why did he pay the prostitute?' – there was one point that bothered me. It was along the lines of feeling sorry for the victim. I considered that question for some time after the events and concluded that I did feel sorry for the victim. I felt sorry for the prostitute. Of all the participants in this media circus, she was the innocent and the one who had behaved with dignity in what, to her, would have been a confusing and frightening episode in her sorry life. After all, she had been an involuntary party to the events. Her 15 minutes of infamy had been cruelly thrust upon her.

'I must, however, confess here to a slight aberration. Initially, I did harbour sympathetic feelings towards Archer, to the point of wanting to tip him off anonymously and tell him not to be so stupid about making an offer to a person he claimed he had not met. These feelings rapidly left me. My task had been to interview the prostitute, obtain her version of events and prove her claims against Archer. In a libel trial against the *Daily Star*, Archer won £500,000.

'That, however, was not my story. I wrote in the *News of the World* that he offered to pay the prostitute £2,000 after her telephone call to his London flat in which she complained she was being harassed, which she was, by people who allegedly had seen him visit her. The figure of £2,000 is one that I contrived for the sake of caution. Archer's friend, Michael Stacpoole, was dispatched to platform three at Victoria station with a brown paper bag stuffed with money, which he was instructed to give to the prostitute so she could go abroad and lie low. Rather than accept the money and involve the newspaper in blackmail charges by Archer, we told Coghlan to decline his offer after counting the money. She reckoned the cash in the paper bag amounted to around £5,000 but we will never know the true sum because Archer readily accepted my conservative 'guesstimate'.

'The burden of proof imposed by the editor was formidable. Only if there was an outright admission by Archer about his activities would Montgomery consider publishing the story. Approaches were made to Rupert Murdoch, the paper's proprietor, for guidance, but he left the matter to the editor's judgment. Montgomery's apprehension was that Archer would turn the tables on the newspaper and he was terrified that the investigation would go wrong.

'Tape-recorded conversations were, and will continue to be, a normal part of investigations, despite the abhorrence from some quarters about their use. It is the best form of protection for a journalist defending his story, particularly where the subject has difficulty in reconciling an earlier version of events. Who would a court of law believe? The word of the deputy chairman of the ruling Tory party or the word of a hack from the gutter press? But it need never have gone so far. Had Archer put the phone down and refused to speak to Coghlan, the investigation would have been nipped in the bud. Had he called the police and said he was being set up in a blackmail situation, as Montgomery feared he might do, the newspaper would have given him an abject and profuse apology. But Archer did not. Despite the fact that he was a top Tory, that he had been an MP and best-selling author, Archer did not smell a rat.

'Here was a former trainee policeman, author, promotions man, public speaker and fixer, willing to pay money to a woman whom he had never met, telling her after one or two conversations, "You'll have to say very firmly that you made a mistake, it certainly wasn't me and don't tell them you've been in contact (with me) or there'll be even more trouble... You say, 'I don't even know who he is.' ... otherwise you'll find it will never end."

'Curiously, while the *News of the World* investigation continued, Archer got wind that something was up and was in a position to be advised by journalist friends in executive positions on what to do. Winning his action against the *Star* gave him the confidence to continue in public life.

'However, scandal and Jeffrey Archer would remain a close alliance. Given his past experience of investigations, it was all the more surprising that he became embroiled in a fiasco over shares – but when the Department of Trade and Industry opted not to prosecute, despite him buying shares in Anglia TV when his wife was a director at a crucial takeover period, his Teflon reputation was sealed.

'Until that is, a former friend rang him, turned on a tape recorder and discussed their plan of 13 years earlier to give Archer a false alibi. All he had to do to get off the hook was to hang up. But some lessons are never learnt.'

9

PUBLISH AND
BE DAMNED

Investigative journalism is a double-edged sword. It can give rise to a conflict of interest that touches personalities and commercial interests. The worst scenario for a journalist is when the target of the investigation is a friend of the proprietor or involves exposing a company that could trigger a substantial drop in revenue for the paper.

A pragmatic decision needs to be taken in those circumstances. It is perfectly natural for people to protect their friends and that is acceptable, providing nobody is harmed by abandoning an inquiry. But I still regret the decision made many years ago by the editor in Adelaide who spiked my investigation into asbestosis and the danger it presented to workers involved with the raw material. He withdrew the feature fearing loss of advertising revenue from companies involved in the industry and there were no other media outlets where I could place it. Of course, if there had been, a different conflict would have arisen. Would it have been disloyal for me to go elsewhere with the story?

The benefit of media plurality is obvious when one outlet turns down a story and it has been one of the joys of working in Fleet Street. Unreasonable proprietorial interference could always be countered with a quiet word to a colleague working on a different newspaper. Most proprietors pay lip service to the principle of democratic rights and freedoms, and we can all live with that while there is choice. But monopolies remove that choice. The article I had written with the help of doctors and scientists on diseases emanating from asbestos was an early warning that could have saved many lives.

If I had learned my lessons from the past, perhaps I would have been more careful when targeting high fliers in an investigation. But you can hardly approach a proprietor and ask if he is a friend of the person you are about to expose. When I began my inquiry into car-maker John Zachary DeLorean I had no idea he was a neighbour and friend of Rupert Murdoch. But DeLorean said he was and the result would be that my story on him would lead to a ban on me dealing with any Murdoch-owned media around the world. So would I do the same again today? Probably.

It started in September 1980. I received a transatlantic call from DeLorean, who had been given my details by his personal assistant Marian Gibson. I didn't know her personally, but we had a mutual friend in the north of England and that was how this American entrepreneur had got hold of me. A former engineer at General Motors, DeLorean had obtained funding from the UK government to build his dream car. The DeLorean DMC-12 would find cinematic fame with its distinctive gull-wing doors opening from the roof in the

Back to the Future franchise. Unknown to me, DeLorean also happened to be Murdoch's neighbour in an exclusive Fifth Avenue apartment block in New York.

The car-maker wanted a favour. He asked if I would fly to New York at his expense to set up an interview with a Detroit motoring journalist who had written a book about General Motors and was critical of DeLorean. For this simple task I was offered £25,000 plus expenses. There had to be a catch. I'd never had an offer like this and alarm bells immediately rang. 'Why?' I asked. To my surprise DeLorean was quite candid about the reason. He wanted to lure the author to New York in order to serve him with a writ. He wanted to stop the publication because he was furious, thinking the book would show him in a bad light. Serving papers in New York was simpler and faster than serving them on someone living in another state like Michigan, he said. I rejected his offer and told him it would be unethical for me to do it.

DeLorean's assistant tried to convince me to come over. Marian was English and had worked for DeLorean since 1979. At that time she was enchanted with her boss. She said he had worked really hard and that publication of the book could prejudice his dealings with the UK government if publication went ahead. A week or so earlier our mutual friend, Eddy Koopman, also met me to discuss DeLorean. He told me that money was being spent hand over fist on plush New York offices on the 42nd and 43rd floors of the prestigious skyscraper building at 280 Park Avenue. Eddy said the huge cost of fitting out the premises had been borne by the UK government, or more accurately, by the British taxpayer. Expensive paintings, stylish furniture, sculptures and jewellery were all put on the same bill, which we were picking up.

Having refused DeLorean's offer, I asked Marian to keep in touch. Some time later I was contacted again by a DeLorean executive, who wanted to know if I would like more information on the company. I asked if I could visit their factory and Belfast headquarters, which had recently been built at great cost on a green field site. My request was refused on the basis that DMC was experiencing a few difficulties and it was not a good time. I spoke to Marian and asked her to contact me if her situation should ever change.

From that time on I began taking a close interest in DeLorean and his business. It was obvious, both from the amount of money he was willing to pay me and from what I was told by my friend Eddy about his spending and extravagant lifestyle, that there would be a lot more to this story. I also asked Eddy to keep in touch with Marian and to keep me abreast of events.

Back in London, 1981 had been a busy year for Murdoch. He had bought the *Times* and *Sunday Times* from the Thomson Corporation, installing Harold Evans as editor of *the Times* (he was previously editor of the *Sunday Times*). Mrs Thatcher was then prime minister and Murdoch was able to avoid a monopolies and mergers commission inquiry into the takeover as Thomson had threatened to close their papers if they were not sold by a certain date. Undertakings about editorial independence were given by Murdoch because as with other takeovers by the mogul, there had been considerable opposition to his ownership. The new titles gave Murdoch control of four national newspapers. Adding the *Times* group immediately raised his profile and he was able to reach an important class of reader and debate serious issues and influence opinions on his pet hates – the EU, the euro, the

BBC, and any form of regulation that would adversely affect the News Corp empire.

Harold Evans recommended Barry Askew to Murdoch. He was an award-winning editor from the *Lancashire Evening Post* and was appointed editor of the *News of the World* in April 1981. Askew was the liveliest, and in my opinion could have been the best ever, editor of the *News of the World* if only his career had not been dramatically curtailed following my story on DeLorean. Unfortunately, Barry did have some faults. He loved drinking to excess with fellow journalists and was ready to engage in a pretend brawl with anyone who disagreed with him. He talked freely about his sexual conquests and worried management when a bed was brought into the anteroom of his Bouverie Street office. *Private Eye* gave him the monicker 'Beast of Bouverie Street'. But perhaps the quality that was least appreciated was his independence. Murdoch did not value independence in his editors. Askew wanted to report on serious issues as well as entertainment and crime, and he particularly wanted to develop a solid investigations team at the paper. He had a strong reputation for campaigning and had won awards for exposing a corrupt chief constable in the north of Britain and for his campaigns for the underprivileged.

Given Murdoch's disregard for royalty, Rupert should have been pleased with Barry's performance at the palace. The Queen was not amused when she admonished a group of editors for hounding Princess Diana while she was shopping and Askew commented, 'She was simply drawing attention to herself. Why doesn't she send a servant to do her shopping?'

To which the Queen's curt response was, 'I think that's one of the most pompous things I have ever heard.'

It had also been a busy year for me as I covered a range of major stories that would later prove to have relevance when it came to tackling DeLorean. Among the articles were a series that Bill Rankine and I had worked on, exposing professional misuse of drugs. I had also written a two-part series in the *Sun* on Judah Binstock, a multi-millionaire former lawyer who had conned the government out of millions with a fraudulent VAT scheme and was now living in Spain. Additionally, I had published a series about clubs in Paris, one on classroom problems and a third on Lord Lichfield for the *Sun*.

This had followed a number of *News of the World* exclusives. One involved organising a psychiatrist to administer truth drugs to test their effectiveness on public figures. It was my task to question Peter Hain, a future Labour cabinet minister, about a set-up by the South African government in which he was wrongly accused of snatching a woman's handbag in a Putney bank. He passed the truth-drug test with flying colours but revealed a number of personal matters, which we did not print. I was also sent by the paper to the Philippines and Australia to investigate brides for sale and my name had received exposure in nearly all the newspapers in which Murdoch took great interest.

Further, I had obtained an exclusive interview with Sex Pistols bassist Sid Vicious in 1979. He was in Rikers Island prison, New York, accused of the murder of his girlfriend Nancy Spungen. I was allowed to see him in his cell just before his release on bail. It was the last interview he did. On the night of his release he died of an overdose of heroin.

Then there was the time that I was able to give the *Sun* a running commentary on the Iranian embassy siege in 1980. The paper was ecstatic. That followed a visit to Iran I had made investigating child slavery. Children of the Baluch tribes were sometimes sold by their parents to carpet-makers, so their tiny fingers could tie the smallest knots needed for expensive Persian rugs. I had travelled along the eastern borders of Iran from Sarakhs on the Russian border to Meshed, bordering Afghanistan, then down to Zahedan, on the Pakistan border, into the mountainous lands of the dead cities where I visited Baluch nomads in desert tents before going further to Bandar Abbas on the Persian Gulf. It was the most dangerous bus journey in the world along rough mountain roads where wreckages of buses littered the valleys below.

On my return I used my knowledge of the country to interview Dr Gholamali Afrooz, a senior diplomat at the London embassy following the downfall of the Shah of Iran. My interview with Afrooz was published in both the *News of the World* and the *Observer*. So when armed Iranian men with demands on their government took the embassy, I telephoned Afrooz's direct number. A Special Branch officer replied and left the phone unhooked on his desk. In the shooting and panic that followed, my call was overlooked and I heard everything that was taking place during the siege and relayed this on my other line to the *Sun* as breaking news.

Meanwhile, John DeLorean was attracting huge amounts of publicity. He was a good-looking man (aided by plastic surgery to his chin), tall and charismatic and he had a beautiful young wife, Cristina Ferrare. They were a dream couple: glamorous and wealthy – thanks partly to British tax payers – and feted wherever they went. He had been featured on the cover of *Time* and she in upmarket glossy magazines. I warmed to her sense of humour when she was photographed sitting among cushions embroidered with the words 'I'd rather be riche than nouveau'. Before marrying her, DeLorean had dated actresses Ursula Andress and Candice Bergen. He was an American idol. Admired as a successful industrialist and brilliant engineer bringing a new concept car to the public, he was a friend of chat show host Johnny Carson and his style was pure Hollywood.

But the reality was quite different. DeLorean was a conman, crook and thief who, with his henchman Roy Nesseth, robbed a number of people of their life savings. Nesseth and DeLorean were also complicit in their dealing with the DeLorean Motor Company – DMC. And the DMC-12, the dream futuristic sports car, was not the 'brilliant invention' DeLorean would have everyone think it was. In fact, his car was very similar to one made by Malcolm Bricklin, a rich young car dealer who had imported Subaru cars to America and manufactured the Bricklin SV1, a gull-wing sports car. To get funding, Bricklin went to a high unemployment area of Canada and talked the state government into backing his idea in the early 1970s. They gave him $20 million by way of grants and incentives but the project folded and the government lost its money.

DeLorean followed suit. He went to underprivileged areas of America to get funding by offering to establish factories and give work to the unemployed. His project was rejected. He then went to Puerto Rico in the hope the government would fund his dream. They too considered his scheme unworkable and rejected it. He then tried to get funding from a Saudi multi-millionaire who asked an American bank to check DeLorean's credentials and assess the feasibility of his venture. They advised their client not to go near him or his car. Ireland proved equally uninterested but, finally, the UK government welcomed him to Great Britian and Northern Ireland, and both Labour and Conservative governments filled his coffers with nearly £85 million of the public's money.

Marian Gibson telephoned me at 7am on 1 October 1981. It was the call I had been waiting for because I was aware she had visited Britain at the end of September to discuss DeLorean with Sir Nicholas Winterton, the Tory MP for Macclesfield and another friend of our mutual contact, Eddy. In the meantime I alerted Barry Askew to the possibility of a story on DeLorean. I suspected DeLorean was a conman who had persuaded the UK government to hand over millions which he was now spending on luxuries and sumptuous offices in New York, that it was doubtful the enterprise would be a success and that DeLorean was more interested in enriching himself than producing a good product. Further, while he claimed to have invested $4 million in the project, there was no evidence of this.

This was exactly what Barry Askew wanted: a proper story to investigate that had an international element and was of national importance. Barry could not have been more supportive. I had enjoyed a very good relationship with the newspaper and Barry and I trusted each other sufficiently to agree we would negotiate a reasonable fee on publication. Barry had mentioned a substantial figure but there was no written agreement. As a freelance journalist I accepted there was always a risk that a story would not stand up but in this case I was confident of a positive outcome. Askew wanted an assurance that I would give him the exclusive and once that was assured, I had use of the company's resources.

Marian had recently become disillusioned with DeLorean

when she saw how ruthlessly he treated his staff. DMC executives had emphasised to her the huge personal losses they would suffer through DeLorean's greed. They were furious he was intent on changing the structure of the company to give himself the lion's share of equity and drastically reducing theirs. They were also aware that payments that should have gone to Lotus, at least on paper, were sent to a Swiss-based Panamanian company. In total, they estimated some $17 million was unaccounted for. Additionally, DeLorean spent the least time possible in Belfast. He would only go there to attend board meetings and would nearly always fly by Concorde. After the meeting, he would immediately return to New York or spend the night in London at Claridge's or another top hotel before going home.

Marian had been privy to documentation showing that Northern Ireland Development Agency (NIDA) money was being spent on projects that had absolutely nothing to do with DMC and everything to do with DeLorean's private ventures. UK taxpayers' money even paid the salaries of DeLorean's personal employees. Marian maintained that one of the main reasons she became a whistleblower was out of loyalty to Britain and because of DeLorean's callous disregard for his fellow executives and staff.

Her call to me that morning was one of despair. She had been banking on Sir Nicholas Winterton, in his capacity as MP, taking immediate action to block DeLorean from restructuring his company. But she was beginning to lose faith. However, Winterton had not sat on the case. He wrote to Margaret Thatcher's parliamentary private secretary informing him that the government was being ripped off, but did not mention the culprit. Action was held up because Mrs

Thatcher had flown to Australia to attend a meeting. Impatient for a result, Marian first complained to Eddy about lack of progress and then called me. Could I come straight away? She told me she had loads of material about company abuses and that a 'top investigative reporter' in the Murdoch empire was helping her with evidence. She was referring to Bill Haddad who had worked for Murdoch's *New York Post* and was now a vice president at DMC.

I flew to New York the same evening, arriving by taxi from Kennedy airport at Marian's flat at 11pm and interviewed her throughout the night. Time was of the essence. The editor wanted to publish the story on Sunday and, apart from long hours of interviewing, I would need time to examine bundles of documents and meet with her lawyer. A draft of the story would have to be ready by Friday night or, at the very latest, Saturday morning. Further checks would also need to be made in London and Belfast. I planned to have a showdown with DeLorean on Saturday. Others had been trying to reach him but for the past two days he had been incommunicado. Word had got out that Margaret Thatcher had been contacted and that police might be asked to intervene in the matter. I would not sleep for three days.

On Friday morning, I asked Marian to show me around the DeLorean offices in Park Avenue. In the afternoon, we went to DeLorean's office so I would know where I might find him on Saturday. With all the activity that was taking place, I had figured there was a good chance he might go there. Marian's lawyer, Clarence Jones, met me at a nearby restaurant before lunch and we went through some of the evidence. I then went to the News International offices at 730 Third Avenue for a meeting with the company's New

York correspondent, Stuart Higgins. I telephoned London and went through the material I had obtained so far. Barry Askew was adamant about getting the story in the paper that weekend and asked me to liaise with assistant editor Bob Satchwell. Bob's job was to make sure my copy was legally safe and had personally taken it to the St John's Wood residence of Murdoch's legal consultant and barrister, Charles Gray (now Sir Charles Gray QC, a former High Court judge appointed by NI to act as an independent adjudicator for hacking victims seeking compensation from the newspaper group). He approved the copy.

By late afternoon I was receiving many calls from England. Eddy rang to say Marian was upset and scared of what DeLorean might do to her. Sir Nicholas Winterton was unhappy with my involvement. I felt he wanted to take the credit for exposing the fraud rather than have a journalist get there first. Sir Nicholas called me on Friday night to say the matter was in hand and could I hold off. But I was determined to get the exclusive. At that stage I had not been told that Winterton had been warned that I was planning to release the story on Sunday. He put some pressure on the PM's secretary and said the government would look silly if we printed the story first.

Mrs Thatcher asked the attorney general, Sir Michael Havers (who had defended Bernie Silvers, the Soho crime boss), to begin a police inquiry into the allegations. Winterton was contacted by the solicitor general and gave him a detailed briefing of Marian's allegations. The MP was assured a police investigation would be authorised by the prime minister. Two detectives were promptly appointed to examine the evidence and flew to New York. But they were ill equipped for the job.

It needed a legal expert and forensic accountant to untangle DeLorean's web of deceit.

Meanwhile, on Friday evening I had a somewhat farcical battle with Marian. I had still not slept and was working away in her living room typing additions to the story. As Marian did not have a landline I had to find a public phone. The caretaker's number was given to the *NoW* if they needed me and, unfortunately, it rang most of the night. Winterton had not helped matters by telling Marian that the matter was now in police hands and that I should leave it to them. I told her it was too late to stop it as the paper had already planned the first three pages and, anyway, I was not going to abandon it just because an MP wanted to win brownie points.

Marian was not happy and every so often she would rush in and tell me to stop writing. 'You don't have a story,' she screamed. I thought it quite unreasonable of her as she had virtually begged me to drop everything to work on this. Moreover, had I not been involved I doubt whether matters would have progressed so quickly. As it turned out, my presence may have saved the government many millions because DeLorean had already put in a bid for further funds as well as scheming to reduce the government's equity in the project.

The police investigation, if you could call it that, would prove to be a waste of time. It was over almost before it began and DeLorean would be cleared of any malpractice. The police were not to blame, however. They had no judicial standing in New York, they could not force people to talk to them and they were not trained for the job. In other words, the investigation was a whitewash to save the government embarrassment. DeLorean must have had a laugh. He even wore a vest at a barbecue with 'I am a con man' printed on the front. Had the government done its homework thoroughly they would not have entertained DeLorean for a moment, let alone showered him with £85 million of taxpayers' money. This was going to be a great story.

But I had not reckoned on one very important ingredient that was to turn my world upside down. Rupert Murdoch, the owner of the *News of the World,* killed my story stone dead. And not only did he kill it, he later helped DeLorean find a solicitor, Lord Goodman, to sue me and others for libel and to demand damages of $250 million.

If that was not bad enough, Mr Murdoch also used his recent purchases, the *Times* and *Sunday Times,* to attack me and denigrate my work in an effort to support his friend and neighbour John DeLorean. Articles supporting the fraudster were also published in the *Sun* and the *New York Post.* It was particularly galling as the stories detailed earlier in this chapter could not have escaped his attention and to call me an 'unemployed writer' seeking to capitalise was plainly ridiculous.

The first inkling of what was to happen came at around 4pm on the Saturday. I entered the skyscraper on Park Avenue, eerily empty apart from a few security men, and took the express lift to the 43rd floor. I walked straight in to DeLorean's office and came face to face with him. He did not act surprised or perturbed. I detailed the allegations and asked him for a comment. I gave him every opportunity to reply. Instead he attacked the government and the Northern Ireland office and abused them for not giving him more money and help. He denied everything but explained nothing.

Towards the end he became irritated that I was asking so

many questions and got up to leave. He then looked at me and said, 'John, you're never going to get this story published.'

I asked him why I wouldn't.

'I know who you are and where you are from and you will not get it published because I am a friend of Rupert Murdoch.'

Ouch! That hurt and I had been there before. Lord Goodman was one example and there would be others in future. But the news was worrying. If DeLorean knew Murdoch as well as he professed, I would have a problem.

I made a hasty retreat from the skyscraper, worried that one of the security men would grab me. I returned immediately to Marian's – my bags had remained unpacked – and we went to the airport. She was as happy as I was to leave New York. I then called the *NoW* office, to be told the story had indeed been killed. Several hours before, I had been telephoned by the editor and congratulated over the same story. He had considered it to be the best story the newspaper had had in many years.

Bob Satchwell explained that all had gone well and that the lawyer had made some amendments, but there had been a change of mind in the afternoon following Rupert's arrival at the office. He had been to lunch in Oxford with Lord Goodman and telephoned the editor to ask what was going to sell the newspaper on Sunday. I suspect he knew what the answer was going to be.

Askew described what happened in a *Press Gazette* article some years later when discussing the importance of the proprietor-editor relationship. 'There is only one winner. The proprietor. With Murdoch I scored an own goal. It began with the Yorkshire Ripper ... Murdoch had authorised me to get the Yorkshire Ripper story at almost any cost ... Murdoch said

£80,000 would buy it [from Sutcliffe's wife, Sonia] but was prepared to offer more. Then the furore about paying "blood money" exploded in a welter of public debate. Suddenly, the coffers clanged shut. Money I had offered for Sonia's story was not "available". I got the front-page exclusive for nothing ... But the souring of my relationship with Murdoch had begun. I did not like being left in the lurch in Bradford and said so.

'The final crunch with Murdoch came over the central issue of investigative journalism ... A fine investigative journalist, John Lisners, was camped up in New York in the flat of a disaffected secretary of DeLorean. He had interviewed her at length, liberated the files and cracked the story. We had a world exclusive. I read the raw copy, word by word. I memorised it, subbed it, "legalled" it and passed it on to Henry Douglas, our resident legal manager, for further scrutiny. I was very happy with the story. As the ultimate failsafe I placed a call to Margaret Thatcher ... in Australia. She ordered a police inquiry.

Bearing in mind the law of libel, you cannot get much safer than the prime minister calling in the police. Murdoch rang in at midday from Oxford where he was lunching with Lord Goodman. What had I got that was going to be selling the paper well next day? I told him of the DeLorean exclusive and the Thatcher phone call. The upshot was unbelievable. He was back in the office in Bouverie Street by mid-afternoon. Soon afterwards he had summoned counsel from St John's Wood. Murdoch said it was legally unprintable. John DeLorean would "sue us for every penny we're worth. It was clear and obvious libel." I stood my ground and argued my corner. He won.

'He would let me print a watered-down version which, by

the time Murdoch and counsel had finished with it, was not worth the paper it was written on. I scrapped the splash, the two inside pages of back-up material and, with John Smyth [a chief subeditor], found a pale substitute. Early the following week, Lisners' account formed the basis for a splash in a Fleet Street daily tabloid. No doubt there would have been legal repercussions. Writs always fly when dynamic and highly personalised material is printed. But I know of no subsequent court hearings for defamation. In any event, I hope John Lisners got a fat cheque. He had earned one. World exclusives don't grow on trees.'

Askew said he had been warned by Peter Stephens, the editorial director, and Bruce Matthews, the managing director of NI, 'Don't take on Rupert – you cannot win.' Barry was editor for less than a year. Sadly, he died in April 2012.

On my return to the UK I was a hero for a week. The *NoW* deputy editor Phil Wrack told me it was a nonsense not being able to publish the story. He said Murdoch told him that what DeLorean had done was normal business practice. Barry Askew apologised again and said he felt gutted by Murdoch's decision. I was invited to lunch by several Fleet Street editors keen to hear the inside story. As far as most of them were aware, we were inhibited from publishing for legal reasons, although the *Observer* had referred to the story but without much detail.

I sold the story to the *Daily Mirror* and each day for the rest of the week it dominated the newspaper. I felt quite pleased that, although I had received far less than I would have got from News International, I nevertheless had it published with maximum effect and retained my integrity. DeLorean had been wrong to say I'd never see the story in print.

For whatever reason, Murdoch was furious. I went to Bouverie Street on the Friday to consult executive staff at the *NoW*. Kelvin Mackenzie was notified that I had entered the building. The *Sun* editor had been given orders to have me seen me off the premises and his news editor, Tom Petrie, who I had often dealt with, apologised profusely as he escorted me from the building with orders never to return. I was later told that I had been banned from every Murdoch-owned newspaper, television and media outlet in the world.

That came as quite a shock. As a freelance there would be no lump sum pay-off, no redundancy. In an instant I had been axed by a media group which had been my main source of income for 11 years and who had considered me to be a star performer. Why? Nobody would give a reason. The following week things got so bad on the south side of Fleet Street that colleagues would cross the road rather than be seen with me. I received messages of support and sympathy but little hope of retrieving the situation. My only consolation was that there was a principle at stake and I was prepared to fight for it. The story was true. DeLorean was a fraudulent conman who had wrecked many lives and I was later proved correct in every detail.

On 11 October the *Observer*'s Public Eye column featured Murdoch pulling the story with the headline: THE SCOOP THAT WAS PUT INTO REVERSE. It said that journalists at the *NoW* were 'still miserable at losing their front-page exclusive last Sunday ... the story was ready to print ... when proprietor Rupert Murdoch ... gave orders that it should be "killed".' It noted that the story made headlines everywhere else on the Monday – including the *Sun*. Murdoch's *New York Post* had prominently carried an 'exclusive interview' on the previous

Friday with DeLorean's wife Cristina. She said the allegations were 'all nonsense' and declared that her husband would never do anything wrong. 'It's so unfair,' she said.

Remarkably, the *Times* and *Sunday Times*, papers of record guaranteed to be free from proprietorial interference, waded in to apply a second coat of whitewash to the corporate crook and conman. Lord Goodman was already planning DeLorean's libel action.

On Monday 12 October 1981, the *Times* front page headline ran, ATTORNEY GENERAL TO CLEAR DELOREAN. It began, 'Mr John DeLorean, American founder of the newly launched sports car company, gave a warning in London last night that the present allegations of financial irregularities could break the company. In an interview with the *Times* he maintained that the group had been the subject of an organized campaign to destroy it.

'Sir Michael Havers, the attorney general, is expected to make a statement today, after police inquiries, which clears Mr DeLorean of any impropriety.' The article was continued later under a photograph of a smiling John DeLorean, standing with the Northern Ireland minister of state and Roy Mason, secretary of state for Northern Ireland, who had agreed the major part of the government's loan. Mason had written his own article under the photo, headlined: DELOREAN IS A WINNER, DAMN IT!

Mason's justification for the loan and support for DeLorean in his article bears little resemblance to what we know today about the case although, to give him some credit, he was trying to alleviate poverty and bring much-needed employment to Belfast. However, his intentions do not excuse the blind faith and unquestioning belief he showed in handing over more than £50 million as the first tranche of the loan. But even that is beside the point: the *Times* was ensuring good PR for the fraudster, even if at that time it was unaware of his fraud. In its editorial, heavily slanted in favour of DeLorean, it said, 'He is too successful...'

The next day's report gave a sizeable chunk of the front page to DeLorean's declaration of innocence and propriety. The piece again emphasised the result of the farcical 'police inquiry' by two Scotland Yard officers, who should be featured in *Guinness World Records* for managing, in just a week, including return travel to New York, to solve a complicated company fraud stretching between two continents and over three discrete areas of Europe.

That Harold Evans, former *Sunday Times* campaigning editor and winner of many awards, and then editor of the *Times* allowed this story to progress is a mystery to me. The article again emphasised the fact that the two policemen had found DeLorean innocent. It began: 'Mr John DeLorean, cleared by a police inquiry of any criminal conduct, said yesterday that his Belfast-based sports car company would survive despite a week of lies and accusations which had virtually destroyed the enterprise. He repeated that there was a conspiracy to bring down the firm. The director of public prosecutions announced that the police inquiry ... had found no evidence to support any allegations of criminal conduct on the part of Mr DeLorean or the company ... Mr DeLorean flew to Belfast to reassure his 2,500 employees at the factory in Dunmurry, "We are here to stay. What you see is a miracle and we are proud of it. Nothing is going to stop us."

'Mr DeLorean said the company would be filing libel writs against a number of people who were the most serious perpetrators "of this terrible crime against this company". The people would not be named until today.' DeLorean said the allegations had always been 'untrue, unfounded, and nonsense'. The article stated that, 'Mr DeLorean described Miss Gibson [Marian] as a troubled, disturbed typist who with an "unemployed writer", Mr John Lisners, had attempted to sell a sensational story to the *News of the World*. The story was not published because it could not be supported.'

I wrote to Evans the same day demanding a front-page apology for repeating libellous remarks DeLorean had made about me. I invited Evans to contact virtually every editor in Fleet Street who could vouch for the work I had done. The *Sunday Times* itself had telephoned me at home asking me to assist their business team with the story on DeLorean. In addition to all the major stories I had covered, I had also been interviewed at length by the Canadian Broadcasting Corporation. 'I would have thought you would be the last person,' I wrote, 'to criticise a fellow journalist for investigating a story of such import.'

I received no reply from Evans although a grudging 'correction' was published on the second page of the *Times* on Friday 16 October. It simply said, 'Mr John Lisners, who was described by Mr John DeLorean last Monday as an "unemployed writer who had attempted to sell what he termed a sensational story about his car firm to the *News of the World*," said yesterday that he has been self-employed as a freelance journalist for 11 years in Fleet Street with an established reputation. Mr Lisners added that what he offered the *News of the World* was a "responsible story of great national interest" which other national newspapers took up –

"and also a statement of fact: that a police inquiry had been ordered into DeLorean Motor Cars."

A recent *Guardian* article written by Evans shows his own sensitivity about not receiving a response to a correction. 'When Murdoch lied about the circulation of the *Times* in my editorship, the *Times* published the falsehood, and then [Charles] Douglas-Home [his successor as editor] refused to publish my letter of response or any form of correction.' Even top journalists can be guilty of double standards.

I accept the difficulty any new editor would have in going against the wishes of a proprietor intent on defending the interests of a high-profile friend attacked in another newspaper. In the *Guardian* article, Evans, a superb journalist, provides a telling insight into his former boss and one that could explain Murdoch's sympathetic approach to DeLorean and to UK politicians who were taken for a ride. Evans wrote of his old boss, 'He is remarkably prescient about how politicians will swallow the most gigantic fiction with barely a gulp. At the time I did not know what he was saying privately while he was trying to buy Times Newspapers, but it turned out to be spot on both about insouciant cynicism and the attention deficit order of political leaders: "You tell these bloody politicians whatever they want to hear," he said to biographer Thomas Kiernan, "and once the deal is done you don't worry about it. They're not going to chase after you later if they suddenly decide what you said wasn't what they wanted to hear. Otherwise they're made to look bad, and they can't abide that. So they just stick their heads up their asses and wait for the blow to pass."'

On 13 October 1981, a libel writ with a massive claim for damages was issued against me and others involved in the

DeLorean story by Goodman Derrick & Co. The claim was prepared by Richard Rampton, 'king of the libel bar'. Other newspapers began querying whether they could in future rely on my stories because of the positive publicity given to DeLorean by the Murdoch press. To their credit, the *Mirror* stuck by me and employed counsel to fight DeLorean's expensive bluff.

Goodman was notorious for stifling comment by issuing writs and he succeeded in this case – for a time. Eventually parliament found that DeLorean was even more culpable in his dishonesty than we had imagined. The following year he was involved in a drugs entrapment case in which he agreed to buy cocaine. Video evidence showed him holding a pack of cocaine saying it was better than gold. He was charged with trafficking but was acquitted on grounds of entrapment. He was declared bankrupt in 1999 and had fought over 40 legal battles by the time of his death in 2005.

In the meantime, executives at the *NoW* were trying to make amends and encouraged me to 'make up' but, without Murdoch's agreement, that would be impossible. It was having an impact on my earning capacity and I could not fight someone in Murdoch's position. I wrote to him a year later, on 26 October 1982, shortly after DeLorean's arrest on drug charges. Could he let me know one way or another about my standing? I phoned editorial director Peter Stephens to let him know I had sent the letter and on 11 November Stephens confirmed the ban had been lifted and it was OK to submit copy. Within 15 minutes the *NoW* assistant editor, a friend who had championed me, was on the phone offering work.

I was back on board the Murdoch train, still a freelance, and once more able to pursue stories ranging from showbiz to serious features and the occasional investigation. When a News Corp publication wanted a promotion, money was no object. I was flown by Concorde to New York with actor Stacy Keach on his release from Reading prison after serving time for his drugs conviction. Despite the first class travel afforded to Concorde passengers, it was the most harrowing trip I had experienced. The flight itself was fine, if a bit squashed, but a problem arose over an overweight banker who occupied his favourite aisle seat next to me and made it virtually impossible for me to speak to Keach. He refused to change seats so I could be closer to Keach. This was my only chance to interview him before we got to New York. In desperation I warned the banker that I had a medical condition that might require fast evacuation to the toilet. The problem was immediately solved. I got my interview.

As far as I was aware, only one other journalist from the paper was privileged to fly to America by Concorde: editor Wendy Henry, who wassummoned to New York by Murdoch. The story was that Murdoch had been incensed about an Arnold Schwarzenegger story that mentioned that his Austrian father may have had Nazi connections. At that time the actor was riding high and appearing in films in which Murdoch had an interest. The published story was a threat to his commercial interests and Henry was given a dressing down.

At one special TV preview at London Weekend Television, I was with a roomful of TV writers who had come to interview actor Anthony Hopkins. Not one of the questions being asked by the press interested me but I knew Hopkins would have something unusual to say if approached in the right way. I took him aside and asked if he had experience of demons in his mind. Why had I asked that question, he wanted to know. Just a feeling, I replied and he expanded his answer leaving me with an exclusive feature story that was sold around the world.

There is no great secret about getting stories. Phone hacking and the like is not only illegal but quite unnecessary. There has always been a core of highly skilled and professional journalists ready to undertake any task. They were able to do it in the past and it is disappointing that some staff reporters, despite the pressure on them to produce, resorted to unlawful means for their stories. It seemed that a few had become too dependent on being fed information acquired through the wrong channels. Yet so much can be achieved through initiative and interaction with people.

The *News of the World* was part of the rich tapestry of British life. Its stories were loved or loathed but rarely dull and it was a diverse range of people that came through its doors. Respectable citizens from Pinner or Tunbridge Wells might possibly have hidden the newspaper between the pages of the *Times* if in public but it was widely read and enjoyed until the disclosure of methods used in the past decade. It was a tragedy for the majority of honest journalists, subeditors and other staff that a newspaper as highly successful as it was could become so toxic.

Distancing himself from the *News of the World*, Rupert Murdoch told Lord Leveson the newspaper was an aberration that he wished he had closed years earlier. To a question about standards at his newspapers between 1968 and 1981 he said that, in 1968, when he came to London, 'I didn't really have enough to do with the *News of the World*. That was my fault...' However, it's difficult to reconcile that statement with

Murdoch having specifically come to London and fought tooth and nail in his battle for the *NoW*.

At that time the opportunity to buy the *Sun* had not arisen and Murdoch's future empire building then rested on the enormous profits produced by the *NoW*. Even so, Murdoch accepted the principle that the buck stops with him explaining to the inquiry, 'I'm not disowning it or saying it wasn't my responsibility to, but I was always closer to the *Sun*. It was a daily paper, there was something more urgent about it.'

To me, as a professional observer and contributor to his newspapers, the only notable difference between them was that the *Sun* was Murdoch's daily newspaper and the *NoW* was Murdoch's Sunday newspaper. The management was the same, the culture was the same and the executives were interchangeable and both papers carried the same political and social messages. There were times when editors of both newspapers competed for my stories and on one occasion editors Kelvin Mackenzie and Wendy Henry tossed a coin as to who would buy my article. Wendy Henry had also been a deputy editor of the *Sun* before Murdoch made her editor at the *NoW*. Neil Wallis had also been deputy editor at the *Sun* and was later hired as deputy editor of the *NoW*. Andy Coulson had been a top executive at the *Sun* before his appointment as deputy and then editor of the *NoW* and Rebekah Brooks had gone from editor of the *NoW* to the *Sun*.

If all these people had been in tune with Murdoch, who told the Leveson inquiry, 'If you want to judge my thinking, look at the *Sun*,' then was there really any huge difference between the ethos of the newspapers? And if Mr Murdoch thought so much less of the *NoW*, then commercial considerations would dictate that he apply even greater scrutiny to a paper which obviously continued its existence because it had always been valuable and whose executives were in the main appointed by either Murdoch or his right hand man Les Hinton.

The Sun on Sunday is a tame imitation of the *News of the World* it replaces. Commercially it is far cheaper to run a seven day newspaper than two separate titles so much of what News International lost on the swings it will gain on the roundabout. But, like roast beef and Yorkshire pudding, it was another British tradition that may not always have been approved of but nevertheless was mourned in its passing.

EPILOGUE

Towards the end of April 2012, Rupert Murdoch and his son James were called to give evidence at the Leveson inquiry at the High Court. Particular emphasis was placed on their relationship with politicians, although James was again questioned about the extent of his knowledge of hacking. He insisted he had not been aware that the practice had spread further than one rogue reporter until it became public knowledge. Like his father, he laid the blame firmly on his executive staff and denied that his legal manager and the *NoW* editor Colin Myler had notified him earlier or if they had, that he was sufficiently aware of it. The question of how effective his governance might have been was not examined. James agreed with Lord Leveson that, with hindsight, the culture at the paper was cavalier in regard to risk taking.

Rupert Murdoch admitted his failing with regard to governance but said he had been let down by executives and lawyers. He wished he had questioned Clive Goodman himself and decided whether or not he was telling the truth in the letter which Goodman had sent alleging that hacking was widespread within the paper. Murdoch said if he had known this that he would have torn the place apart and apologised again.

To the surprise of many in the courtroom, James revealed the extraordinary relationship that existed between the Murdoch family and the prime minister, David Cameron, and members of the cabinet. Rebekah Brooks features large in this cosy arrangement. James admitted he and Cameron had discussed News Corporation's bid to buy BSkyB at her country home. His admission was an embarrassment for the prime minister, who went on television to defend his position, insisting that no deal had been done or ministerial code breached.

In his witness statement James Murdoch said, 'I recall speaking briefly to the prime minister on one occasion about the proposal ... at a dinner hosted by Rebekah and Charlie Brooks and attended by a number of other people. It took place two days after responsibility for the matter had passed to the secretary of state for culture, media and sport, Jeremy Hunt, from the secretary of state for business, innovation and skills, Vince Cable.

'On 21 December, the prime minister's office had issued a statement saying that, "The prime minister is clear that Mr Cable's comments were totally unacceptable and inappropriate." I recall concurring with that view and believe I would have appreciated assurances that the process would be handled objectively in the future. I recall one conversation with the chancellor of the exchequer, George Osborne, about the bid.'

Cameron's 'chat' may have infringed the ministerial code of conduct in relation to conflict of interest as no decision had been made about the BSkyB takeover. The prime minister has always denied having an inappropriate discussion about this matter. James Murdoch also admitted that he personally told David Cameron that the *Sun* would switch allegiance from Labour to the Tories. He had discussed the matter with Rebekah Brooks and the editor and political editor and told Cameron of their decision over drinks.

Rebekah Brooks' career was astonishingly successful. She appears to have had little or no formal journalistic training, although she had shown initiative and determination when she appeared at the features desk of *Today* newspaper. Later she worked on the *NoW* magazine after a stint as secretary and then rose to the position of features editor before being appointed editor in 2000. On the several occasions that I was in her company, Brooks networked brilliantly with the most important people present, exuding charm and attentiveness towards those she met. With female associates she could be just as engaging. The wife of one executive told me that although she had nothing in common with her, Brooks had admired her shoes and said, 'I've got similar ones to you. We can be shoe sisters...' She made an immediate impact. But that was not sufficient expertise to run a huge enterprise like News International. Murdoch should not have entrusted someone with as little experience to be in charge, impressed as he may have been with her new political 'friends'.

Had it been earlier in his illustrious career there is little doubt that Murdoch would have been the first to sort out the mess after Clive Goodman was sent to prison for hacking. It was not sufficient excuse that he had taken over the *Wall*

Street Journal. He had the staff to help him examine in detail what was going on in his London newspapers. Or had the organisation become so powerful that nobody would dare touch it? Murdoch was a boss to be feared. Did this stop other staff from blowing the whistle? Nobody would dare criticise Brooks to Murdoch. She had become another 'favourite daughter'.

And some staff at the paper had become lazy. It was far simpler to sit back and let someone else do the dirty work in obtaining information than getting out there to seek stories. They would still get the byline justifying their high wages. Also the drive for results made people take chances. Some people would do anything for Murdoch, even if it meant putting themselves in danger without realising the potential damage they were doing to the organisation. Who turned a blind eye to what was going on?

Whatever Murdoch says about being let down by his executives he still kept in touch, particularly with the Brooks. She was the most powerful media person in the UK. Other Murdoch executives were constantly in touch with their boss. Les Hinton was virtually family, having served Murdoch for over 50 years. In America, the top people were on his doorstep. In Australia, John Hartigan, recently retired as chief executive, had been with the organisation for about 45 years and had also worked on the *Sun* in the UK, as had Les Hinton.

James Murdoch could be forgiven for his ignorance concerning events at the paper. It appears nobody told him what was really going on. A novice who knew little about the dark secrets of newspapers, he was more involved in digital media and taking over BSkyB. Hinton and Hartigan, however, were on the ball. They did not lock themselves away in an ivory tower but mingled with staff and other executives. They would often be seen on the shop floor, talking to journalists and to editors. They were Murdoch's eyes and ears.

Rebekah Brooks peaked too early. She made editorial errors for which she was publicly criticised and professional mistakes when she told parliament that News Group paid policemen. Although Andy Coulson immediately offered an explanation to mitigate the damage, it was too late. Murdoch or Hinton should have stepped in at that stage and investigated. So why didn't Murdoch do anything? Was it because the organisation had become too powerful and too complacent while keeping the bank happy? Or had Rupert begun to relax his tight control and did not want to hurt his 'handmaiden', as Kelvin Mackenzie described Brooks? Whichever it was is immaterial. In the past, Rupert Murdoch would not have thought twice about firing someone for a similar mistake.

There were further opportunities to nip illegality in the bud when news first came out about hacking. But the opportunity to do so was not taken. It was all very well saying, as Murdoch did, that one has 52,000 employees and can't be expected to monitor them all – but here was an organisation where every editor appointed in London had been first approved by Murdoch and anyone above that level was on first name terms with him. Murdoch did not have to read their staff files.

On 1 May the House of Commons culture media and sport select committee issued a damning report into hacking, declaring, 'Rupert Murdoch is not a fit person to exercise the stewardship of a major international company.' He was accused of turning, 'a blind eye and exhibited wilful blindness,' to what had gone on. It was a symptom of a culture that permeated from the top and 'speaks volumes about lack of effective corporate governance,' the report said. Some members considered the personal criticism against the mogul unfair, but the majority agreed that parliament had been misled by by Les Hinton, Murdoch's right-hand man, Colin Myler, editor and Tom Crone, the *News of the World*'s legal chief.

The fallout threatens to spread beyond the shores of the Murdoch's UK operation as a magnifying glass has been applied to the entire global organisation. Toxicity spread from *News of the World* employees to the Murdoch family name itself. It will take years to cleanse the stain by which time it is unlikely Murdoch will be in the driving seat. The family will not suffer financially. But their power base has been seriously eroded. Politicians will in future be very careful about getting too close. Individual political writers working for their papers may still curry favour with those in power – who were equally to blame for having sought the mogul's patronage – but it will never be the same.

Murdoch was unable to conquer China because its leaders had studied his methods and they were unimpressed. They did not want to subjugate themselves to the media barbarian at the city gates. Perhaps one day even that entrance may open for his Chinese-speaking daughters. But Rupert Murdoch himself will find that access through many gates from now on will be severely restricted.

THE RECKONING

Fittingly inscribed in stone at the entrance to Crane Court in Fleet Street is a plaque commemorating the printing of Britain's first daily newspaper, the Daily Courant, published on Wednesday March 11, 1702. At a cost of one penny, readers were regaled with bland accounts of second hand stories copied from European newspapers. A situation that would t appeal to opponents of Press freedom. Controversy and opinions were studiously avoided in the Courant even though a rich seam of events capable of filling every page was taking place. Europe was in turmoil. The Duke of Marlborough was in the throes of battle on the banks of the Danube, preparing for the War of the Spanish Succession against French and Bavarians troops in southern Germany. Thankfully the Courant's anodyne style of reporting was short-lived and over the next 150 years, the Press revealed its mettle in critical pamphlets, periodicals, and newspapers, although not without their editors suffering imprisonment and fines.

Opposition to establishment views began with spirited writers like Jonathan Swift, Henry St John Bolingbroke, and Daniel Defoe, author of Robinson Crusoe. Defoe, like others, faced prison on several occasions over publication of his views as did fellow pamphleteers and editors who refused to toe the official line. Today, post Leveson newspapers face the threat of draconian penalties for transgressing strict new rules presently under consideration. The effect may be similar to that achieved by 18th and 19th century politicians who partially succeeded in inhibiting press freedom by the imposition of a range of taxes. A tax of 1 penny on each printed sheet was imposed followed by taxes on advertisements. Recalcitrant publishers were warned that government owned post offices would refuse to distribute their newspapers. But it was not all one-way traffic. Newspapers also profited and conspired in corruption and venality practised by politicians. British statesmen, particularly Sir Robert Walpole, 1st Earl of Orford and William Pitt, 1st Earl of Chatham increased their popularity by bribing publishers to give them a good press, funded by the tax payer. Some might even draw comparisons about the propriety of relationships that existed between press and parliament two centuries ago with the present.

Certainly the relationship between the press and politicians was an area examined in the Leveson inquiry and there is now a growing anxiety that freedoms won long ago are in jeopardy. Misconduct by a few are threatening the freedoms of many in the wake of ugly truths exposed in the hacking saga. But while penalties already existed to curb the excesses of unlawful behaviour by journalists, it has given opponents of press freedom the opportunity of attempting to impose fresh restraints against newspapers and the media in general. That does not excuse proprietors, however innocent, who must take responsibility for the unlawful conduct of their employees nor limit the importance of much of what Lord Justice Leveson recommends. His recommendations for a statutory based regulation are questionable. Regrettably, they pander to sectional rather than general interests and risk playing into the hands of politicians who are all too ready to stifle dissent or criticism. It is doubtful that Prime Minister David Cameron who ordered the inquiry into the Media would have fully appreciated the extent to which it would evolve. He was against statutory control of the media while favouring more stringent regulation than that which existed. However, his coalition deputy, Liberal leader Nick Clegg sided with Labour's Ed Milliband in demanding statutory involvement. Eventually an unhappy compromise was reached with each party declaring a dubious victory after a Sysyphean struggle that is yet to be properly resolved.

So what now for battle-hardened Rupert Murdoch, who will be 83 next birthday? Despite his allegiance to the stars and stripes on becoming an American citizen he is still the most powerful figure in Australia capable of influencing state and federal governments through his vast media holdings. Eldest son Lachlan who is on the board of News Corporation has added to the family pile in Australia with investments in television (Channel 10) where he is a joint shareholder with two other mega rich Australians, James Packer and multi billionaire heiress Gina Rinehart. In 2012 Lachlan completed purchase of DMG Radio Australia, owner of the Nova and Smooth FM networks for which he paid around $200 million through his private investment vehicle Illyria. Both Lachlan and dad Rupert were included in the list of 50 most influential people in Australia in 2013.

But reputational concerns over hacking and further investigations into past illegal activities in Murdoch's British newspapers following closure of the *News of the World* continue to plague the mogul despite his continuing financial success. Police activities are far from over and further court appearances of top News International executives are due in September 2013 and will once more serve to remind the public of the toxic aspects of News Corporation subsidiaries.

Separating News Corporation's publishing and entertainment divisions will please American shareholders but will not wipe out the memory of past misdemeanours that have done so much damage to the company's UK holdings and threatened Murdoch's American interests. However, Murdoch is not one to give up easily – only recently the octogenarian put in a bid for the Los Angeles Times but fears that US Democrats will use the Federal Communications Commission's rules against cross ownership of TV and newspapers. A sympathetic administration could concede a waiver and perhaps that might explain an extraordinary story recently published by Watergate journalist Bob Woodward in the Washington Post last December (2012). Woodward's source was a taped recording he obtained of former CIA boss General Petraeus's meeting with Fox defence analyst K T McFarland. The Watergate journalist's story was followed up by other media under banner headlines alleging that while Sir Brian Leveson was investigating the phone hacking scandal in the UK, Rupert Murdoch made a '…brazen bid to hijack the [US] presidency.' The Guardian newspaper published an article written by Woodward's fellow investigative journalist Carl Bernstein on 20 December 2012. It read:

'So now we have it: what appears to be hard, irrefutable evidence of Rupert Murdoch's ultimate and most audacious attempt – thwarted, thankfully, by circumstance – to hijack America's democratic institutions on a scale equal to his success in kidnapping and corrupting the essential democratic institutions of Great Britain through money, influence and wholesale abuse of the privileges of a free press.

In the American instance, Murdoch's goal seems to have been nothing less than using his media empire – notably Fox News – to stealthily recruit, bankroll and support the presidential candidacy of General David Petraeus in the 2012 election.

Thus in the spring of 2011 – less than 10 weeks before Murdoch's centrality to the hacking and politician-buying scandal enveloping his British newspapers was definitively revealed – Fox News' inventor and president, Roger Ailes, dispatched an emissary to Afghanistan to urge Petraeus to turn down President Obama's expected offer to become CIA director and, instead, run for the Republican nomination for president, with promises of being bankrolled by Murdoch. Ailes himself would resign as president of Fox News and run the campaign, according to the conversation between Petraeus and the emissary, K T McFarland, a Fox News on-air defence "analyst" and former spear carrier for national security principals in three Republican administrations....'

THROWN TO THE WOLVES

Damage limitation at News International's London newspapers took a heavy toll on staff morale. Many journalists at the *News of the World* and the *Sun* felt they had been abysmally treated by senior executives, and by Murdoch himself. The majority had done no wrong and had shown great loyalty to their boss over many years. The same courtesy was not offered to them. The company's management and standards committee (MSC) appointed to assist the authorities with information which could lead to the arrest of those who were engaged in illegal activities or had the slightest connection with guilty parties went into overdrive. Expense sheets were scrutinised, hundreds of thousands of emails examined and passed to police, letters and recordings and details of phone accounts were checked and the smallest piece of evidence deemed even remotely relevant was surrendered to prosecutors. This resulted in a number of arrests on scant evidence which later proved to be wrong. In the meantime, a number of innocent reporters had been arrested at their homes in the early hours of the morning and held for questioning at police stations in the capital. Many felt they were being unfairly sacrificed to save News Corporation's skin.

They were particularly angry when it was announced that their former chief executive Rebekah Brooks had been paid nearly £UK11 million as compensation following her resignation. The situation became so wrought that Rupert Murdoch eventually flew to Britain and visited a number of his employees at their private addresses to express his regret and sympathy. There was also a feeling that Murdoch had regretted the closure of the *News of the World* and that it could have been avoided if top executives had accepted responsibility and resigned immediately. The whole matter had been very poorly handled by News International and resulted in severe criticism against leading figures in the company. For James Murdoch, it was a complete disaster. Although he had very little to do with the UK newspaper titles, concentrating instead on television and new media, he was nevertheless held responsible for company shortcomings. Even so, he won the respect of fellow professionals for his contribution to television and digital media but had fallen foul of governance issues. As a result there was serious doubt about his suitability, at least in the immediate future, to succeed his father and it seems his older brother Lachlan now appears to be the more likely successor as head of the family firm.

For Rupert Murdoch himself, the failure to take over Sky is a huge personal loss as is the loss of his influence with the UK government after the shutters came down at 10 Downing Street. Imagine how different things would have been if the hacking problem had not arisen. British Sky Broadcasting would now be fully owned by News Corporation. James Murdoch would be chief executive of the London subsidiaries and a prince in waiting to inherit his father's crown. Downing Street, advised by the former editor of the *News of the World*, Andy Coulson, would be continuing its close relationship with the Murdochs and Rebekah Brooks. She would also be in line for a peerage for services to the media and News Corp's interests would grow from strength to strength in the USA with further takeovers while forging close ties with the next Republican to hold office. No other tycoon had ever succeeded in attaining his degree of potential influence with governments and leaders in the English speaking world and beyond.

In terms of financial loss, the hacking saga is virtually an irrelevance to News Corporation. The company is rich enough not to be affected by the $360 million plus that it has cost them to date. Its profits have increased and revenue of both divisions, newspapers and entertainment, have been healthy. The company reported in February 2013 that revenue was up 5 per cent in its last quarter to $9.43 billion with profits of $2.38 billion.

News Corporation's biggest loss, which has yet to be quantified, is reputational damage and the consequent loss of influence in the UK and USA. This September further trials will take place involving practices at News International newspapers. Meanwhile investigations on the fallout from hacking and the suborning of state employees are continuing and involve journalists from other newspapers as well as the *News of the World* and the *Sun*. To date over 100 arrests have been made as a result of linked police operations investigating phone hacking allegations (Operation Weeting); corruption and/or payment of bribes to public officials (Operation Elveden); and allegations of computer hacking (Operation Tuleta). Additionally, seven people were charged with conspiracy to pervert the course of justice. Scotland Yard has reported that 169 officers and staff are working on the three linked investigations: 91 officers on Weeting; 61 on Elveden; and 16 on Tuleta.

Lord Justice Leveson reported his findings at the end of November 2012. His general statement about the press was fair and measured.

'...I know how vital the press is – all of it – as the guardian of the interests of the public, as a critical witness to events, as the standard bearer for those who have no one else to speak up for them. Nothing in the evidence that I have heard or read has changed that. The press, operating properly and in the public interest is one of the true safeguards of our democracy. As Thomas Jefferson put it: "Where the press is free and every man able to read, all is safe." As a result of this principle which operates as one of the cornerstones of our democracy, the press is given significant and special rights in this country which I recognise and have freely supported both as barrister and judge. With these rights, however, come responsibilities to the public interest: to respect the truth, to obey the law and to uphold the rights and liberties of individuals. In short, to honour the very principles proclaimed and articulated by the industry itself (and to a large degree reflected in the Editors' Code of Practice). The evidence placed before the Inquiry has demonstrated, beyond any doubt, that there have been far too many occasions over the last decade and more (itself said to have been better than previous decades) when these responsibilities, on which the public so heavily rely, have simply been ignored. There have been too many times when, chasing the story, parts of the press have acted as if its own code, which it wrote, simply did not exist. This has caused real hardship and, on occasion, wreaked havoc with the lives of innocent people whose rights and liberties have been disdained. This is not just the famous but ordinary members of the public, caught up in events (many of them, truly tragic) far larger than they could cope with but made much, much worse by press behaviour that, at times, can only be described as outrageous. That is not to conclude that the British press is somehow so devoid of merit that press freedom, hard won over 300 years ago, should be jeopardised or that the press should be delivered into the arms of the state. Although the Inquiry has been reported as having that aim, or likely to have that result, even to suggest it is grossly to misrepresent what has been happening over the last 16 months. I remain (as I started) firmly of the belief that the British press – all of it – serves the country very well for the vast majority of the time...It is not necessary or appropriate for the press always to be pursuing serious stories for it to be working in the public interest. Some of its most important functions are to inform, educate and entertain and, when doing so, to be irreverent, unruly and opinionated. It adds a diversity of perspective.'

Leveson's main recommendations include the appointment of a new independent regulatory body underpinned by statute and overseen by the broadcast watchdog Ofcom which in turn is controlled by Government. This is seen as too great a threat to the principle of free speech as such regulation could inhibit the Press from criticising members of parliament or investigating abuses of power. It would also impact heavily on Article 10 of the Human Rights Act which guards free speech and eases the burden of investigative journalists undertaking exposés of public interest matters such as the *Telegraph*'s investigation into MPs expenses. However Leveson did advocate that the new legislation should 'place an explicit duty on the government to uphold and protect the freedom of the press.' But recommending fines of up to £1 million for breaching a new press code would also represent an unwelcome gag on newspapers.

Leveson is minded that celebrities have a right to privacy and concluded that parts of the press considered actors, footballers, writers and pop stars were 'fair game, public property with little if any entitlement to any sort of private life or respect for dignity.' The judge said there was a perception that senior

Metropolitan police officers were too close to News International and that politicians of all parties had developed 'too close a relationship with the press in a way which has not been in the public interest.' He criticised the *News of the World* saying that apart from phone hacking, there was a failure of systems of management and compliance and a general lack of respect for individual privacy and dignity.

Meanwhile, Rupert Murdoch planned to visit his Australian interests over Easter 2013. News reports said that his former chief executive at News International Rebekah Brooks and husband Charlie would be visiting Australia at the same time. There was no word on whether the old friends would meet.

British and American regulators will not be the press mogul's only headache. Australia's Prime Minister Julia Gillard is planning to introduce wide-ranging changes to media rules. A new regulator is due to be appointed to oversee print and online news content as well as introducing a public interest test for mergers. Understandably News Ltd CEO Kim Williams considers this a retrograde and unbalanced measure.

Murdoch will not be amused that his Foxtel pay television business would be included in a public interest test administered by a Public Interest Media Advocate (PIMA) who may approve or reject media acquisitions. Perhaps Mr Murdoch's first point of call might be to the PM's office in Canberra. The last time he called on her she obliged him with an article for his London *Sun*.